Magic Guidebooks:
Walt Disney World Resort®
2017 Guide

*Secrets, Money Saving Tips, Hidden Mickeys, and
Everything Else You Need to Know!*

Want even more tips and stunning photos of Disney Parks? Sign up for our Free E-Mail List on our Website:

www.magicguidebooks.com

You can also follow us on social media:

Instagram
@magicguides

Facebook
facebook.com/MagicGuides

Twitter
@magicguides

We'd LOVE if you hashtag us!
#MagicGuidebooks

Magic Guidebooks:

Walt Disney World Resort
2017 Guide

The Absolute, Best Advice from the Experts!

- Insider tips on using FastPass+ and other tricks to skip the lines!

- Save on Walt Disney World hotels, flights, and park tickets.

- Reviews on every restaurant, the best food, and advice for the value of the Disney Dining Plan.

- Covers all four theme parks, water parks, hotels, Disney Springs, and beyond.

- Honest, real, and often humorous insight into Walt Disney World Resort. We love these Parks and we put our years of knowledge and insider secrets in the palm of your hand.

6

Table of Contents

About This Guide...11

Chapter 1: Introduction to the Walt Disney World Resort...12

    Walt Disney World: A Brief History 13

    What to Expect During Your Vacation 14

    Why You Need This Guidebook...17

Chapter 2: Words and Phrases for the WDW Resort.............18

Chapter 3: When to Visit..24

    New Attractions 26

    Recommended Travel Months...29

    Theme Park Breakdown..32

    Best Days to Visit..34

    Tips for Beating Crowds on Busy Days 46

Chapter 4: Booking Your WDW Vacation 48

    Booking Discounts 52

    Annual Passes..55

    Disney Vacation Club 56

Chapter 5: Traveling to Walt Disney World 58

    By Airline..60

    Disney's Magical Express..63

    By Car..64

    By Bus 65

    By Private Car App 66

    By Shuttle or Taxi 67

    By Train...68

    Transport Inside of the Walt Disney World Resort............68

Chapter 6: What to Wear and Bring – And What Not To! 70

    What to Wear and Bring..71

    What *Not* to Wear or Bring 74

Chapter 7: the Magic Kingdom Park 78

    Main Street, U.S.A..81

    Adventureland 84

Frontierland 88
Liberty Square..91
Fantasyland 92
Tomorrowland...100
Chapter 8: Epcot..104
Future World 106
World Showcase 111
Chapter 9: Disney's Hollywood Studios............................119
Hollywood Boulevard 122
Echo Lake 122
Muppets Courtyard 124
Pixar Place 125
Animation Courtyard 126
Mickey Avenue...128
Sunset Boulevard..128
Chapter 10: Disney's Animal Kingdom 133
The Oasis 136
Discovery Island...137
Africa...140
Rafiki's Planet Watch..144
Asia..145
DinoLand U.S.A 148
Chapter 11: Disney's Water Parks 151
What to Bring..154
Disney's Typhoon Lagoon 156
Disney's Blizzard Beach 160
Chapter 12: Hotel Reviews 165
Disney's Animal Kingdom Lodge and Villas 172
Disney's Beach Club Resort and Villas 174
Disney's Boardwalk Inn and Villas 176
Disney's Contemporary Resort and Bay Lake Tower......178
Disney's Grand Floridian Resort and Spa 180
Disney's Polynesian Village Resort 181
Disney's Wilderness Lodge 183

Disney's Yacht Club Resort 185
Disney's Fort Wilderness – Cabins and Campgrounds...187
Disney's Caribbean Beach Resort 188
Disney's Coronado Springs Resort.......................................190
Disney's Port Orleans Resort...192
Disney's All-Star Resorts...193
Disney's Art of Animation and Pop Century Resorts 195
Disney's Old Key West Resort 197
Disney's Saratoga Springs Resort and Spa.........................199
Walt Disney World Swan and Dolphin 200
Shades of Green..203
Chapter 13: Disney Springs..204
La Nouba by Cirque du Soleil 208
Chapter 14: Restaurant Guide 210
Disney Dining Plan: Is It Worth It?.....................................208
Chapter 15: Bringing Kids: From Toddlers to Teens...........280
Tips for Visiting with Kids...282
Visiting with Babies and Toddlers..283
Attraction Tips with Babies and Toddlers..........................285
Rider Switch..285
Kids (Ages 3-9)...286
Tweens (Ages 10-12) 287
Teens (Ages 13-17) 289
Chapter 16: Adults, Things to Do...290
Parents' Evening Out...291
The Best Restaurants and Bars for Adults 294
Chapter 17: Non-Rider Guide 302
Chapter 18: Hidden Mickey List 308
The Magic Kingdom 310
Epcot..312
Disney's Hollywood Studios..314
Disney's Animal Kingdom 315
The Resort Hotels...316
Disney Springs...317

Chapter 19: FastPass+ Tips 318
Chapter 20: The Very Best of WDW – Top 7 Lists 326
Chapter 21: Pre-Planned Ride and Attractins Guides.........330
   Create Your Own Attraction List...343
   WDW Resort Vacation Checklist 346
Chapter 22: Character Locations 347
Index 353
Conclusion...349

About This Guide

When writing and designing this book, we had *you* in mind. Maybe you're a first-time visitor to the Walt Disney World Resort or perhaps, you've frequented for many years. Wherever you come from and whatever your experience, we wanted to provide a complete guide from start to finish, while giving a critique of the attractions and restaurants in the resort. In fact, the entire purpose of this guide is to inform, critique, and recommend to you about the many attractions, restaurants, hotels, and more from the Walt Disney World Resort.

Keep in mind that this guide is an "unofficial edition" meaning that we are in no way affiliated with the Walt Disney Company®, the Disneyland Resort®, the Walt Disney World® Resort, and nor have we ever been. We are simply fans of the Disney Parks who are giving an honest opinion on what it has to offer.

Magic Guides

Chapter One

Introduction to the Walt Disney World Resort

Walt Disney World: A Brief History

Nine years after opening his iconic Disneyland Resort in Southern California, Walt Disney started a new dream. It was to create something even bigger to enchant the globe. In essence, he wanted to create more than a *land* – Mr. Disney wanted a *world*!

In 1964, that dream was planted like a seed which would eventually grow into the massive, enchanting tree of reality. Originally nicknamed the covert "Florida Project" Disney secretively bought nearly 30,000 acres of marsh, swamps, and groves in central Florida. Unfortunately, the next year, Walt Disney passed away. You'd think that his ghost could haunt this project, but the opposite happened: his brother, Roy, kept the *spirit* of Walt Disney alive.

By 1969, the secret was out, and construction began on the Magic Kingdom, Florida's version of Disneyland. Orlando's massive 189-foot (56 meters) Cinderella Castle towers California's Sleeping Beauty Castle – which is only 77 feet (23 meters). In October of 1971, Walt Disney World opened its gates to visitors, bringing classic attractions like Peter Pan's Flight, "it's a small world" and the Jungle Cruise to world in the biggest park ever.

The flat, Floridian lands just outside of Orlando, now had a center of magic for all to behold. It wouldn't be long until thousands of visitors turned to millions, making it the most successful theme park resort in history (and still is today). Nearly 20 million people visit the Walt Disney World Resort annually to live the stories from classics like *Snow White and the Seven Dwarfs*, experience the frosty magic of *Frozen*, and to meet Mickey Mouse himself.

For Disneyland lovers, they will notice the wider streets of the Magic Kingdom and the spacious, interactive queues. Orlando rains more than Southern California, so indoor lines and some of the rides (like the Mad Tea Party or teacups) are better with covers than exposed to the tropical, Floridian air. However,

Florida makes an ideal spot for the Walt Disney World Resort as there is plenty of space for the twenty-eight Disney hotels, four world-class theme parks, shopping center, water parks, golf courses – you get it. With warm weather nearly year-round, it's the ideal spot vacationers of all ages to experience the massive, endless magic that Walt Disney has brought to the world.

Soon, Walt Disney World continued its mission to become the massive theme park resort that it is today by adding the futuristic EPCOT (which stands for Experimental Prototype Community of Tomorrow) in 1982, followed by MGM Studios (now called Disney Hollywood Studios) in 1989 and Disney's Animal Kingdom in 1998. Walt Disney World also has two themed water parks, Disney's Typhoon Lagoon (opened 1989) and Disney's Blizzard Beach (opened 1995). There is also a downtown shopping area known as Disney Springs, a boardwalk, ESPN Wide World of Sports Complex, a Cirque du Soleil show, and an NBA Experience.

What to Expect During Your Vacation

Orlando, Florida is an ideal location for the WDW Resort because of its year-long sunshine. Likely, as your plane lands or car or bus arrive, you'll see the sun shining with white tufts of cottony clouds. Many times, especially in the late afternoon, it'll be cloudy and gray for an hour or so. Thunderstorms, especially in the summer months, will sweep by and leave as quickly as they came. It's not uncommon for it to rain each day at the Walt Disney World Resort, but, fortunately, it doesn't last for long. Meanwhile, half of the year in Florida, the humidity is high. Sometimes even 100% saturating the air. It can feel a bit stifling, but the Resorts and Parks know this. Air conditioning pumps in every car, Hotel, and indoor ride to help you enjoy your stay.

If you're flying into Orlando International and staying at the Disney World Resort, you'll arrive at your hotel via Disney's Magical Express. This is a complimentary Disney charter bus with comfortable seats, air conditioning, and cartoons playing on several television screens. After a stop or two at other hotels, you'll be at your new home.

The MagicBands feel like gifts that Disney provides to its guests staying on Resort. These are light, waterproof bracelets that you customize on the internet before your stay. These special bands are your room key, your ticket into the Parks, and even a payment method. If you've checked in ahead of time, you continue directly to your room without stopping at the front desk. Disney delivers your bags from the luggage pickup at the airport within an hour after your arrival.

Soon you'll be at the Parks or the pool, enjoying your stay. The Parks are massive and filled with people happy to enjoy Walt Disney World. You'll see all types of people here from all over the world. The magic of Disney overtakes them, and they instantly act happier than maybe they would at Walmart or the grocery store. Walt Disney World is a different place, and while it's not cheap, they give you countless memories for your dollar!

The employees of Walt Disney World are also generally friendly and have been properly coached to show you a good time. They keep the Parks and Hotels especially clean, setting the WDW Resort apart from the typical feel of a carnival or other theme parks. You and your family or group will feel safe and welcome everywhere you go. There are several delicious items to eat throughout the Resort as well as picturesque scenes that come to life before your eyes.

Walt Disney World's four main Parks have completely different feels as they transport you into their themes. The Magic Kingdom has all of the classic Disney rides from Peter Pan's Flight to Pirates of the Caribbean. The iconic Cinderella Castle also serves as a centerpiece in the magic-filled Park. Epcot is massive with futuristic rides and delicious world cuisine. It won't feel as "Disney" to you like the Magic Kingdom does, but adults will love it for the mature atmosphere. Hollywood Studios is a place for teens and Star Wars fans, as it's filled with movie-themed thrill rides. Disney's Animal Kingdom will transport you into the wilds of Africa and Asia where you'll see breathtaking animals and adventure on stunning thrill rides. There's no place in the world like the Animal Kingdom, and Disney's attention to detail has never been so flawless.

You'll also notice that there is *a lot* to do on your vacation. Within the Resort, there are nearly countless activities and attractions, while outside of the Resort there are several other amusements. You could be tempted to visit Universal Studios in Orlando to see Harry Potter or visit a local attraction like Gatorland–and we recommend it!

You'll see the sights, feel the magic, and live instant memories on your trip. Walt Disney World is the perfect place for those looking to get away, no matter the style. There are world-class rides, stunning shows, fantastic fireworks, beautiful hotels, boat rides, unforgettable dining experiences, relaxing spas, sparkling pools, and even golf courses. Walt Disney World has it all, and we are thrilled that you're planning a vacation!

Why You Need This Guidebook

Truthfully, you'd need to stay an entire month (or more) to do everything in Walt Disney World – it's *that* massive. Think of it as a playground for the whole family, where you'll feel safe, accommodated, and in awe as you make your adventure through the Magic Kingdom and beyond. However, as there is so much to do in Disney World, people often wonder: where do I start? Where should I stay? How long should I stay? Is this going to cost me an arm and a leg?

That's where we come in! At Magic Guidebooks, we are more than just some people who write about Disney and other theme parks–we love them! Better yet, we visit all of the time and know the ins and outs of theme park travel. Not only can we help make your vacation more enjoyable, but we can save you time waiting in lines, money on travel, tickets, and hotels. We also recommend the best of where to eat, how to get from place to place, and where to stay.

So, how do we do it? Why is this guide important? We're glad that you asked! As you read this guidebooks, we'll show you all of the tips, tricks, and secrets to maximize your vacation! We've done Disney World on the cheap and never felt like we were uncomfortably frugal. With careful planning and our help, you can have the time of your life with your family and build everlasting memories!

Chapter Two

Words and Phrases for the WDW Resort

Introduction

If you are new to the Disney theme parks or just haven't been in some time, you'll instantly notice the vibrant lingo that arises at the resort. Most of the time these come from well-seasoned guests and Disney employees (known as cast members). Sometimes they will say something like "Snow White is a classic dark ride" and if you're not up on the knowledge, you might feel lost at the start. Whether you're talking to a fellow guest, cast member, or reading signs by rides, it helps to know the terms first.

We have our own terms that we frequently use throughout this book. They are fairly intuitive, but so that we are all on the same page (ha! – we used a book pun), we invite you to familiarize yourself with the section to help with reading this guide.

Disney World: Words and Phrases

The Walt Disney World Resort – The area that encompasses all of its theme parks (Magic Kingdom, Epcot, Disney's Hollywood Studios, Disney's Animal Kingdom, and the water parks), the Walt Disney World hotels, the Disney Springs shopping area, parking lots, and more.

Cast Member – A term for all Disney employees. They often wear themed costumes when they work in the Resort, but the behind-the-scenes employees will typically wear business casual or engineering jumpers.

MagicBand – This amazing (and stylish) piece of technology allows WDW hotel guests to do it all with a simple bracelet. The MagicBand allows you to unlock the door of your hotel room, use it as your ticket into the theme parks, activate your FastPass+, and even purchase with it!

Park Hopper – A ticket that allows you to visit multiple parks, as many times as you'd like during that day. You can purchase Park Hopper tickets for WDW that will allow you to hop between the four theme parks, while others allow you to visit the water parks in addition to the theme parks.

FastPass+® – Said "Fast Pass Plus", it's an easy and free way to cut the lines! FastPass is your way to pre-reserving your tickets online up to 60 days before your vacation begins. The "Plus" comes from the adopted system of being able to swipe your MagicBand to activate your FastPass. It's *really* cool!

PhotoPass and Memory Maker – a paid Disney service to have professional photographers take your picture around the WDW Resort. We *highly* recommend adding this feature so that you can download quality photos when you get home or on your mobile device!

Single Rider Line – A fast way to get on the rides as long as you don't mind riding by yourself.

My Disney Experience – WDW's stunning app that works with your phone or tablet. You can change FastPass+ reservation times, schedule and check dining reservations, see line wait times, and much more!

Extra Magic Hours – Special extended hours for WDW Resort Hotel guests. You may enjoy getting into the parks early or stay after they are closed to enjoy the attractions. These hours change daily, so check the WDW website to see which times will give you the most enjoyment.

"Dark Ride" – An indoor ride where the vehicle is guided along a track. Typically, these are family-friendly rides like "it's a small world" and "They also have air conditioning to escape the heat on hot days!

Disney Dining Plan – Pre-purchased meal plans to select eateries around the Walt Disney World Resort.

Passholders – Those who purchased Annual Passes. Typically, Disneyland Annual Passholders call themselves just "passholders", while Walt Disney World Resort Passholders will call themselves "WDW Passholders".

3D – The use of 3D glasses during the ride or attraction.

4D – The use of 3D glasses with added effects like splashing water and rumbling seats.

Animatronic – Robotics brought to life for music and narration, typically used in stage shows and rides.

Closed for Refurbishment – No one likes seeing this sign as it means that the ride is closed for restoration. Some refurbishments can last a couple of days, while others have lasted two years. The Walt Disney World Resort plans their refurbishments carefully and will post these on the attraction schedule: https://disneyworld.disney.go.com/attractions

Rope Drop – The ceremony that begins minutes before the Park opening. These are sometimes short shows or a simple announcement.

WDW – The Walt Disney World Resort. By this, we mean the entire resort from theme parks to hotels to Disney Springs and more.

*MK – The Magic Kingdom. It's our little shortcut that we don't use very often, but it sometimes comes in handy.

*DHS – Disney's Hollywood Studios.

*FW – Stands for Future World which is part of Epcot (and Epcot doesn't have an acronym because, well, isn't it short enough?)

*AK – Disney's Animal Kingdom. This is just the park (not the Animal Kingdom Lodge), but it's the official WDW shortcut so most use it instead of DAK.

MGM – some people still call Disney's Hollywood Studios by its old name. MGM Studios and Disney's Hollywood Studios were fairly similar and many of the same attractions still exist, so it's understandable why people want to get nostalgic with this.

*We don't use these in this guide, but they are found around the WDW Resort.

Contact Information

Here are a list of phone numbers and websites to call for Walt Disney World booking and information. These are the official contact channels for Disney. We recommend booking online instead of calling because wait times can be long with WDW (and often the automated phone line doesn't tell you how long the wait will be). If you feel it's necessary to speak with a cast member, they are very friendly, courteous, and knowledgeable. However, keep in mind that they are sales people and they might be so friendly that you end up buying more than you bargained for!

General – Visit for booking and reservations.
www.DisneyWorld.com

Hotel Reservations
(407) 939-1936
https://disneyworld.disney.go.com/resorts

Disney Dining – Book your restaurant reservations in advance.
(714) 781-DINE
https://disneyworld.disney.go.com/dining

Ticket Booking – Book your tickets in advance.
(407) 939-7679
https://disneyworld.disney.go.com/tickets
Existing Tickets: (407) 939-7523

Group Reservations – For 10 or more guests.
(407) 939-1942
https://disneyworld.disney.go.com/tickets

Help with My Disney Experience, MagicBands, and FastPass+
(407) 939-4357

Annual Passholders
(407) 560-7277
https://disneyworld.disney.go.com/passes

Cirque du Soleil La Nouba Reservation
(407) 939-1929
https://disneyworld.disney.go.com/entertainment/disney-springs/cirque-du-soleil-la-nouba/

Other Booking Websites with Discounts

DisneyRewards.com – If you have a Disney Visa® Card, earn points and claim special rewards.

Orbitz.com/deals – For special promotions (look for codes up to 15% Off hotels).

Bookit.com/coupon-codes – Search here for discounts on flights, hotels, and ticket bundles.

Amextravel.com – If you have an American Express Card, this can save you, plus earn more rewards.

AAA.com – Members of the American Automobile Association receive special discounts on tickets and hotels.

Words and Phrases for this Guide

We pride ourselves on insider information and are happy to share it with you in the guide.

Look of the words: ★ **Magic Tips** ★ in throughout the chapters. These are special tips and secrets from our personal experience after frequently visiting the Walt Disney World Resort. Magic Tips are designed to:

• Save time waiting in lines for rides and character greetings
• Get the best viewing areas for shows and parades
• Save money booking, etc.

Ride Levels by Interest and Age

Everyone – Perfect for anyone of all ages, even many Thrill Riders enjoy these attractions.

Family – Suited for anyone of all ages, both kids and adults. However, these rides may not interest Thrill Riders.

Kids – Children ages 6-9.

Young Kids – Children 2-5.

Tweens – Children ages 10-12.

Teens – Young people ages 13-17.

Adults – People ages 18+ (we often specify typical age recommendations, those not everyone will fall under these)

Thrill Riders – Those looking for the maximum thrill of the rides. Whether it's a ride with loops like the Rockin' Rollercoaster or the high-dropping Tower of Terror, we guide you to the biggest thrills of the WDW Resort!

Chapter Three
When to Visit

Visiting in 2017

Walt Disney's vision of his parks is that they would be changing all of the time. From new attractions to hotels and dining experiences, the Walt Disney Resort is packed full of things to do. However, as millions flock to the mega-theme park each year, they'll be expecting the classic old as well as the brand new. The Walt Disney World Resort has been gearing up for 2017 for quite some time. Most notably (and anticipated) is the Pandora–The World of *Avatar*. Based on the James Cameron film, Disney is finalizing their enormous expansion to the Animal Kingdom park. Pandora will have the magic of the movies with glowing and floating worlds, new rides, and, of course, blue aliens.

But that's not all! 2016 launched some dazzling new attractions, and now that their highest buzz is over–it's your turn to enjoy the shorter lines!

New Attractions

Pandora–The World of Avatar

As we mentioned above, Disney and James Cameron set out to recreate the breathtaking world of the film series, *Avatar*. Set to open sometime in 2017 (we'd like to be more specific, but we can only speculate summer or fall), Pandora will be home to two new rides and several original attractions. When construction began on this land in 2014, park attendees could already see how massive it would be. Set over 12-acres, Pandora will be home to the iconic, blue-costumed characters, holograms, rides, dining experiences and more.

So far, Disney has announced two rides. The first will be a thrill ride where guests ride over the terrain of Pandora on a mountain banshee. The second will be a family-friendly boat ride at night where guests will see plants and animals that come to life in the bioluminescent world of Pandora. There is also rumored to be a "mess hall" type eatery, several shops, and animatronics for guests to interact with. We're excited to see Pandora come to life in 2017 and you should be, too! Both Disney and James Cameron promise that there will be nothing else like it on the planet–or any other!

Ride the New 2016 Attractions with Shorter Lines

In 2016, the Walt Disney World Resort launched popular new attractions like Epcot's *Frozen Ever After*. The craze was so intense at Epcot to lines so long that WDW had to limit riders to those with FastPasses. In fact, some people waited over five hours in long, hot lines just to ride.

Luckily, in 2017, you'll miss that initial craze. While the excitement of the ride will still be there, the lines will have diminished to something less intimidating. However, if you want to ride Frozen Ever After, we still highly recommend using your FastPass+ to reserve your spot in advance.

Beat the Crowds Before Star Wars Land

Star Wars is coming to the Walt Disney World Resort in the largest way imaginable. Several acres of the Hollywood Studios theme park have gone under construction to make way for likely the most-anticipated themed land since the Wizarding World of Harry Potter at Universal Orlando.

Star Wars Land (which is just a code name because Disney hasn't announced the official title yet) isn't set to open until around 2020. However, we don't recommend waiting until then. WDW has so much to offer that it'll blow your socks off! Visit now before the insane crowds take over during the Star Wars Land launch. Plus, there are plenty of Star Wars-themed attractions at Hollywood Studios like Star Tours the ride and the Jedi Training: Trials of the Temple.

When to Visit the
Walt Disney World Resort

Wanting to go to Walt Disney World is easy– planning *when* to go can be a whole other animal! As we've said before, there's *so* much to do at WDW that it can feel impossible to wrap your mind around the seemingly limitless possibilities. We completely understand your headache!

Depending on the dates you choose, whether it's the Awaken Your Summer events, the Halloween themes in the fall, the Food and Wine Festival at Epcot, or Disney's holiday events, there are several unique attractions in store. In short, whether you have a set of dates in mind or you're looking for the best times to go–we're here to help.

We've picked up TONS of useful tips for you during our vacations, our friends' vacations, and by talking to the cast members. This is one of our most vital chapters as we walk you through how to plan your amazing WDW vacation.

In this chapter, we will walk you through the choices of travel and our recommendations for saving time and money. Choosing a time for your vacation may not be entirely up to you. It could depend on your work schedule, your travel schedule, or your children's vacation days from school. Whether you have flexible travel days or not, we have laid out a month-by-month breakdown of what to expect when you visit WDW. We also give you tips on how to avoid the long lines and more to save you time and make your stay a magical one!

Most Recommended Travel Months

There are times when the WDW Resort isn't as crowded (or hot) as others. This is usually when the kids are in school or the holidays are nowhere in sight. Yet, these are the best times to see the resort in its full glory, without the packed parks. To see our full descriptions of these months, continue reading the rest of this chapter.

1. **September** – Summer continues throughout September in Central Florida. Expect hot days and far less crowds than in June, July, and August. Halloween decorations will spread throughout the Magic Kingdom most of the month. Mickey's No-So-Scary Halloween Party also premieres. While the weekends can get a bit packed, the weekdays have the thinnest crowds.

2. **October** – The WDW parks continues to come alive during Halloween with typically perfect weather. Decorations, desserts, special rides, and Mickey's Not-So-Scary Halloween Party await you! Like in September, the weekdays are the best time to book your reservations to avoid the local crowds who come for the Halloween décor (especially at the Magic Kingdom). Expect warm, humid weather for most of the month.

3. **February** – The WDW Resort typically has fewer crowds at this time, though weekends can be busier. Still, we find that this is one of the better months if you are looking for cooler weather and thinner crowds.

Least Recommended Travel Months

1. **July** – Massive crowds from all over the world flood WDW. Expect long lines, and the hottest, most humid weather of the year.
2. **December** – While park guests are treated to the holiday decorations, treats, and special rides, the crowds are some of the most massive. If you must go in December, we recommend the first week.
3. **June** – Similar to July with the crowds, but June doesn't get as busy until after the first week (though that can be busy for many other reasons like graduation parties). Keep in mind that the weather is blazing hot in Central Florida at that time.

More Dates to Consider

1. **Weekdays:** This might not seem like much of a secret, but weekdays are the best times to plan trips to the more popular parks like the Magic Kingdom and Disney's Animal Kingdom. If you must go on a weekend date, we would recommend saving Hollywood Studios and Epcot for those dates, since those parks don't attract as many visitors.
2. **Marathons**: Many vacation planners don't even consider one of the *run*Disney marathons. *run*Disney is an awesome event (with an extra fee) for runners to marathon around the resort. Though these take place in

the early hours on the weekend, the crowds flock to the parks afterward. Sometimes guests will stay for a few days after the run, making it extra crowded on dates you might not otherwise think would be packed. RunDisney.com has released some of the 2017 dates already, and here they are:

> January 4th – 8th, 2017: Walt Disney World® Marathon Weekend
>
> February 23rd – 26th, 2017: Disney Princess Half Marathon
>
> April 20th – 23rd, 2017: Star Wars Half Marathon – The Dark Side
>
> November usually has a marathon on the first weekend at WDW that is TBA for 2017.

If you want to participate in the marathon, visit: rundisney.com for information. To avoid the crowds, plan your stay after the marathon. Many guests report the week after the marathon to be the least crowded dates to visit!

3. **Holidays:** These are usually the dates that families all over the world have available for vacations and that's why they can be some of the most packed. The Resort is open every day, including holidays, and many people assume that it won't be busy–but it will!

The order of the busiest holidays:

- Christmas (all week)
- New Year's (all week)
- Thanksgiving (all week)
- Easter (all week)
- The 4th of July (all week)
- Memorial Day weekend
- Labor Day weekend
- Martin Luther King Jr. weekend
- Presidents' Day weekend
- Columbus Day
- Veteran's Day weekend
- Mother's Day and Father's (more crowded on Mother's Day)

Are you planning to be at the resort during one of our least recommended months? Don't worry! This guide will help you avoid those long lines.

Be sure to follow one of our pre-planned attraction lists–we use them ourselves and they can save you hours of time waiting in lines (or avoid them altogether). Tips for beating the crowds are at the end of this chapter.

Theme Park Breakdown

Magic Kingdom
This is Walt Disney World's most crowded theme park. During the holidays and weekends, this park is a crowd favorite and draws the most visitors. In fact, the Magic Kingdom pulls in roughly 20 million visitors a year, doubling the number of guests for Disney's Animal Kingdom.

Epcot
Built over a decade after the Magic Kingdom in 1982, Epcot is one of Walt Disney World's most iconic parks. With a world-travel theme and massive, golf ball-like centerpiece, Epcot brings in over 11 million visitors annually. Epcot is popular for its food and unique attractions like Soarin' Around the World and the new Frozen Ever After ride. Epcot picks up at night with locals looking to drink along it's beautiful lake. We expect Epcot to be even more popular in 2017.

Disney's Animal Kingdom
With popular rides like Expedition Everest, stunning shows, and beautiful animals, AK is the third most popular destination (but nearly tied with Hollywood Studios). It's the resort's latest theme park, and it pulls in over 10 million visitors annually. We predict

that Animal Kingdom could surpass Epcot in popularity once the Avatar attraction opens later in the year.

Disney's Hollywood Studios

WDW never quite hit its expectations for success with its movie-themed park. However, it still pulls in over 10 million visitors a year, making it the least popular of the three main parks, and perfect for popular dates when guests might flood to the Magic Kingdom or Epcot.

Day Breakdown

These days always depend on the month, but this is a general idea of how to avoid the largest crowds. Also to consider are our theme park breakdowns. The Magic Kingdom tends to get the most packed on these dates, while Hollywood Studios and Animal Kingdom might not be as busy.

Sunday – Busy weekend crowds, but far less than Saturday.

Monday – Often these can be just as crowded as Sundays because people take off extra days to avoid weekend traffic. On Monday holidays, expect larger crowds, sometimes busier than weekends.

Tuesday – Our most recommended day for fewest crowds and the shortest lines.

Wednesday – Our second most recommended day for fewest crowds and shorter lines.

Thursday – Third most recommended day for fewest crowds.

Friday – Less busy in the morning, but busiest in the evening after school when the locals tend to visit. Epcot can be open later but swamped with Floridians looking for nightlife.

Saturday – By far busiest day at the resort. If you stay on a Saturday, make sure to use the FastPass+ system in advance to avoid the lines.

Best Days to Visit

• The 1st or 2nd weeks in February (especially Tuesdays and Wednesdays)
• The last week in January (unless it's near the Martin Luther King, Jr. Day Holiday on the 3rd Monday of January)
• 2nd week of September (the week after Labor Day)

★ **Magic Tip** ★
Walt Disney World's new tier pricing will be higher (Peak pricing) on more crowded days and lower (Value pricing) on less crowded days.

Month Breakdown

January

January is busy in the first two weeks, and generally less busy after that. The first week will be crowded from and filled with holiday rides, treats, music, and decorations lighting the resort.

Weather: mid-70°F during the day and chilly at night (sometimes in the 40°'s). The humidity is low.

Least Crowded Days: The last week in January

Most Crowded: The first two weeks (especially around New Years) and Martin Luther King Jr. Weekend (Friday through Monday). January 4th – 8th, 2017 for the Walt Disney World® Marathon Weekend.

Holiday Rides and Attractions:

1. "it's a small world" Holiday (Magic Kingdom)
2. Jingle Cruise, the Jungle Cruise Holiday (Magic Kingdom)
3. Meet Santa Claus (Disney Springs)
4. Holidays Around the World (Epcot)

5. A *Frozen* Holiday Wish (Magic Kingdom)
6. Wishes Nighttime Spectacular fireworks (Magic Kingdom)

New Year's Dining:
Enjoy special campaign dinners at the finer restaurants at the WDW resort's Signature Dining locations.

★ Magic Tips ★
1. Holiday rides typically continue through the first week of January.
2. WDW parks may have ride closures for refurbishments after the holiday decorations come down.
3. The hours may also be shorter after the holidays, so we recommend getting to the parks at opening so that you can get everything done.

February

Possibly the least crowded month to visit the WDW Resort. Like January, the weather is cooler, and some of the rides may be in refurbishment.

Weather: Mid-70°F during the day and chilly at night (low 50"'s). Also expect far less humidity than in the summer and fall. The humidity is low.

Least Crowded Days: Any week except near President's Day Weekend (Friday through Monday)

Most Crowded: President's Day Weekend (Friday through Monday). February 23rd – 26th, 2017: Disney Princess Half Marathon.

Mardi Gras: WDW will hold a Mardi Gras event on February 28th, 2017. Expect to see celebrations and delicious New Orleans food at the Magic Kingdom, Disney Springs, and Disney's Port Orleans Hotel.

★ **Magic Tip** ★

> The WDW theme parks may have more ride closures for refurbishments in February than other months.

March

March's popularity has increased recently as spring breaks spread throughout the month. If you visit in March, be sure to do so during the week, Tuesday through Thursday.

Weather: mid-70°F (21°C) during the day and chilly at night. However, March has been known to have occasional heatwaves, bringing the weather above 90°F (32°C). The humidity is medium.

Least Crowded Days: the first Tuesday, Wednesday, and Thursday of March.

Most Crowded: Last two weeks of the month.

Events:

Flower & Garden Festival (Epcot) – Bring in the spring with spectacular Disney-themed hedges and flower designs that will make your jaw drop!

St. Patrick's Day: On March 17th, come in green to the WDW resort for some fun, Irish treats:

1. Green beer cider at the United Kingdom Pavilion in Epcot
2. Chocolate Mint Cupcakes sold at various carts throughout the Resort theme parks.
3. Get a pair of St. Patrick's Day Mickey ears at the hat shops in Disney Springs, Hollywood Studios, and the Magic Kingdom's Le Chapeau on Main Street.

★ **Magic Tip** ★

> Like February, The WDW theme parks may have some ride closures for refurbishments. Usually, these are far less than in January and February.

April

With spring breaks continuing through April, the end of the month tends to be the least crowded. We love visiting in April because the weather feels a lot more manageable (though it may not be very ideal for the water parks). Also there usually isn't very much humidity in the air. Lately, WDW has been more crowded in April. We believe that this is because of schools changing their spring break schedules.

Weather: Low-80°F during the day and cooler at night (mid-60°). The humidity is medium.

Least Crowded Days: The last two weeks of the month.

Most Crowded: First two weeks of the month. April 20th – 23rd, 2017 for the Star Wars Half Marathon.

Events: *Flower & Garden Festival* (Epcot) continues throughout April.

May

Spring at WDW is beautiful and hot almost from the start. To most, it will feel like the Floridian summer has begun. Storms tend to pick up during this time and it might rain during the day for an hour or so. However, the rain is tropical and WDW is set up for the short showers, so it shouldn't put a damper on your vacation.

Weather: Mid-70°F (21°C) during the day and sometimes chilly at night. The humidity is medium/high.

Least Crowded Days: The first two weeks of the month.

Most crowded: Memorial Day weekend (Friday through Tuesday).

Events:

•*Flower & Garden Festival* (Epcot) continues through Memorial Day weekend.

•*Disney Gay Days* runs from May 30 - June 5th, 2017. See June for details.

June

The warm June weather perfectly suits the WDW Resort.

Weather: Mid-80°F (27°C) during the day. Typically keeps warm at night. The humidity is medium/high.

Least crowded days: Tuesday, Wednesdays, and Thursdays and the first week of the month.

Most crowded: The last week of the month.

Events:

• *Sounds Like Summer Concert Series* – Bands and musicians take over Epcot's World Showcase as they perform covers of your favorite songs and tributes to your favorite artists. The 2017 dates haven't been announced yet, but Sounds Like Summer usually runs from the first week of June through the middle of July.

• *Gay Days* runs from May 30 – June 5th, 2017. A massive, unofficial event for LGBT families and singles to wear red in the parks. Visit www.gaydays.com for more information about the week of events.

July

The weather heats up (often, unbearably so) and crowds from all over the world venture into the WDW Resort during July. Even though July is crowded, it does make a great opportunity to visit the water parks and ride the many water-themed attractions, like Splash Mountain, throughout the parks.

Weather: Low-90°F during the day, but the humidity can make July feel even warmer. The weather typically stays warm and humid at night. The humidity is high.

Least Crowded Days: Tuesday, Wednesdays, and Thursdays (unless one is July 4th)

Most Crowded: July 4th

Events:

Sounds Like Summer Concert Series – Bands and musicians take over Epcot's World Showcase through the middle of July. See June for more details.

Fourth of July "Concert in the Sky" – Stunning nighttime fireworks all around the Magic Kingdom.

★ **Magic Tips** ★

Florida is hot during this time, so you'll need plenty of water! Bottles at the WDW Resort can cost up to $4.00! To avoid paying these high prices, you can pack your own. Just make sure that the bottles are sealed before you enter the Parks.

Note:

As we've said before, July is the busiest month. If you are planning to visit during this time, see our tips for beating the crowds at the end of this chapter.

August

Just when you think Florida couldn't get any hotter than in July, August comes around. This is most likely the hottest month all year round. The weather continues to heat up even more in August as crowds continue to pour in until school begins around mid-August. However, August rarely feels as crowded to us as July does, so if you want to get away during the summer, this is the month to pick.

Weather: Mid-90°F (32°C) during the day with usually near 100% humidity. Nights are sometimes just as warm and balmy. Showers typically occur once a day for an hour or two, but the queues for most rides have coverings. The humidity is very high.

Least Crowded Days: Tuesday, Wednesdays, and Thursdays and the last two weeks of the month.

Most Crowded: The first 2 weeks of the month.

★ **Magic Tips** ★

Don't forget the water! Bring your own sealed bottle!

September

More hot weather typically all month long with Halloween rides and treats beginning after labor day.

Weather: Low-90°F during the day and humid. Typically keeps very warm at night. The humidity is very high.

Least Crowded Days: Tuesday, Wednesdays, Thursdays, and Fridays (except for Mickey's Not-So-Scary Halloween Party nights). See October for details on this event.

Most Crowded: Labor Day weekend.

Special Days: *Epcot's Food & Wine Festival* (Mid-September through Mid-November) – Enjoy tasty meals and drinks from all around the world in this unique and popular attraction. If you are a foodie, we highly recommend coming around this time. We recommend visiting other parks during the day and heading to Epcot at night. Make your dinner reservations early so that you can taste the world!

October

October is a favorite time of ours at the WDW Resort! The weather cools down (though it can still feel like summer) as the Halloween party kicks into full gear.

Weather: High-80°F during the day, cools a bit at night. The later you go in October, the more likely tropical storms can come into play. If you are planning a visit, we recommend somewhere in the first couple of weeks. The humidity is very high.

Least Crowded Days: Tuesday, Wednesdays, and Thursdays

Most Crowded: Halloween and Mickey's Not-So-Scary Halloween Party on select dates.

Halloween at the Magic Kingdom:

Mickey's Halloween party begins in the Magic Kingdom! A perfect time to dress in costume (all ages) and get some treats. Many adults love visiting as much as the kids because they can finally wear their costumes into the park (Disney has a ban on anyone over 13 from entering the park dressed as a character for safety reasons). You must purchase a separate ticket for this event. See WaltDisneyWorld.com for dates (they are usually not released until Spring, but often fall on the weekends and select other dates in September and October).

Halloween Attractions (during Halloween Parties only):

    • *Hocus Pocus* **Villain Spelltacular** – The best of Disney Villains take over the Magic Kingdom from Maleficent to the Sanderson Sisters.

    • **Parade and Fireworks** – See the nighttime stunning parades and spectacular fireworks starring Disney Villains and your favorite characters dressed in costume!

Decorations – See Mickey-shaped pumpkins, try delicious treats, and see your favorite characters dressed in their Halloween costumes!

Halloween Dining – Enter one of these dining areas for a Halloween-themed dining experience.

We highly recommend a reservation first at https://disneyworld.disney.go.com/dining.

    – Be Our Guest in Fantasyland (our top choice!)
    – Cinderella's Royal Table in Fantasyland
    – Crystal Palace (character buffet) in Main Street, U.S.A.

Special Days:
•*Epcot's Food & Wine Festival* (Mid-September through Mid-November) – See September for details.
★ **Magic Tip** ★
Mickey's Not-So-Scary Halloween Party can be packed! To avoid some of these crazy times, book your tickets during the first half of the event dates, preferably in September.

November

The holidays begin mid-November at the WDW Resort. Expect larger crowds beginning Veterans Day and forward.
See for December for WDW Holiday details.
Weather: High-70°F during the day, cools at night to High-50°F. The humidity is medium.
Least Crowded Days: The first week of the month.
Most Crowded: Veteran's Day weekend and Thanksgiving week. The first weekend of the month for the marathon.
Special Days:
Epcot's Food & Wine Festival (Mid-September through Mid-November) – See September for details.
Thanksgiving at the Walt Disney World Resort
It's be a busy day, but there are plenty of places to enjoy a delicious turkey dinner (and many other Thanksgiving favorites). Restaurants all over the Resort offer fine meals:
Magic Kingdom – Liberty Tree Tavern.
Epcot – Akershus Royal Banquet Hall, Biergarten, Coral Reef, Le Cellier Steakhouse, Restaurant Marrakesh, Rose & Crown, Sunshine Seasons.
Disney's Hollywood Studios – 50's Prime Time Café
Disney's Animal Kingdom – Tusker House
Disney Springs – Raglan Road, Fulton's Crab House, Planet Hollywood, Portobello, Wolfgang Puck Café
Resort Hotel Dining:
• Disney's All-Star Sports – End Zone Food Court

- Disney's Animal Kingdom Lodge – Jiko, Sanaa
- Disney's Beach Club – Cape May Café
- Disney's Boardwalk Resort – Flying Fish Café, Trattoria al Forno
- Disney's Caribbean Beach Resort – Shutters at Old Port Royale
- Disney's Contemporary Resort – California Grill, Chef Mickey's, The Wave
- Disney's Fort Wilderness Resort – Mickey's Backyard Thanksgiving Feast, Trail's End Restaurant
- Disney's Grand Floridian – Citricos, Grand Floridian Café, Narcoossee's, Victoria and Albert's
- Disney's Old Key West Resort – Olivia's
- Disney's Polynesian Resort – Kona Café
- Disney's Port Orleans Resort – Boatwright's Dining Hall (Riverside)
- Disney's Saratoga Springs Resort – The Turf Club Bar & Grill
- Walt Disney World Dolphin and Swan Hotels – Garden Grove, Fresh Mediterranean Market, Il Mulino, Todd English's Bluezoo
- Disney's Wilderness Lodge – Artist Point, Whispering Canyon Café
- Disney's Yacht Club – Captains Grille, Yachtsman Steakhouse

More than any other time of the year, we recommend a reservation, otherwise you may not get a chance: https://disneyworld.disney.go.com/dining.

December

The holidays are in full gear at the WDW Resort. See decorations all around with special treats, fun holiday-themed rides, and a chance to meet Santa Claus!

Weather: Low-70°F during the day, cools at night to Low-50°F. The humidity is low.

Least Crowded Days: The first week of the month.

Most Crowded: The last two weeks, especially Christmas Day and New Year's Eve.

Holidays at the WDW Resort

See the glittering lights decorating the WDW Resort. From magnificent Christmas trees to endless strings of lights and ornaments, you'll be in awe of the resort's holiday transformation around the resort.

Holiday Rides and Attractions:

- Mickey's Very Merry Christmas Party (Magic Kingdom) – Mickey and his friends (and Santa!) bring their Christmas spirit with special costumes, shows, fireworks, and even snow! Like Mickey's Halloween event, this is a night with a separate admission cost. Once you see Cinderella's Castle lit in magical, icy blue, you'll be glad that you came!

- "Jingle Cruise" (Magic Kingdom) – The Jungle Cruise get a Christmas layover with holiday humor and decorations around the riverboat ride.

- "it's a small world" holiday – See the wondrous holidays celebrated all around the world set to holiday music.

- A Christmas Fantasy Parade (Magic Kingdom) – Mickey, Santa, Disney Princesses celebrate Christmas aboard stunning floats.

- Meet Santa Claus in Disney Springs (and the Magic Kingdom) and greet Mickey and his friends in their holiday clothing.

- Holidays Around the World (Epcot) – From stunning fireworks displays at night to the holiday traditions from Epcot's 11 countries, you'll feel the magic of the holidays! There is also a Candlelight Processional with a massive orchestra and choir.

- A *Frozen* Holiday Wish (Magic Kingdom) – Mickey's Very Merry Christmas party celebrates with the wintery fun of

Frozen. See your favorite characters and sing along with them during this nighttime show.

- <u>Wishes Nighttime Spectacular Fireworks</u> (Magic Kingdom) – Feel the magic of the holidays with Disney's unique wishes fireworks display, hosted by your favorite characters!

Epcot Holiday Treats

Tour around the Epcot World Showcase and taste the delicious holiday cuisine of nearly a dozen countries!

- American Adventure – Gingerbread and eggnog
- Canada – Pecan maple bark
- China – Kaikouxiao, a type of fried cake
- France – Buche de Noel au Chocolate with cinnamon ice cream and caramelized pecans
- Germany – Artisanal cheese plate
- Italy – Prosecco sparkling wine
- Japan – Kurobute pork sausage served with pineapple and onions
- Mexico – Sweet tamales
- Morocco – Honey chocolate baklava
- Norway – Frozen Peppermint Trifle
- United Kingdom – Hot applejack cider Or cruise over to the Future World for a Mickey Santa Hat Cupcake!

Holidays at Hollywood Studios and Animal Kingdom:

These Parks are light with their decorations, however, they both place fantastic Christmas trees in the center hubs. Look for unique ornaments hanging from the branches. Hollywood Studios does a holiday fireworks show. Animal Kingdom uses African vibes to decorate their tree, giving it an exquisite, animal-themed appearance.

Holiday Dining Events

- Nearly every resort hotel dining features holiday treats from Mickey caramel apples to holiday macaroons. With Christmas décor all around (even on the cups!), the holidays are a treat for your sights and your taste!
- Epcot's Promenade Refreshments hosts annual Christmas quick service savory treats like a turkey sweet potato waffle, holiday teas, hot chocolates, and ciders.

Tips for Beating Crowds on Busy Days

1. **Use FastPass+** – As early as possible (beginning 60 days ahead of your reservation), get passes to the rides that you want to experience.

2. **Be Early** – Get to the park at open before the crowds. If you are staying at a Walt Disney World Resort hotel you can get "Extra Magic Hours" which allow you to arrive early (or stay late) on selected days. Check the WDW website for hours: https://disneyworld.disney.go.com/calendars

3. **Plan Your Day** – Follow one of our pre-set day plans (or make your own). We use these planners ourselves and it will save you hours of time waiting in lines (many times you'll miss the long lines altogether).

4. **Book Dining Reservations Early** – We can't stress this enough. Many of the more popular restaurants will be booked full, like the Beauty and the Beast Be Our Guest dining experience in the Magic Kingdom. Luckily, WDW allows you to book your reservations 180 in advance!
   Book Early: https://disneyworld.disney.go.com/dining
   or call (407) 939-3463

5. **Avoid Typical Meal Times** – If you don't have a restaurant reservation, these are the times to avoid on the busy days:
   a. Lunch: Dine before 11.30am and after 2.30pm
   b. Dinner: Dine before 5.00pm and after 7.30pm
6. **Plan Your Parks** – We recommend avoiding the Magic Kingdom and Epcot on the weekends as they can pull the most crowds. Instead, head over to Animal Kingdom or Hollywood Studios. If you can, it's best to save the Magic Kingdom and Epcot for the weekdays.
7. **You Might Have to Wait** – Waiting in line isn't the end of the world. Sometimes we all have to do it for the best attractions. The trick is to wait the *shortest* amount of time for the *fewest* rides possible. You can avoid the longest lines by following our planned out ride lists.
8. **Take a Break** – If you are feeling worn out, take a break at your hotel or visit Disney Springs for some shopping. If you're not near your resort hotel, head to the nearest one for dinner or to look around. The WDW Resort offers so many surprises that you might have blast drinking a cup of coffee while you listen to music near Starbucks rather than surrounded by a swarm of people. After you and your group have recharged, take a free bus back into the parks.

Chapter Four

Booking Your WDW Vacation

Introduction

We're going to be straight forward about booking: if you've never been to Walt Disney World, booking a vacation there can make you go crazy. Okay, not literally, but it can be a taxing event. While WDW is extremely helpful and their website (and third-party websites) have a bunch of cool pictures, they don't really give you a feel of what it's like to stay there or visit the Parks. There are dozens of choices in and out of the Resort, and they all seem to be fun and full of magic.

Depending on your plans, personality, and needs, some of the Resort Hotels will fit you better than others–that's where this chapter comes into play. Here, we outline how to save yourself money when booking so that you can pick your favorite hotel with ease (we get into the Hotel breakdown in another chapter).

You also might be wondering which Parks to check out and which ones you could afford to skip. If you are planning a week, we highly recommend getting a Park Hopper so that you can visit any location when you want (more on that later). Here is a breakdown of the Theme Parks we recommend, in order:

1. The Magic Kingdom – It's very similar to Disneyland in California, but it's the world's most visited theme park for a reason. With more attractions than anyone can do in a day, this is the classic resort location for anyone looking to have a magical time.

2. Disney's Animal Kingdom – If theme parks are your thing, there's nothing like Animal Kingdom. It's over 500 acres of rides, lush foliage, and exotic animals.

3. Epcot – This is one of those parks that doesn't look very good on paper as it does when you're there. The 21+ crowd will love Epcot for its food and adult beverages, while under-agers will be entranced by its unique rides

from the racing Test Track to the magical Frozen Ever After.

4. Disney's Hollywood Studios – Though we've placed Hollywood Studios last, it shouldn't be forgotten. There are dozens of attractions from stunning shows starring Indiana Jones or the characters from *Beauty and the Beast*, also thrilling rides like Twilight Zone Tower of Terror and the Rock 'n' Rollercoaster. However, with all of the construction for Toy Story Land and "Star Wars Land" you might feel that it wasn't worth taking an entire day.

5. The Water Parks – Again, just by putting these at the end of the list doesn't mean that they're not great. In comparison to the other unique Parks, these might be passible (especially since nearly every Resort Hotel has a pool and waterslide without the additional cost to use them). If you are deciding which of the two water parks to visit, we recommend Typhoon Lagoon since the attractions are generally more fun.

We find that people look to our guides to help make the right choices, avoid waiting in lines, and also how to save the most money. There are several tricks that we outline throughout this guidebook, and here we help you save money on your initial booking.

Tips for Before You Book

Pre-book your Flights, Hotel, and Transport:
The further out you book your vacation, the less expensive it tends to be. This is almost always true with flights, but the car rentals

and hotels sometimes have better deals that fluctuate. If you are booking with the WDW Resort, they give you lots of wiggle room. You can change your bookings to add more date or even completely change your hotel without penalty even days before your travel dates. However, if the price goes down or you cancel, you may have to pay a fee (usually around $50 for each package).

Fly into Orlando International Airport:

If you are planning to fly, we recommend Orlando International because it tends to be the least expensive and easiest to travel from. The airport is located right next to highways that will take you to WDW. We review more of that in the next chapter.

Bundle:

Sometimes purchasing a flight/hotel/car package from WaltDisneyWorld.com or third party travel website can save you a lot of money. If you collect points with airlines like Southwest or Alaska, you can get even better points with this.

Know the Ticket Pricing Structure:
- Park tickets vary in pricing for each day.
- Tickets are broken into 3 categories:

    Value: $97 (typically Monday – Thursday, not during holidays or summer)

    Regular: $102 (typically Friday – Sunday, not during holidays or summer)

    Peak: $114 (holiday weeks, summer, spring break)
- Park Hoppers – These allow you to visit any or all of the 4 Theme Parks in a single day (or days, depending how long you book). Park Hoppers are an extra $50 - $60 for a single day, or package. We highly recommend the Park Hopper option. Since the Parks stay open later, you can take a break in the middle and head out at night to Epcot or the Magic Kingdom for more fun. Park Hoppers can also include the water parks for an additional cost that is usually a very good deal.

- You can save on all parks by booking consecutive days. The difference between booking a 4-day pass and a 5-day pass is often only $20 per ticket.
- Visit: https://disneyworld.disney.go.com/tickets for specific pricing for the dates you've chosen.

   In this chapter, we outline how to save money on tickets, but for standard pricing, book at https://disneyworld.disney.go.com.

Booking Discounts

There are many ways to save on booking your stay at the WDW Resort. Some are better than others depending on the offer. Here are our most recommended choices based on how much they can save you:

Bookit.com **(877-742-9891)** – *highly recommended!*
- Perfect for flying/hotel packages with ticket options.
- Pros of Bookit.com:
   - Payment plans available with a down payment (no credit check required).
   - Often big discounts on flights and park tickets when you book a package.
   - WDW Resort Hotels Available (get all of the benefits including MagicBands and Extra Magic Hours even when you book through a 3rd party site).
   - We tend to notice that Bookit.com has a different selection of available hotel rooms than other 3rd party sites.
   - Lists WDW's "Good Neighbor Hotels" so you can see the closest hotels for what Disney recommends.

- ° Bundle park tickets for discounts. Save on multiday park hopper tickets and to other parks including Universal Studios Orlando and Islands of Adventure.
- ° Discounted car rental options and inexpensive travel insurance available.
- Cons:
  - ° When you just book a hotel without airfare, this website can sometimes be more expensive than other 3rd parties.
  - ° Some of the better deals cannot be cancelled.
  - ° Often the cancellation comes with a fee. Many other companies offer free cancellation without a fee. Bookit.com sometimes offers free cancellation, too.
  - ° Discount Code Link: www.bookit.com/coupon-codes

WaltDisneyWorld.com (407-939-1936)

- Check the website for discounts on hotels and more. Here you can book any of the Resort hotels, purchase Theme Park tickets, and add features like Disney Memory Maker.
- Summer Time (June – August) and Fall (September – October) typically have the lowest fares. However, WDW will offer discounts even for Spring and Winter getaways. Look for deals when booking on the website.
- When WaltDisneyWorld.com has sales, usually the 3rd party websites will as well.
- Benefits of booking at WaltDisneyWrold.com
  - ° Just put $200.00 down when you book for your entire package. The balance is typically due 30 days before your trip begins.
  - ° Typically, a larger selection of rooms that are not available on third-party sites (though the other way around can happen, too).
  - ° Bundle park tickets (though it doesn't save you any money this way).

- ◦ You can add flights, transportation, character dining, and tickets to Theme Parks and Water Parks.
- ◦ Knowledgeable Disney cast members will be able to answer any of your questions about the park over the phone or via online chat.
- ◦ WaltDisneyWorld.com often has flexible cancellation policies for full refunds.
- • Cons:
  - º No discounts on park tickets.
  - ◦ The travel insurance is a lot pricier than most 3rd party sites.
  - ◦ You may save money booking with 3rd party sites.

Special Discounts
Always check this link before booking to see if you're getting the best deal. This link provides discounts for Military, Group, and more:
https://disneyworld.disney.go.com/special-offers

Other great 3rd Party Sites:
Orbitz.com – *highly recommended!*
- ◦ Vacation packages available for Walt Disney World Hotels and other close resorts.
- ◦ Promo codes: www.orbitz.com/deals (often 15% off).
- ◦ Earn Rewards when you sign up for their discount plan.
- ◦ Note: We find that booking separate hotels on Orbitz.com and a separate flight on Southwest.com (or another airline) are the least expensive options.

Priceline.com
Great hotel selections and vacation packages on an easy to use site. It's hard to find promotional codes for Priceline, but they have great prices.

AAA.com, AmEx Travel, etc.:

There are almost countless other options. We've listed our favorites, but depending on your work discount or credit or club membership, you often can get discounted tickets. The best deals are typically a bundle of them together. Make sure that you check more than just one third-party site to ensure you are truly getting the best discount out there.

★ **Magic Tip** ★

Still can't decide between the places you really want to stay? Why not book both? We've done it before and it was a great idea. Disney allows for a smooth transition from one hotel to the next. If both of your hotels are in the WDW Resort, tell bell services that you need your bags transferred to your new hotel.

They will pick them up for you before you head to the Parks for the day and your bags will be waiting at your new hotel's bell services for when you arrive. You can still check in and out quickly online, so the process feels seamless. If you've book a flight, make sure to call the front desk to inform them that you will need Disney's Magical Express to pick you up and give them your flight information. They will print out a sheet to give to the bus driver for your departure.

Annual Passes

Annual Passes – The Walt Disney World Resort offers 3 annual passes for its theme parks. Platinum Passholders receive MagicBands as well as discounts on dining, merchandise, and Resort hotels. All Annual Passes are for ages 3 and up. To qualify, you must be either a resident of Florida (with documentation like a driver's license) or a Disney Vacation Club Package.

1. Disney Platinum Plus Pass ($829) – Visit any park on any day, including the water parks. Also gives admission to Disney's Oak Trail Golf Course and the ESPN Wide World of Sports Complex.

2. Disney Platinum Pass ($749) – Visit all 4 of the theme parks any day of the year, but not the water parks, golf course, or ESPN Sports Complex.

3. Water Parks ($115) – Visit the water parks any day of the year (that they are open). Does not include any additional discounts or access to other Parks.

More Information on Annual Passes:
https://disneyworld.disney.go.com/passes

Disney Vacation Club

We're only touching on this lightly because we feel that an entirely new book can be created based on the Disney Vacation Club. DVC members get access to special offers and point-based pricing for the WDW Resort, Disneyland Resort, Aulani in Hawaii, Disney Cruise Line and many other exciting Disney and non-Disney destinations around the world. Many people ask if it's worth it. There are a few things to consider before deciding to go with the Vacation Club:

1. It's not cheap. Disney is a premium company with premium prices, meaning that you will get the quality experience for the money that you pay.

2. How often do you plan to vacation at Walt Disney World? If you said every year or every other year, the DVC may be a great option for you that can save you money.

3. Many times the DVC doesn't feel worth it until pricing goes up in a few years. This means that you may see a wash at first (or close to it), but when the prices for Resort Hotels start to climb and your DVC points buy the same, you'll be happy that you went there.

If you are interested in joining the Vacation Club, we highly recommend checking out one of their presentations. They give you extra FastPass+ selections just for attending.

For more information, visit:

https://disneyvacationclub.disney.go.com

Chapter Five

Traveling to Walt Disney World

Introduction

With the planning out of the way, it's time to bring your vacation to the Walt Disney World Resort. Getting there doesn't have to be tricky, but if you don't plan correctly, it might feel like a mess. Contrary to what many believe, WDW is not exactly the heart of Orlando, Florida. The Resort is located in Lake Buena Vista, Florida... which is about 20 miles southeast of the Orlando International Airport.

It appears that most people who visit the Resort either drive or fly into Orlando International. If you have a family or three or more and live within a comfortable driving distance, then going by car might be your best bet. However, if you live on the other coast or the Midwest, driving might be a bit taxing. Thankfully, WDW has you covered no matter your form of transport. In fact, you can even arrive at the Resort via bus, train, shuttle, or even taxi!

When we visit WDW, we typically fly into Orlando International (though we have driven there before). Flying is great because as soon as you arrive, there are plenty of options to get to your hotel. If you've booked a WDW Resort Hotel, Disney's Magical Express is a free bus service that takes you to your Hotel. We enjoy the Magical Express because it's located inside of the airport and the staff is extra friendly. WDW even mails you Disney-themed luggage tags to strap to your belongings so that it's easy for you to load and unload.

The Magical Express feels like any other bus, but it has its Disney touches with cartoons playing on small television screens. If you have kids, it's a great way to distract them as their excitement builds for the destination. The downside to the Magical Express is that you have to drop others off at their neighboring Resorts first. Sometimes this can be a little annoying, especially after a day of travel. However, for a free transport, it saves you a lot more than if you opted for a private shuttle or car.

If you aren't staying at a WDW Resort Hotel, check with your hotel or vacation spot to see if they offer a shuttle. To better compete with Disney, they are often they are free. However, they tend to run less than the Magical Express, since those busses go all day and night. Otherwise, there are several options to get there.

We've tried the private car and the rideshare apps like Uber. These are nice because the drivers tend to know the areas very well and they get you quickly to your hotel without stopping anywhere else. Typically, we've saved about 10-15 minutes in travel time. Expect, however, to be charged anywhere from $30 or more each way. This is a standard price for these rideshare apps, and the private cars can cost up to $100. Whichever way you choose, we highly recommend planning ahead and having a back-up plan just in case. Taxis are always available in front of the airport to help get you to your destination. Just make sure to ask the driver if he or she has a flat fee.

If you are driving yourself, the coastal routes are extremely scenic. We even love driving up the middle and seeing Florida's flat, lush landscapes, many lakes, and even wildlife along the route. By the time that you get to the Resort, you'll be ready to hit the pool for relaxing–or the bed for some much-needed sleep. In this chapter, we review the several different methods of getting to the resort. How you get there is entirely up to you, but if you're feeling indecisive (or just need more information to choose), read thoroughly to get the best choices.

By Airline

If you aren't planning a road trip and live far away from the WDW Resort, flying will likely be your best option. While airlines can be expensive at times, there are several ways to save money:

1. Compare airlines to see the best pricing.
2. Check baggage fees and allowed carry-on items (we like Southwest because they give you 2 free checked bags). If

you live on the east coast, Spirit Airlines is an al-a-cart option that can save you hundreds of dollars, especially on last-minute flights.

3. Book early to get the best discounts.

Our Top Choice Airlines

Southwest

We love Southwest. If you grab their "Wanna Get Away" deals, you can score some really great rates. Southwest works perfectly if you book ahead. However, if you are late to the game, they can get pretty pricey. We love Southwest because the staff is friendly, the aircraft are generally comfortable for long flights, they include snacks and soft drinks for free, and you get 2 free checked luggage bags per person. This can be a *very* sweet deal if you plan on your Disney World vacation being longer than 5 days. This airline also does not charge for change fees, meaning, if you have to change your flight for whatever reason, you can do so without charge during an allotted time period. Because Southwest offers first-come-first-served seating, we highly recommend paying the extra money to get the "Early Bird" option. This will allow everyone in your party to pick seats together for your flight. You can also ask any of their helpful flight attendants to assist with seating your family together, though it can't be guaranteed.

Alaska

We also love Alaska. This is a great airline that is great with customer service. Book early enough and their rates are very affordable. Alaska gives you the free option to select your seat, but checked bags are often a moderately priced additional charge. They also offer free soft drinks and snacks for the flights. If you've never flown Alaska, we invite you to give them a try!

Delta

Delta is a premium airline that excels in what it does. While it's not as innovative with its deals as Southwest, it does deliver fantastic flights and aircrafts. This is usually our third choice above other airlines like United or American because of its quality. However, Delta is often more expensive that Southwest or Alaska.

Budget Options

Spirit Airlines

This airline is an a-la-cart, so the general price you see is just for a seat on the plane–everything else is an extra cost. The extra costs include: picking your own seat, checking a bag or putting a bag in the overhead compartment, drinks, and snacks. If you don't mind where you sit and that you only need to bring a personal item, Spirit can save you some big bucks. However, once you pick a seat and opt to bring another bag (even carry-on bags are extra), the prices begin to stack. Also, Spirit Airlines doesn't have much of a customer service department in our opinion. We've had an issue with a delayed flight and no one was there to assist at the gate. However, we've also had a good experience with them as well. Just understand that you usually get what you pay for and Spirit is no exception to that rule.

Frontier Airlines

Works similarly to Spirit and can get to be very pricey. We find that Spirit tends to have more comfortable seats than Frontier. If you're only on a two-hour flight or less, you may not mind.

We Post Fresh Discounts!

Want the best new deals? Visit our website and we'll keep you updates: www.magicguidebooks.com/waltdisneyworld

Flying into Orlando International

We recommend Orlando International because it tends to be the least expensive and easiest to travel from. The airport is located right next to highways that will take you to the Walt Disney World Resort. This is also the airport where Disney's Magical Express is stationed.

Disney's Magical Express

If you've opted to fly into Orlando International and you're staying at Walt Disney World Resort, you can take the Magical Express coach from the airport to your hotel. The Magical Express is a bus with service on the baggage claim floor in the airport. To reserve your spot, you need to opt in when making your reservation, giving your flight times (you can also add this information later).

During peak seasons, lines for the Magical Express can be long. However, most of the time, you'll only wait about 15 minutes, and 30 minutes maximum for you bus to arrive.

These are the reasons we love Disney's Magical Express:

1. It's included with your WDW Resort booking at no additional cost.
2. The bus is efficient, entertaining, and it doesn't cost the hefty fees of a taxi, Uber, or rental car.
3. It's air conditioned!
4. Before you arrive, Disney sends you free luggage tags with codes to your hotel (if you change hotels last minute, the tags still get to your hotel).
5. Conveniently located in the baggage claim area in the Orlando International Airport.
6. Comfortable charter bus seats.
7. Quick check-in using your Magic Band.

8. The bus has television screens that show fun things to do on your trip as well as Disney cartoons and quizzes.
9. Disney picks up your luggage for you at the airport and bell services deliver it straight to your hotel room.
10. The Magical Express drop your party off right in front of the lobby.
11. When you leave to return to the airport, the Magical Express will drop you off in the same location before you leave for your flight.

If the Magical Express doesn't sound amazing enough already, there's even more. If you are flying with Alaska, American, Delta, JetBlue, Southwest, or United, most WDW hotels will allow you to drop off your luggage and print your tickets for you inside of the hotel. It's fast and friendly service that takes a lot of the stress off of your departure. Keep in mind that the Magical Express picks up about 3 hours before your flight and that the Orlando International Airport lines can be long, even domestically.

★ Magic Tips ★

1. Have everyone in your party wear their Magic Band on the plane. You don't want to pack it away otherwise it's much harder to check in.
2. Your bags will get to your room *after* you check in (usually within an hour they arrive). Because of this, we recommend bringing anything you might need with you to the hotel.

By Car

Whether it's a road trip, staying in a neighboring city, or you live close enough to drive to the Resort, this can be a great method to take in the beautiful sights of Florida's wetlands before you head to the WDW Resort.

Car Rental: We recommend Enterprise.com or Dollar.com for car rental as they typically have great selection and the best pricing. Pre-booking before you arrive at the airport is advised.

★ **Magic Tip** ★

If you are just planning on staying at the WDW Resort, we don't recommend a rental car. Parking can cost daily at certain Resort hotels (like the Walt Disney World Swan and Dolphin), and there are free transports around the Resort. If, however, you plan on visiting Universal Studios or any other parts of Florida, it may be worth doing.

Popular Car Rental Companies:
- www.Enterprise.com: You can visit the company's website or see typically better deals on Priceline.com (or bundle with your airfare and hotel booking).
- www.Dollar.com: click the "specials" tab for deals.
- www.Budget.com: click the "deals" tab for offers.

By Bus

There are a few great options to take the bus to the Walt Disney World Resort. Here are a few reasons you may opt for the bus:
1. Saves Money – This is usually the top reason you might want to go with the bus. Airfare and the train can cost ten times the amount.
2. It's Relaxing – The bus can be a calming, easy way to travel from your home to WDW.
3. A Discount – Seniors and students can receive discounted rates on Greyhound.

We recommend Greyhound as our top pick for busses. They have a great reputation and are often the fastest way with the most options to get to Orlando. Keep in mind that the Orlando Bus Station is not near Orlando International or the Walt Disney World Resort. You'll need to take a private car into the Resort or to your hotel–and that might cost you a lot of money.

By Private Car App

With ride-sharing apps like Uber taking off, it may seem like a top choice. Uber offer private drivers in clean cars (these are not cabs). Here are a few ways you can book:

Uber (mobile application):

To download the application, open the App Store (Apple Devices) or GooglePlay Store (Android Devices) and search for "Uber" in the store.

- Many times you can only select an Uber Black car, which is a quality experience in a town car, but is also more expensive. A ride like this will be around $75-$90 each way (depending on traffic).
- Promo codes (typically only for first time riders):
    - Uber: uber.com/promo (often a free ride)
- When you are ready for your car to arrive, activate it on the app. The pickup spot is in the Express Pick-Up tunnel located on Level 1 (subject to change). The application should signal where to go. Your driver also will alert you when he/she has arrived.

Notes:

1. Uber doesn't require a tip and the drivers won't ask you for one (it's not customary as the diver gets a cut of each ride).
2. The estimated costs are just that–estimations. The time of day and traffic *does* matter. In the app you can select an estimated fare by entering your destination.

By Shuttle or Taxi

Hail a taxi in front of the airport and ask for a flat rate. The typical price is usually around $45 each way.

For a shuttle, we recommend Mears:
http://www.mearstransportation.com (they also have an app). They usually cost about $23 each way, per person. You can also pay up front for the round trip cost of $37 and they will pick you up from your hotel and return you to the airport at the end of your vacation.

Discount Code: WEB10 (to save 10%) with Mears.

Notes:
1. It is customary to tip your taxi driver 15–20%, depending on your experience with the route.
2. If you are planning on traveling outside of the WDW Resort (especially if you plan to visit Universal Studios Orlando), you may want to consider renting a car over getting a shuttle or taxi. It can save you a lot of money to rent a vehicle to make your family or group feel more comfortable.

By Train

Taking the train can a be relaxing and beautiful way to travel to the Walt Disney World Resort. The trains let out at the Orlando Station (or Kissimmee) and you will need to have a second transport from the train station to the resort which is roughly 20 minutes away by car. We recommend renting a car for the best value. Taxis work great, too.

Amtrak – Perfect for longer distances.
Website: www.Amtrak.com
Check the "Deals" tab for discounts.

Transport Inside of the Walt Disney World Resort

If you are staying off of the Resort property and haven't elected to rent your own car, many hotels will offer a free or paid shuttle to the Walt Disney World Resort. Once inside of the Resort, Disney offers a free bus transport to the hotels, Parks, and parking lots. These are clean, standard busses that run day and night. After 1AM, they will only service to the Disney World Hotels. Look for the Bus Stop signs outside of each Hotel, Theme Park, and Disney Springs. There are usually multiple locations outside of the gates from the Parks. The bus line you desire will have your location marked on the display in front of the bus. Sometimes you may have a stop or two before your destination.

We sort of have a love/hate relationship with the WDW bus system. On one hand, it's free and has excellent air conditioning. On the other, it can feel crowded at times and slow to arrive. Sometimes you have to do a bit of walking to get to your stop. We much prefer using the boats and the monorail system when they are available because they are much more enjoyable to ride. WDW also offers free ferries between some of the parks and Disney Springs as well as a monorail system around the Magic Kingdom Park and Epcot. The monorail takes you to Disney's Contemporary Resort, Disney's Grand Floridian, and Disney's Polynesian Village. The ferries travel to all of those locations with trips to many other resort hotels and to Disney Springs.

Want an Easy Way to Book?

We post all of these links on our website to make it easier for you: www.magicguidebooks.com/waltdisneyworld

Chapter Six

What to Wear and Bring - And What Not To!

Introduction

Now that you've planned your vacation, it's time to figure out what to wear! Luckily, this part is easy (and to experience theme park travelers, it's common knowledge). WDW is filled with people from all walks of life, style, and attitude. But everyone is there for the same reason: *to have fun!* The important thing is to be yourself!

Here we explain how to maximize your fun through comfortable clothing and bringing the right items. Did you know that a bottle of water at the WDW Parks can cost $3 or more? In this section, we review tips and tricks for a comfortable and cost-effective stay at the resort.

Note: Be aware that the WDW Resort inspects your bags before you enter the parks.

What to Wear and Bring

For a quick listing of these items, visit our website that you can order instantly for Amazon.com:
www.magicguidebooks.com/waltdisneyworld

1. **Comfortable Clothing** – Shorts, t-shirts, sneakers (trainers), and tank tops are seen all around the Resort for a good reason: they are comfortable. You'll be standing in the hot (and often humid) Florida sun all day, so we recommend that you dress comfortably.

2. **Hats and Sunglasses** – Again, the Floridian sun! It's a wonderful thing, but you don't want to get burned. Be careful of hats and sunglasses on rides (most high-speed attractions will have a compartment on the ride to store your items).

3. **Sunscreen** – Even on a cloudy day the ultraviolet rays from the sun can give you an uncomfortable burn. Be

careful and stay protected–you don't want to ruin your vacation by looking and feeling like a boiled lobster.

4. **Stroller** – Kids can get tired and WDW has zones to park these with attendants that watch them while you ride. You can bring your own or rent one at one of the parks. If you're even worried a little that your child may be too tired to walk around all day, it's best to use caution and set aside extra cash for a stroller rental. For longer stays, the WDW Resort gives a bit of discount.
Stroller Rental Cost:
Single – $15 per day / $13 for multi-day
Double Stroller – $31 per day / $27 for multiday
Disney Springs requires a $100 credit card deposit in addition to the daily cost. This is done for theft preventative reasons since anyone can walk in and out of Disney Springs and take the strollers they've rented.

5. **A Jacket or Sweater** – Even on a hot day the WDW Resort can get chilly at night. We highly recommend having a jacket or sweater to keep you warm.

6. **Water Bottles and Snacks** – You can save money (or help any picky eaters in your party) by bringing your own snacks. WDW will allow you to bring sealed bottles of water into the parks. Save yourself money and bring your own. If you don't mind fountain water, you can refill at water fountains near any restroom for free.

7. **Hand Sanitizer** – Though we know that science tells us not to use hand sanitizer on a daily basis, it's virtually a must-have at the Parks. Sometimes you've gone to the restroom a half hour before eating, and the lines are long. You'll likely touch handrails, seat cushions, and many other things that will require you to disinfect before eating.

8. **Extra Phone Charger and Waterproof Cellphone Bag** – If you have a smartphone, we highly recommend an extra

portable charger. We also recommend becoming familiar enough with your smartphone so that you can change on the battery-saver mode in the settings. This will prevent you from running out of juice too early while you take pictures and use the My Disney Experience app. Also, if you plan on riding the water attractions like Splash Mountain or Kali River Rapids, you're likely to get soaked. The last thing you want is to accidently drench your cellphone! We *highly* recommend the Frieq waterproof cellphone bags and we use them ourselves. They are often $9 or less and they come with a lanyard. The case is clear (so you can touch the screen and take photos). Since it's completely sealed, we've taken photos underwater and on the wettest rides without worrying about getting our phones drenched.

9. **A Standard Backpack** – Carry your items in one of these. Make sure it's not too large to fit on the rides. Also keep in mind that your bag will be checked by security before entering the park area. If you don't feel like lugging it around all day, rent a locker and store it in there.

10. **Money** – The WDW Resort accepts all major credit cards and cash. However, if you are staying at a WDW Resort Hotel, you can link your MagicBand to your credit card for easy paying.

11. **Identification** – For adults, make sure you plan on bringing your government-issued ID if you plan to drink alcoholic beverages. At times, you may be asked to present ID when purchasing at shops in Disney Springs.

12. **Water Resistant Clothing** – Even on the sunniest days, rainclouds can show up at WDW. Typically, the rain will last under two hours, but you don't want to wear something that can't get wet. Leave the suede shoes and stick to cotton shirts. Just in case you really don't want to

deal with the rain, this is what we recommend bringing with you:

   a. Compact Umbrella – On rainy days, this is very handy. Don't bring a full sized umbrella, as it won't fit on rides and will be difficult to carry around.

   b. Poncho – It might be a bit of a fashion *faux pas* to some, but a poncho could keep you and your belongings dry. Many visitors love wearing these for the water rides as well!

What *Not* to Wear or Bring

1. **Selfie Sticks** – It seems like it would be so much fun to take photos with one of these, but WDW bans them for the safety of other guests.

2. **Adult Costumes and Masks** – Children under 14 are allowed to wear costumes, but as not to trick people into thinking a non-cast member is a character, WDW bans these for adults. During Mickey's Not-So-Scary Halloween Party, you may dress in costume. For safety reasons, adults are not allowed to wear masks to the park.

3. **Skateboards, Rollerblades, Bikes, Roller skates** – WDW bans these for safety reasons. Even those skates that slide out from kids' shoes are banned. If you need a vehicle, you may rent a scooter or wheelchair from Guest Services to the right of the WDW entrance gates.

4. **Remote Control Toys and Drones** – Sorry, but not allowed.

5. **Your Pet** – Animals are not permitted in any of the six parks, Disney Springs, Hotels, or any of the transportation at the WDW Resort. If you need a place for your dog or cat during your stay, the Resort offers pet boarding and kennels at the Best Friends Pet Care, located

near Disney Springs and the Port Orleans Resort Hotels. The facility is huge, air conditioned, and a premium resort for your pet. They offer dozens of trained pet caregivers to accommodate your family's furry member when   you   enjoy   the   resort. They offer play and grooming services for both dogs and cats, and depending on your length of stay will determine the   pricing.   For   more   information,   please   visit: https://disneyworld.disney.go.com/guest-services/best-friends-pet-care   or   call   (877)   493-9738. *Note: You must book this in advance at the number above. Your pet will also require proof of certain vaccines before boarding.*

6. **Alcoholic Beverages** – These are not allowed in the parks (though adults 21 and over with a valid ID may purchase alcoholic drinks at all Theme Parks except for The Magic Kingdom).

7. **Lawn Chairs** – You might be tempted to bring these to watch a parade, but WDW bans them. We assume it's to keep the resort's aesthetics away from looking like a 4th of July picnic.

8. **Glass Bottles** – Another safety precaution. However, small glass containers of baby food are allowed.

9. **Bags with Wheels and Hiking Backpacks** – It's okay to bring these into the hotels, but you'll need to leave them out of the parks.

10. **Wrapped Gifts** – For inspection reasons, you cannot bring wrapped gifts into the parks. If you plan on giving someone a present, choose a gift bag or wrap it when you get to the park.

Backup Plans

Rent a Locker – We suggest renting a locker to everyone. There's no need to tire yourself out with a hefty backpack when a locker that fits your belongings starts at just $8/day plus a $5 key deposit. Larger lockers are $10/day with a $5 key deposit. You get the deposit back when you return the key.

The water parks have a different cost at $10/day for regular-sized lockers and $15/day for large-sized lockers. The water park lockers work with a 4-digit pin that you create in order to keep your belongings safe and secure.

- Lockers are located just outside of each park, to the left of the gates.
- Inside the park, lockers are to the right:
- Magic Kingdom – Just before Main Street, U.S.A. outside of the gates
- Epcot – Bus Stop outside of the park, International Gateway at the entrance, and there are lockers near the Camera Center.
- Hollywood Studios – at the entrance and near the bus stop
- Animal Kingdom – Expedition Everest and Kali River Rapids

- Typhoon Lagoon – There are two: at the entrance and just after the entrance
- Blizzard Beach – There are two: at the entrance, and to the right after you enter.

Plan a Midday Return to Your Hotel – If you don't want to rent a locker, make a plan to return to your hotel midday. There you can eat, refill on drinks, and maybe take a power nap. When you're refreshed, head back to the parks for more fun!

Get Park Hoppers – Sometimes you don't get everything done in one day and if you can afford the extra cost, the Park Hopper is the way to go. This pass allows you to visit any of the four main theme parks any time you want (though there is a water park option as well).

★ **Magic Tips** ★

1. If you forget any of these items, The Resort sells them. Check the shops near the entrances to any of the parks for some of these item.

2. Don't forget that we have a pre-made list of these items: www.magicguidebooks.com/waltdisneyworld

Chapter Seven
The Magic Kingdom Park

Introduction

The Magic Kingdom is Walt Disney World's epicenter and most beloved theme park. Designed after the original Disneyland concept, the Magic Kingdom offers a world-class experience into the heart of Disney.

With 20 million annual visitors, the Magic Kingdom is the most-visited theme park in the world! It opened in 1971 and has over 100 square acres of classic rides, roller coasters, themed lands, delicious food, beautiful scenery, a massive lake, and, of course, the iconic Cinderella Castle.

The six sizeable lands are all differently themed and have their own set of rides. Main Street, U.S.A.® is the gateway into the stunning park. Though Main Street feels like a tempting beginning, the allure of the distant castle will have your feet moving toward Fantasyland® with rides designed for families with young kids. Adventureland is like walking into a dense jungle, and Frontierland places you in the heart of the Wild West! Liberty Square rounds the classic experiences with its unique, American attractions, and Tomorrowland pulls guests into the future where anything is possible!

There are nearly countless things to do in the lands of the Magic Kingdom, but we've reviewed every single one of them to give you the best planning opportunity. In this section, we explore everything from the rides to the spectacular shows that bring the magic Walt Disney's Kingdom!

Notes:
1. The Magic Kingdom may be the smallest of the four parks, but it's the busiest. Because of this, we recommend visiting on a weekday.
2. Please be sure to read the ★ **Magic Tips** ★ in this section. They are designed to help you avoid long lines and bring fun activities in focus. Follow these and they will make your time at the Magic Kingdom Park even more enjoyable.

Speaking of Magic Tips, here's our first one:
★ **Magic Tip** ★
The best time to ride an attraction is right at opening or in the evening after sunset. If you didn't get a FastPass reservation for one of your favorite rides, we highly recommend visiting it first to avoid the long lines (Peter Pan's Flight is perfect for this).

Magic Kingdom Rope Drop
We recommend getting to the Magic Kingdom 30-minutes before opening. This will allow you to get through security, head to the hub before Main Street. You'll see a crowd forming with the train tracks in sight. About 10 minutes before the rope drops to allow you into the Park, Walt Disney World's best opening show starts. There's a song, dancers, and a dozen characters, including Mickey Mouse, swooping down on the train. It all ends with a *bang* before you start your day.

"The Kiss Goodnight"
Nope, this doesn't mean that Mickey and Minnie are going to kiss you (though Minnie has kissed one of us on the cheek before). Instead, the Cinderella Castle dazzles late at night, sending guests

back to their hotels after the night ends. Disney worked carefully on this special announcement, making certain that you'll feel the last bit of magic it has to offer before you leave. While the Kiss Goodnight isn't as spectacular as the Rope Drop ceremony, it still leaves you with some good feelings.

Main Street, U.S.A.

The Magic Kingdom's iconic grand entrance filled with shops, dining, and a magnificent view of the castle. The first thing you'll notice is the train station, beautiful flower arrangements, and smiling faces. Choose the left or the right side of the entrance to find yourself in a hub of horse-drawn street cars, carriages, unique shops, and Disney characters waiting to greet you. You'll feel the magic of good ol' small-town American life as you stroll down a street with carriages and shops for clothing and mouthwatering candies and ice cream.

Theme: Turn-of-the-century American town–specifically, Walt Disney's hometown of Marceline, Missouri in the early 20th century.

★ **Magic Tips** ★

1. Main Street makes a great viewing spot for many of the parades and nighttime fireworks displays. Crowds line up along the streets typically 30-60 minutes before each show to get a great view. If you'd like to avoid the parades and shows, it's best to stay clear of Main Street around the show times.

2. Get souvenirs here on your way out of the park. They have everything from character antennae balls to clothing to candy.

3. If you are staying at any of the WDW Resort Hotels, always check the Extra Magic Hours while planning your

trip. Sometimes you can get into the park before all of the other guests or are able to stay later to ride using your MagicBand as a pass.

Rides

Walt Disney World Railroad
Best for: Young Kids, Adults 50+
Description: All aboard the iconic steam train that moves around the perimeter of the park. It's a 20-minute ride over a mile and a half of track. Guests love the relaxing feel of riding on one of the four locomotive passenger cars. Other stops include Frontierland and Fantasyland.
Level: Everyone
Recommendation: Best if you are looking for a way to stay out of the sun and an enjoy a leisurely experience. Tweens, Teens, and Thrill Riders may not enjoy this experience as much.
Line Length: Short / **FastPass+:** No

Main Street Vehicles
Best for: Young Kids, Adults 50+
Description: Ride a horse-drawn streetcar, horseless carriage, or a double-decker bus that will take you down to Cinderella's Castle.
Level: Family
Recommendation: A nice stroll for small children and guests who enjoy the classic appeal of Disney attractions. However, Thrill Riders might rather skip this and head straight to a ride like Space Mountain or Big Thunder Mountain Railroad.
FastPass+: No

Shows and Attractions

Town Square Theatre
Best for: Young Kids, Kids, Family
Description: Meet Mickey Mouse in this stunning theatre.
Level: Family
Recommendation: If you're looking for a photo with Mickey Mouse, this is your best opportunity. Other characters like Tinker Bell and Disney Princesses show up throughout the day. Check the My Disney Experience app for character times on the day of your visit.
FastPass+: No

Wishes: Nighttime Spectacular Fireworks
Best for: Everyone of all ages!
Description: A fireworks show starring Jiminy Cricket, Peter Pan, Ariel, and many more as Disney Villains attempt to stop the wishes from coming true. Luckily, we have the Disney heroes on our side!
Level: Everyone
Recommendation: Conclude your day with this stunning fireworks display that dazzles the sky. See an array of colors over Cinderella's Castle that will surely make your trip a memorable one.

★ **Magic Tips** ★
- The best viewing is at the end of Main Street before the center "Hub" with the statue of Walt Disney and Mickey Mouse. Here you can see the entire display. However, we recommend getting their early, either an hour on less-busy days and two hours early on busy days.
- If you don't have time to get there early, the second best viewing is on Main Street near the entrance. You'll also be able to beat the crowds out of the park at this time.

- Grand Floridian Hotel guests can see the Magic Kingdom fireworks from the hotel's beach. Some of the rooms also have perfect views of the theme parks and the nighttime fireworks.
- Contemporary Resort Hotel guests also have fantastic views from select rooms. We recommend eating at the California Grill on the top floor for fantastic viewing. The restaurant even plays the Wishes theme music and dims the lights when the show starts.

Harmony Barber Shop

Description: Get a haircut in this charming barbershop. Look for the famous barbershop quartet, the Dapper Dans, singing in four-part harmony! Haircuts start at $19 for adults and $18 for kids. Harmony isn't a salon, so those with long, stylized hair may not prefer to visit this location.

For Reservations, call (407) 939-7529

Even More:

You can also discover the many shops, City Hall, and the Main Street Chamber of Commerce.

Adventureland

Theme: Enter the jungle, explore ruins, and ride iconic attractions like the Pirates of the Caribbean, in this lush and wildly designed land.

★ Magic Tips ★

Adventureland is the place to find Disney's famous Dole Whip desserts! These are perfect treats for a hot day and not to be missed!

Rides

Jungle Cruise
Best for: Young Kids, Kids, Families, Tweens, Adults 30+
Description: Venture down a massive river on a boat with your comedic tour guide. See animatronic Amazonian and African animals from monkeys and crocodiles to elephants and lions on this 7-minute long ride.
Level: Everyone
Recommendation: A classic, humorous Disney ride that most guests will enjoy. Teens, Young Adults, and Thrill Riders may want to skip it.
Line Length: Long / **FastPass+:** Yes
★ Magic Tips ★
> 1. The Jungle Cruise has a completely different feel at night. We highly recommend it!
> 2. The holiday version, Jingle Cruise (early November – early January) offers Christmas lights, new jokes, and animals wearing Christmas hats.

Swiss Family Treehouse
Best for: Young Kids, Kids, Tweens, Families
Description: A climbable treehouse themed after the 1960 *Swiss Family Robinson* film.
Level: Young Kids / Everyone
Recommendation: Kids ages 10 and under will enjoy this attraction that typically has a very short line (or no wait at all). However, the nostalgia may set better with those over the age of 50. Ironically, they may not be the ones who will want to climb the treehouse.
Line Length: Very short / **FastPass+:** No
★ Magic Tips ★
> There are great photo opportunities from the top of the Swiss Family Treehouse!

Pirates of the Caribbean

Best for: Everyone!

Description: Pirate-themed boat ride in the dark

Level: Everyone – Though some young kids may be frightened by the drop, loud sounds, and darkness.

Recommendation: Both thrill riders and families will love this attraction for its stunning scenery, animatronics, and pirate humor.

Line Length: Long / **FastPass+:** Yes

★ **Magic Tips** ★

1. We recommend a FastPass+ selection for this one. The boats load quickly, but this is one of the Magic Kingdom's most popular attractions, so the line can be quite long.
2. Sit near the center to avoid getting splashed.
3. A great air conditioned ride to cool off on warm days.
4. We notice a pattern of people who tend to get wet on this ride. Out of nearly every boat, about one or two people look wet. If you are on the 4th or 5th row, and only on the right side, a cannon blast can send a mighty splash of water your way. Avoid these seats if you want to stay dry.

The Magic Carpets of Aladdin®
Best for: Young Kids, Kids, Families
Description: Looping flying carpets similar to the Dumbo the Flying Elephant ride.
Level: Families
Recommendation: Kids under ten enjoy this ride the most as they control the flying carpets to go high or low.
Line Length: Very Short / **FastPass+:** Yes
★ **Magic Tips** ★

> These are also perfect to ride if your family wants to go on Pirates of the Caribbean, but you have young kids who may be too scared to ride.

Shows and Attractions

Walt Disney's Enchanted Tiki Room
Description: An animatronic show starring birds and Tikis in a tropical island setting.
Level: Family / Everyone
Recommendation: Have a Dole® Whip while you watch the 15-minute long show. Tweens, Teens, Young Adults, and Thrill Seekers will want to skip this one, as it's a classic attraction that can feel a bit dated.
Line Length: Short / **FastPass+:** No

Pirate's Adventure (Treasures of the Seven Seas)
Best for: Kids, Tweens
Description: *Pirates of the Caribbean*-themed walkthrough attraction. Help Captain Jack Sparrow discover all seven treasures in this unique experience.
Level: Kids and Tweens
Recommendation: Perfect for Kids and Tweens, but it may be too complex for Young Kids, and it's not aimed for Adults.
Line Length: Short / **FastPass+:** No

Pirate's League

Best for: Young Kids, Kids

Description: Transform into a swashbuckling pirate with makeup beard and all. Kids can also look undead and learn the swagger of a pirate!

Level: Kids and Tweens

Recommendation: Perfect pirate fans with an extra cost starting at $39.95.

Frontierland

Theme: Immerse yourself in the wild west near the Rivers of America. Ride the high-speed Big Thunder Mountain Railroad or catch a lighthearted show at the Diamond Horseshoe Stage.

Rides

Big Thunder Mountain Railroad

Best for: Kids, Tweens, Teens, Adults, Thrill Seekers

Description: A fast rollercoaster with few dips called "The Wildest Ride in the Wilderness"

Level: Thrill Ride (must be 40"/102cm or taller)

Recommendation: Many families and thrill riders will love this fast rollercoaster with short dips and great special effects. If you're unsure whether to take your child on this rollercoaster, have them ride the family-friendly Seven Dwarfs Mine Train first in Fantasyland.

Line Length: Long / **FastPass+:** Yes

Splash Mountain

Best for: Tweens, Teens, Adults, Thrill Seekers

Description: Water-based log ride starring the singing critters from *Song of the South*. Prepare to hear the classic Disney song, "Zip-A-Dee-Doo-Dah"!

Level: Thrill Ride (must be 40"/102cm or taller)

Recommendation: If you love getting wet and drops, this is the ride for you! However, there are several drops in this ride, including a 50 foot drop at 45 degrees at the end.

Line Length: Long / **FastPass+:** Yes

★ **Magic Tips** ★

1. This ride typically has the longest lines, especially during the hotter days (can be well over an hour wait). This is why we highly recommend making it a FastPass+ selection.

2. Sit near the back to avoid getting as wet (though you will still likely get wet). Ask a cast member at the end of the

line to sit in the back and they will help accommodate you.

3. If you want to get *soaked* – ask a cast member to sit in the front!

4. If it's a cold day or you just don't feel like getting your clothes wet, either buy/bring a poncho or skip this attraction (though it is one of our favorites).

5. Say cheese! The camera for Splash Mountain is on the left side of your log as you plunge down the last drop.

Tom Sawyer Island

Best for: Kids, Tweens

Description: Explore a remote island in the center of the Magic Kingdom's famous river. You must get there by raft!

Level: Family

Recommendation: We recommend this island playground for kids. There are hideaways and trinkets for them to play with, however teens, adults and thrill seekers will likely want to skip this one.

Line Length: Short / **FastPass+:** No

★ **Magic Tip** ★

Tom Sawyer's Island closes before sunset, so make sure that you get this attraction done earlier in the day if it's on your list.

Country Bear Jamboree

Best for: Young Kids, Kids, Adults 50+

Description: A country music-filled jamboree featuring the classic animatronic Country Bears. There are over twelve songs in this nearly 16-minute long show.

Level: Everyone

Recommendation: Perfect for nostalgic Disney World-goers, but the theme may feel lost on others. The Country Bear Jamboree

might be a classic, but the crowds have thinned over the years and the show doesn't have the same excitement from its previous fans.
Line Length: Short / **FastPass+:** No

Shows and Attractions

- Walt Disney World Railroad – A station for the park's iconic train.
- Frontierland Shootin' Arcade – A paid experience where you can shoot targets with laser-guided toy rifles.

Liberty Square

Theme: A colonial America-themed land filed with shops, treats, and one of the park's most popular rides, the Haunted Mansion. Catch sight of a Liberty Bell and Liberty Tree replicas, dine, or catch a parade near the Rivers of America.

Rides

Haunted Mansion
Best for: Kids, Tweens, Teens, Adults
Description: A slow-paced ride through a haunted house. Filled with illusions, animatronics, and creepy sounds, this attraction is uniquely Disney.
Level: Everyone – though young children may become frightened
Recommendation: It's a Disney classic that many thrill-riders may want to skip for it's slow movement and effects that are only scary enough to terrify young kids.
Line Length: Long/ **FastPass+:** Yes

★ **Magic Tips** ★
1. You can fit 2-3 people per "Doom Buggy" chair. We've sat 3 adults together, but it's not very comfortable.
2. A great air conditioned ride to cool off on warm days.

Shows and Attractions

Hall of Presidents
Best for: Young Kids, Adults 50+
Description: Animatronics show hosted by US Presidents.
Level: Everyone
Recommendation: Another Disney classic that may bore some guests uninterested in US History.
Line Length: Short / **FastPass+:** No

Liberty Belle Riverboat
Best for: Young Kids, Adults 50+
Description: Explore a beautiful American-style riverboat over the Rivers of America.
Level: Everyone
Recommendation: For those looking to cool off and ride on a large river boat.
Line Length: Short/ **FastPass+:** No

Fantasyland

Theme: Magic makes memories in this classic kid-friendly land located behind the famous castle. The Magic Kingdom's Fantasyland is divided into 3 sections: the castle courtyard, the Enchanted Forest, and the Storybook Circus. In Fantasyland, you can ride movie-themed attractions, meet your favorite characters, and cruise along to Disney classics.

Rides

Seven Dwarfs Mine Train
Best for: Kids, Tweens, Teens, Adults, some Thrill Riders
Description: A family-friendly rollercoaster through the mines of the Seven Dwarfs. The carts move side to side, creating a unique experience like no other rollercoaster.
Level: Family (must be 38"/ 97cm or taller)
Recommendation: This ride is perfect for kids and younger kids who are craving to ride a rollercoaster because it's not very fast. However, even Thrill Seekers will enjoy this ride.
Line Length: Very Long / **FastPass+:** Yes
★ Magic Tip ★
1. This is one of the Magic Kingdom's newest attractions and its most popular. Above all rides, we recommend the Seven Dwarfs Mine Train to be on your FastPass+ selection list.
2. If you aren't able to get a FastPass+ for this ride, come when the park first opens and ride this attraction first.

Peter Pan's Flight
Best for: Young Kids, Kids, Tweens, Adults 50+
Description: Fly along Peter Pan through London and Neverland on a pirate ship!
Level: Young Kids / Everyone
Recommendation: Perfect for all ages (kids *love* this ride) and a Disney classic that we even recommend to thrill-seekers looking to ride an all-ages ride.
Line Length: Very Long / **FastPass+:** Yes
★ Magic Tips ★
If you don't get a FastPass+ selection for Peter Pan's Flight but want to ride it later, visit after dark for much shorter lines (when the younger kids have gone home).

The Many Adventures of Winnie the Pooh

Best for: Young Kids and Kids

Description: A slow-paced ride through the brightly-colored world of Winnie the Pooh.

Level: Young Kids / Family

Recommendation: Great for Kids of all ages, but Tweens, Teens and Thrill Riders will likely want to skip it.

Line Length: Short/ **FastPass+:** Yes

Dumbo the Flying Elephant

Best for: Young Kids and Kids

Description: Soar high while boarding Dumbo! You control how high or low Dumbo goes.

Level: Young Kids / Family

Recommendation: Perfect for families with Young Kids.

Line Length: Short / **FastPass+:** Yes

★ **Magic Tip** ★

We don't recommend a FastPass+ selection for Dumbo the Flying Elephant because the ride has a pager system. The queue is interactive and perfect for Young Kids to play while they wait. When the pager goes off, it's your turn to ride!

Mad Tea Party (Tea Cups)

Best for: Everyone

Description: Disney's famous tea cups inspired by Alice in Wonderland! Spin with your friends (up to 3-4 adults per tea cup).

Level: Kids / Everyone

Recommendation: Perfect for all ages and a Disney classic that we even recommend to Thrill Riders (the tea cups can spin *fast* or slow, depending on how hard you turn them).

Line Length: Short / **FastPass+:** Yes

★ **Magic Tip** ★

> If you get motion sickness easily, you might want to skip this ride.

Prince Charming Regal Carrousel

Best for: Young Kids and Kids

Description: A classic carrousel with horses from *Cinderella*.

Level: Family

Recommendation: Perfect for families with Young Kids.

Line Length: Short / **FastPass+:** No

"it's a small world"

Best for: Young Kids, Kids, Families, Adults 50+

Description: A boat floats through several counties with children singing the "It's A Small World" theme song in different languages.

Level: Young Kids / Family

Recommendation: Perfect for families with young children. During the holiday season, this ride dazzles with lights and new costumes. Adults may enjoy the ride as they beat the heat in the air-conditioned boat ride.

Line Length: Short / **FastPass+:** Yes

★ **Magic Tips** ★

1. Some find this ride horribly annoying because of the endless singing children (we're not kidding!)
2. The Holiday version (from early November to early January) features a frosty layover with a holiday remix of the classic song.

The Barnstormer

Best for: Kids and Tweens

Description: A kid-friendly outdoor rollercoaster starring Goofy as the Great Goofini.

Level: Family

Recommendation: Like the Seven Dwarfs Mine Train, this is a great introductory rollercoaster.

Line Length: Very Short / **FastPass+:** Yes

Under the Sea ~ Journey of the Little Mermaid

Best for: Young Kids, Kids, and Tweens

Description: Board shell-shaped chairs as you travel underwater to see Ariel and her friends. There's music, special effects, fish, and even Ursula!

Level: Family

Recommendation: Perfect for fans of *The Little Mermaid*.

Line Length: Medium / **FastPass+:** Yes

Shows and Attractions

Cinderella Castle Walkthrough

Best for: Everyone

Description: Walk through the famous Castle! There's also a dining area, Cinderella's Royal Table.

Level: Everyone

Recommendation: Walk through, see the art, and take a picture outside of the castle.

FastPass+: No

★ **Magic Tip** ★

> There is often a photographer outside of the castle. He or she will take your picture for free (though you have to pay for the prints) and afterward, the cast member is happy to take a free photo of you with your camera or phone.

Mickey's PhilharMagic

Best for: Young Kids, Kids, Tweens, Families

Description: A 4-D film show starring Mickey Mouse and his friends. Though, to be honest, it should be called Donald's PhilharMagic because most of the show stars him and Mickey just seems to make a cameo.

Level: Family

Recommendation: Great for show lovers of all ages. Awesome special effects and music.

Line Length: Short / **FastPass+:** No

★ **Magic Tip** ★

> We recommend sitting in the center of the theater. Seats further up can seem blurring in the 3D glasses.

Disney Festival of Fantasy Parade

Best for: Young Kids, Kids, Tweens, Families

Description: An afternoon parade set to Disney music with impressive floats, singing, and dancing.

Level: Family

Recommendation: Great for parade lovers of all ages.

FastPass+: No

Tip: Get there early for the best seating! We recommend being near the Cinderella Castle (on the Main Street side) at least 30 minutes before the parade begins. Maps and WaltDisneyWorld.com keep updated lists on their sites.

Casey Jr. Splash 'N' Soak Station

Best for: Young Kids and Kids

Description: A *Dumbo*-themed water playground for kids.

Level: Everyone

Recommendation: They will get soaked!

FastPass+: No

★ **Magic Tip** ★

> On the hottest days when your kids don't feel like waiting in lines, this can be a memorable attraction. It's best to plan to head back to the hotel afterward or bring a change of clothes. Though, many times, the hot Florida sun may be enough to dry them off.

Bibbidi Bobbidi Boutique (inside the Cinderella Castle)

Best for: Young Kids and Kids

Description: Dress up in princess clothing and makeup

Level: Kids and Young Kids

Recommendation: Perfect for children who are inspired Disney princesses (for pricing starting a $59.95, kids can get their makeup and hair done– and even a gown from their favorite Disney princess).

FastPass+: No

★ **Magic Tip** ★

> There are more packages, including a "Knight Package" and a "Frozen Package".

Character Meeting Spots

Ariel's Grotto

Best for: Young Kids, Kids, and Tweens

Description: Take photos with Ariel from Disney's *The Little Mermaid*.

Level: Family

Recommendation: Perfect for fans of *The Little Mermaid*.

FastPass+: No

Pete's Silly Sideshow

Best for: Young Kids, Kids, and Tweens

Description: Take photos with Daisy and Minnie or Donald and Goofy in this circus-themed meet and greet attraction. The characters are dressed in circus attire.

Level: Family

Recommendation: Perfect for those looking for any of these character.

FastPass+: No

Fairytale Garden: *Brave* "Play and Greet"
Best for: Young Kids, Kids, and Tweens
Description: Take photos with Merida at the Fairytale Garden
Level: Family
Recommendation: Perfect for fans of *Brave*.
FastPass+: No

Princess Fairytale Hall
Best for: Young Kids, Kids, and Tweens
Description: Take photos with Cinderella and other Princesses in this royal hall.
Level: Family
Recommendation: Perfect for fans of Disney Princesses.
FastPass+: No

Enchanted Tales with Belle
Best for: Young Kids, Kids, and Tweens
Description: Take photos with Belle from *Beauty and the Beast*.
Level: Family
Recommendation: Perfect for fans of Disney Princesses.
Line Length: Long
FastPass+: Yes

The Tangled Rest Area

Every Walt Disney World fanatic knows the best rest area in all of the Resort. The Tangled-themed rest area is well-designed and to the west of Fantastyland, near Liberty Square and the Haunted Mansion. These are its benefits:

1. The Best Restrooms – equipped with pristine toilets, sinks, and floors, you'll feel the spotless clean of these new restrooms. The stalls are also well-spread and have a great, private feeling for both women and men.

2. Cellphone Charging – the tree stumps across from the restrooms are free cellphone charging stations. They use regular outlet plugs, so you'll need to bring your own cord.

3. Plenty of Seating – take a break and rest your feet in a tranquil spot in the heart of the Magic Kingdom. There's also a nice waterfall and plenty of Tangled-themed landscapes to admire.

4. Water – fill up your water jugs here. The pipes are newer so they don't have some of the old Florida water taste that areas in Adventureland have in their fountains.

Tomorrowland

Theme: An imagined world of the future with rocket ships that blast you to space and Disney favorites like Buzz Lightyear and Stitch take you to their home planets.

Rides

Space Mountain
Best for: Thrill Riders
Description: A rollercoaster in the dark.
Level: Thrill Riders (must be 40"/ 102cm or taller)
Recommendation: A *must* for Thrill Riders! Space Mountain at the Magic Kingdom feels a little bit dated with its worn carpet in the queue and 70's-style exterior. However, the ride hasn't lost its unique charm as you blast through outer space!
Line Length: Very Long / **FastPass+:** Yes

★ Magic Tip ★

> We highly recommend this unique experience for Thrill Riders, so select this as a FastPass+ (and consider you may want to ride this twice!)

Tomorrowland Speedway

Best for: Kids and Tweens

Description: Where kids can drive cars around a track.

Level: Kids / Family (must be 32"/81cm or taller to ride) (must be 54"/137cm to drive alone)

Recommendation: Designed for kids to tweens, but with height restrictions. Young kids may enjoy riding passenger side more than driving.

Line Length: Long / **FastPass+:** Yes

Buzz Lightyear's Space Ranger Spin

Best for: Everyone

Description: Compete against others in this fun Toy Story-themed ride. It seems like it's for the kids, but it's fun for everyone to blast the laser guns and try to rack up the points.

Level: Everyone (including most thrill riders)

Recommendation: A crowd favorite for everyone to enjoy.

Line Length: Medium / **FastPass+:** Yes

★ Magic Tips ★

There are special targets on the robot and alien enemies that give different points. However, it's not clear how much these are worth unless you know these tips. We picked the ones that will quickly get you the most points:

1. You can hit the targets as many times as you'd like, even the ones worth the most.
2. Blue Robot (first room) – Shoot the inside of its glowing hands for 100,000 points.
3. Volcano (second room) – Aim for the volcano with green lava in the back of the room and get 25,000.

4. Alien Ant – There's an ant with a target on its rear worth 50,000.
5. Zurg's Ship – There's a difficult target at the bottom the crab-like ship that's worth 100,000.
6. Hyperspace Warp – There's a huge spaceship at the end with a target worth 100,000.

Stitch's Great Escape!

Best for: Kids and Tweens

Description: Stitch escapes his special container and pranks the audience in a theatre-in-the-round setting.

Level: Everyone (must be 40"/ 102cm or taller)

Recommendation: Kids and Tweens will love this attraction for its humor and adorable alien, Stitch. Adults and Thrill Riders may find this attraction somewhat disappointing as it's clearly aimed at younger people. Young Kids might want to sit this one out if they don't like being strapped to a chair and lots of darkness.

Line Length: Short / **FastPass+:** No

Note: As of October 2016, this attraction is seasonal and may only be open during peak times.

Astro Orbiter

Best for: Young Kids and Kids

Description: Orbit a solar system model on rocket ships (similar to Dumbo)

Level: Kids / Family

Recommendation: Fun for Young Kids

Line Length: Medium / **FastPass+:** No

Tomorrowland Transit Authority PeopleMover

Best for: Young Kids, Kids, Adults 50+

Description: A futuristic, slow-moving vehicle through Tomorrowland.

Level: Kids / Family

Recommendation: Perfect for those looking for a break. The PeopleMover is a 10-minute long ride and a great way to beat the heat as the ride travels through air-conditioned spaces.

Line Length: Very short / **FastPass+:** No

Shows and Attractions

Monsters, Inc. Laugh Floor

Best for: Young Kids and Kids

Description: A theatre with digital puppetry that allows characters on a screen from *Monsters, Inc.* to interact with the audience.

Level: Kids / Family

Recommendation: Fun for Families with Kids

Line Length: Short / **FastPass+:** Yes

Walt Disney's Carousel of Progress

Best for: Young Kids and Adults Ages 50+

Description: Watch as animatronic characters bring you the future of gadgets in a turning carousel-like building.

Level: Everyone

Recommendation: Another great way to cool down, but there is a lot of standing. The ride is more for those looking for nostalgia, though Young Kids can appreciate the characters more than Tweens, Teens, and Young Adults.

Line Length: Short / **FastPass+:** No

Chapter Eight

Epcot

Introduction

For over 35 years since its opening in 1982, Epcot has been a staple of the Walt Disney World experience. Its name, however, is an acronym for Experimental Prototype Community of Tomorrow. It's a place where "joy, hope, and friendship" are launched into a space of creativity, exploration, and innovation.

We are asked a lot: "is it worth visiting Epcot?" For us, the answer is a clear *yes*. Epcot is like the Magic Kingdom's Tomorrowland, fully expanded over 300 acres. It's a world of tomorrow and today where guests can ride futuristic attractions, try delicious food from all over the world, and even party into the night.

Epcot is divided into two sections: Future World with the most rides and the World Showcase which consists of representations of eleven countries. Whether you are a Thrill Rider looking for unique experiences, a foodie craving something different, or a kid yearning to make some Disney memories, Epcot is the place. With new attractions like Soarin' and Frozen Ever After as well as delicious wine and gourmet delights, there's something for everyone in Epcot!

Notes:

1. Many of the rides in Epcot are slow-paced and informative. However, Test Track and Soarin' give Thriller Riders what they crave.

2. Epcot is often open late, allowing for locals to wine and dine around it's beautiful, massive lake in the center of the World Showcase. Because of this, it's sometimes best to avoid the weekend crowds–unless you're open to them!

3. Don't forget to read the ★ **Magic Tips** ★ in this section! We wouldn't want you to miss out on any valuable information.

Epcot Rope Drop

Epcot has the least exciting rope drop. Perhaps it's because the space is so large and so few guests show up for it. Or it could because they often have Extra Magic Hours before the actual Park opens. However, it has two official rope drops, one for each entrance. The first is in Future World, where you are lead near the Innoventions buildings (which are now closed except for the character greeting spots). Cast members will allow you to move to one of the Future World attractions after that. Many people head to The Land to ride Soarin'. The second rope drop is in the World Showcase entrance between the United Kingdom and France. It's the least climactic one as it opens much later in the morning than the other Parks, so only a tiny of people appear. You might want to head to Frozen Ever After from there, but since it's on the complete opposite side, we recommend accessing it from Future World.

Future World

The first half of Epcot is home to its iconic, golf ball-like centerpiece. This structure is actually considered a "spaceship" and contains the captivating ride, Spaceship Earth. Epcot's many flowers bloom here, especially in the Spring during the Flower and Garden Festival. Future World has a new attraction, Soarin', which now takes guests to choice locations around the world. It's an experience not to be missed by any Disney fan!

Theme: Future World of Tomorrow

★ **Magic Tips** ★
1. Epcot has two entrances: one at the Main Entrance near Spaceship Earth, the second between the United

Kingdom and France sections in the World Showcase on the other side of the park. The second entrance is known as "The International Gateway".

2. Typically, the two sections have different opening times. The Future World opens earlier (usually about two hours) than the World Showcase. This is because Future World has more rides and World Showcase is mostly shops and restaurants. The World Showcase often is open two hours after Future World closes.

Rides

Disney & Pixar Short Film Festival
Best for: Young Kids, Adults 50+
Description: The creative geniuses behind the Academy Award winning Pixar films bring an 18-minute show. Experience Pixar shorts like never before with 4-D effects!
Level: Everyone
Recommendation: A must for Pixar lovers, but those looking for thrills might want to skip this one
Line Length: Very Short / **FastPass+:** No

Ellen's Energy Adventure
Best for: Kids, Tweens, Teens, Adults
Description: A show hosted by comedian Ellen DeGeneres. It discusses energy and how we use it on Earth in our daily lives. At 45-minutes, it's the longest attraction in WDW.
Level: Everyone
Recommendation: An informative and funny show for anyone looking to learn and laugh, if you have a spare 45-minutes–or are just craving the AC.
Line Length: Very Short / **FastPass+:** No

Imagination!
Best for: Young Kids, Kids, and Tweens
Description: Separated into two parts, this pavilion explores imagination for its fun and importance. The first is a ride called "Journey to Imagination with Figment". It's a classic Disney dark ride hosted by a pink dragon named Figment. The second is a show titled ImageWorks: The What-If Labs. Here, guests are able to interact while discussing what they learned on the ride Journey into Imagination.
Level: Everyone
Recommendation: Great for families with Kids. Everyone will love Figment the Dragon!
Line Length: Very Short / **FastPass+:** Yes

Mission: Space
Best for: Tweens, Teens, Adults, and Thrill Riders
Description: A dizzying astronaut training excursion into outer space hosted by actor Gary Sinise (*Forest Gump*).
Level: Everyone.
Recommendation: Thrill Riders should choose the more intense experience, while those who experience motion sickness to choose a stationary option–or skip this ride altogether.
Line Length: Medium / **FastPass+:** Yes

The Land
Best for: Everyone
Description: Explore a pavilion filled with information and rides about humans and their relationship with the land over time–and in the future.

There are three attractions in this building:

• Living with the Land– A slow-paced ride that describes how we harvest the land for food.

• Soarin'– See below

• Circle of Life: An Environmental Fable – A 12-minute film starring characters from

Disney's *The Lion King* that discusses symbiosis.

Level: Everyone

Recommendation: Perfectly informative and fun. Thrill Riders may want to skip the slow-paced "Living with the Land" ride and head straight for Soarin'.

Line Length: Very Short (Living with the Land and Circle of Life)

FastPass+: No

Soarin' (inside The Land)
Best for: Kids, Tweens, Teens, Adults, and Thrill Riders
Description: An all-new update to the park's popular Soarin' ride. Fly over some of the world's most famous landmarks in this unique hang glider simulation.

Level: Kids to Adult

Recommendation: Small children and those with a fear of heights may want to skip this one, though the ride feels very relaxing. A FastPass+ reservation is recommended.

Line Length: Long / **FastPass+:** Yes

The Seas with Nemo & Friends
Best for: Everyone
Description: Learn about the oceans in this Finding Nemo-

themed attraction. The ride loads quickly with seats similar to the "doom buggies" in The Haunted Mansion and clam-shells of The Little Mermaid ride. There are also massive aquariums with live fish and more!

Level: Everyone

Recommendation: A spectacular ride with plenty to see and experience. Thrill Riders may want to skip out unless they are interested in seeing the aquariums.

Line Length: Short / **FastPass+:** Yes

Turtle Talk with Crush (inside The Seas)

Best for: Young Kids and Kids

Description: Interact with Crush the turtle from *Finding Nemo* in this unique and hilarious theatre-like event designed for Young Kids.

Level: Everyone

Recommendation: Young Kids

Line Length: Short / **FastPass+:** Yes

Spaceship Earth

Best for: Everyone

Description: A slow-moving dark ride set inside of the Epcot sphere. The ride has animatronics and more as it discusses human's ability to communicate on Earth from the past and into the future.

Level: Everyone

Recommendation: A ride that is more fun that it seems. Thrill Riders might want to head directly to Test Track instead.

Line Length: Short / **FastPass+:** Yes

Test Track
Best for: Tweens, Teens, Adults, Thrill Riders
Description: Zoom along a simulated test track in a futuristic car. The vehicle races at over 60-miles per hour with turns and movement inside and outside of a building.
Level: Thrill Ride
Recommendation: Perfect for Thrill Riders.
Line Length: Very Long / **FastPass+:** Yes
★ **Magic Tip** ★

> Test Track also offers a Single Rider Line. There is a very small chance that you'll end up riding with another person in your party, but if you don't snag a FastPass+ reservation and the line is long, this might be a great option. To access the Single Rider line, look for the sign next to the regular line queue entrance.

World Showcase

It's rare that a description of Epcot's World Showcase does justice for this half of the park. Many think of the rides, parades, and Mickey Mouse when they think of Walt Disney World. So, when it comes to the World Showcase, it's a completely different vibe– and that's a good thing! While Future World dives us into "what could be" in the universe, the World Showcase is designed to enlighten you about the dining, entertainment, and splendor of the world around us.

Made up of 11 countries (Canada, China, France, Germany, Italy, Japan, Mexico, Morocco, Norway, United Kingdom, and the United States), you can try the food and beverages of these lands, plus ride along to discover their culture. There's even a new Frozen-themed ride in the Norway showcase. There are also fireworks over a massive lake, dazzling gardens, and architecture from Japanese pagodas to Mayan temples!

Year round, there's always something new and exciting happening at Epcot. A fan favorite (and ours, too) is the Food and Wine Festival that takes place in the Fall. Here, guests can try everything from sampled courses at the many restaurants, flights of wine or beer (ages 21+, of course), and many other treats. These meals and beverages come at an additional cost, and there's something fun for all to try. We love the waiters at Epcot, because they are authentically from their respective country (many of the times), and they are some of the happiest employees in all of WDW.

The World Showcase has a popular new attraction, Frozen Ever After. It's a dazzling boat ride with the characters and music of Frozen. There are a couple of small dips and some impressive animatronics. It's also one of the most coveted rides in all of Walt Disney World, so we recommend grabbing a FastPass+ selection for it.

We invite you to step into Epcot with an open mind and heart as you have the opportunity to fall in love with the splendor or the World Showcase. If you're an adult, you might just walk away thinking that this was your favorite land of all.

Theme: A Showcase of Worldly Traditions

★ Magic Tips ★
1. Don't forget about the second, "The International Gateway" entrance right between the United Kingdom and France sections.
2. Come back here at night! Since the World Showcase often is open two hours after Future World closes, it allows guests to dine and drink around this half of the park.

Showcases

There is a lot to do in the World Showcase and you may not have time to do it all. Most of the attractions are family-oriented, though all ages can enjoy them. See the recommendations in each section to see which ones you should explore in case you don't have the time.

Disney Phineas and Ferb: Agent P's World Showcase Adventure
Best for: Kids and Tweens
Description: A scavenger hunt around the showcases.
Level: Family
Recommendation: Unless you have Kids or Tweens who are fans of Phineas and Ferb on the Disney Channel, it's best to skip the Agent P adventure.
Line Length: None / **FastPass+:** No

Frozen Ever After (Norway)

Best for: Everyone

Description: Explore the culture of Norway and the magic of Disney's *Frozen* in this unique boat ride.

Level: Everyone / Family

Recommendation: The World Showcase's most "daring" ride, though it's fun for the whole family. There are some small dips and senses of danger, but the *Frozen* characters keep young kids happy.

Line Length: Very Long / **FastPass+:** Yes

⋆ **Magic Tips** ⋆

This is an all-new attraction and has had record long lines. We recommend choosing a FastPass+ selection for this one.

The Gran Fiesta Tour Starring the Three Caballeros (Mexico)

Best for: Everyone

Description: Explore the culture of Mexico in a boat ride with music.

Level: Everyone

Recommendation: We recommend experiencing the ride for its fun and Donald Duck with his pals.

Line Length: Very Short / **FastPass+:** No

O Canada! (Canada)

Best for: Adults

Description: See the native history of Canada in this North American tribute to the country.

Level: Everyone

Recommendation: Everyone may enjoy this circle-vision 360 movie. Adults will enjoy the lager and handcrafted merchandise.

Line Length: Very Short / **FastPass+:** No

France

Best for: Everyone

Description: Watch a panoramic movie that showcases France's history and famous architecture. There are a few restaurants with the most famous being Les Chefs de France.

Level: Everyone

Recommendation: It's a small pavilion and great to walk through. If you enjoy French cuisine, we highly recommend eating at Les Chefs de France. Many of the employees come from Disneyland Paris to give an authentic French vibe. Just don't forget to make a reservation!

Reflections of China (China)

Best for: Everyone

Description: Explore China in this 12 and a half-minute "circle-vision 360" movie.

Level: Everyone

Recommendation: Perhaps put this at the end of your list. The encounter is well-done, but not as memorable as Mexico or Norway.

Line Length: Very Short / **FastPass+:** No

Japan

Best for: Everyone

Description: Impressive pagodas and traditional structures make this land a temptation for the eyes. Many of this pavilion's employees are from Disneyland Tokyo and they are happy to guide you through their culture.

Level: Everyone

Recommendation: Check out the shops and take photos by the amazing architecture.

The American Adventure

Best for: Everyone

Description: Epcot's showcase of Americana with an animatronic cast on a stage who review the history of the country.

Level: Everyone

Recommendation: It feels like a bit of a repeat from what is shown in Liberty Square at the Magic Kingdom, so it's not as popular as Norway, Germany, Japan, or France.

Line Length: Very Short / **FastPass+:** No

Morocco

Best for: Kids, Adults 30+

Description: Explore a Moroccan city with mosaics and artwork created by Moroccan artists. There are several shops, dining experiences, and musical acts throughout the pavilion. Aladdin and Jasmine also make daily appearances.

Level: Everyone

Recommendation: Adults will love the food and the scenery while Kids will look forward to taking photos with Aladdin and Princess Jasmine.

United Kingdom

Best for: Everyone

Description: Stroll down the streets of London or the old countryside of England while listening to British rock cover bands.

Level: Everyone

Recommendation: Perfect for shop-lovers.

Germany

Best for: Adults 21+

Description: Quaint German towns, food, and Biergarten beverages make up this unique pavilion.

Level: Everyone

Recommendation: Germany feels more like a land for Adults who enjoy beer and classic German food. Kids may want to skip it for attractions like Frozen or to see the shops in Japan.

Italy
Best for: Kids, Adults 30+
Description: See the sweeping scenes of Italy as recreations of its famous landmarks and artwork are put on display in this pavilion. Pinocchio also shows up for photo opportunities.
Level: Everyone
Recommendation: Adults will love the food and the scenery while Kids will look forward to taking photos with Pinocchio.

Shows and Attractions

Illuminations: Reflections of Earth fireworks
Best for: Everyone
Description: A nighttime fireworks and laser show over the World Showcase Lagoon. It's a stunning nightly event divided into three acts: Chaos, Order, and Meaning. All parts flow together to show the history of the Earth and brings a sense of belonging to our journey on our home planet.
Level: Everyone
Recommendation: Conclude your day with this stunning fireworks display that dazzles the sky.
FastPass+: Yes – If you reserve a FastPass for this, you will stand near the entrance to the World Showcase. For many, this is the best spot.

★ **Magic Tips** ★
1. As with all fireworks and parades, it's best to get there early and sit as close to the lagoon by Mexico or the Mitsukoshi Store in Japan. On busier days, you'll want to claim your

spot about 90 minutes ahead of time. If you don't get there that early, find standing room where you can.

2. The crowds pour out of Epcot after the show. Most of the time, the International Gateway will be your exit, between Great Britain and France.

3. There are a few ways out after the fireworks: bus, monorail, boat, or your own car. The first three are much easier as Disney has this system down for getting guests back to their hotels. However, if you don't have a hotel and drove, it's sort of a mad rush to the parking lot. To avoid this, we recommend being one of the first to leave through the International Gateway.

4. You can also request a patio or window seat at any of these restaurants for firework viewing: Rose and Crown Pub (United Kingdom), Bistro de Paris (France), Cantina de San Angel (Mexico), La Hacienda de San Angel (Mexico), Tokyo Dining (Japan).

5. Disney's Boardwalk Inn guests can see the Illuminations fireworks from the hotel's outdoor walkway. It's not the best viewing, but it beats the crowds, and you can see plenty of the fireworks in the sky.

6. If you enjoy fine dining, the Four Seasons Orlando has a Spanish steakhouse called Capa (on the 17th floor). Make a dining reservation around the time of the fireworks, and you'll be able to see not only Epcot's display but also the Magic Kingdom's. As it is a Four Seasons, the meals don't come cheap, but it might be worth the cost!

Chapter Nine

Disney's Hollywood Studios

Introduction

Previously known as MGM Studios until it was revamped in 2008, Disney's Hollywood Studios is a park dedicated to Hollywood's Golden Age in the 1930's. Disney may never admit it, but the Park was likely created in response to the growing popularity of Universal Studios Orlando that brought its visitors to the magic of the movies with its attractions. Hollywood Studios does the same, only with Disney's famous films and characters. Even if the idea for the Park wasn't original, everyone can agree that they are happy Disney did it. With rides like Twilight Zone Tower of Terror and stunning shows like *Fantasmic!*, Hollywood Studios truly does justice to Disney's expansive collection of films in an exciting way.

Even though its revamp was less than ten years ago, there's something about Disney's Hollywood Studios that has always felt lacking. The other three parks are bursting with adventure, but Hollywood Studios felt more like a studio back lot with sprinkles of attractions, no unique food, and while it's a fun place to be, Disney's magic isn't felt here as much as the other Parks.

The good news is that Walt Disney World knows this. In fact, they are putting the Park under massive construction for the next few years to bring exciting new Disney-movie-themed attractions that might make it one of the most popular parks in the world! Coming soon are two unique lands: Toy Story Land and a yet-to-be-named Star Wars themed area. Both lands will bring the fun and adventure of their respective films with unique rides and experiences that will leave guests in awe (opening dates are likely in 3-4 years).

But what about in 2017? Well, fret not because there is still much to do in Hollywood Studios. There is the classic Star Tours ride for Thrill Seekers as well as the Toy Story Mania! that's fun for everyone of all ages. Sure, there will be construction, but

Disney does a great job of disguising this so that it doesn't interrupt your experience.

There are 8 Main Area of Disney's Hollywood Studios, and we review them all, attraction by attraction, in this chapter of the guide.

Thrill Seekers

Disney Hollywood Studios has many shows. So if you are just looking for rides, you might want to consider doing Hollywood Studios and Epcot on the same day. They are just across the road from one another and easy to get to with the bussing system (or by boat and a bit of walking).

Families with Young Kids

There's very little for Young Kids to do at Hollywood Studios. While the Park includes a Disney Jr. show, Frozen show, and Toy Story, that's pretty much the extent for Young Kids. We'd recommend a water park or a revisit to the Magic Kingdom instead of this Park until they finish the Toy Story Land in a few years. However, if you have Park Hopper, it might be worth dropping by for a few hours to experience the unique attractions.

Hollywood Studios Rope Drop

Hollywood Studios has one of the more expansive pre-opening areas. Guests are allowed to stroll down Hollywood Blvd as well as parts of Echo Lake. We recommend getting there 30 minutes early for the security and onto the street. There is a welcome announcement with cast members. Most guests head toward Toy Story Mania! so we recommend just grabbing a FastPass+ selection for it and avoiding the unnecessary hustle.

Hollywood Boulevard

The grand, golden age-themed entrance of the Park. You'll feel like you're walking down a glamourized version of the real Hollywood Boulevard in the same way that Walt Disney experienced it when he first moved to Los Angeles.

Theme: Golden Age Hollywood entrance mostly made of shops and dining.

Rides:

The Great Movie Ride®
Best for: Young Kids, Kids, Tweens, Adults 30+
Description: The outside looks like the iconic Chinese Theatre where many films have their debut (though Disney films usually premiere across the street at the El Capitan). The ride is a slow-paced dark ride that explores the movie history of Hollywood.
Level: Everyone
Recommendation: Kids of all ages and adults over 30 will enjoy this attraction for its glitzy appeal. However, Teens and Thrill Seekers might find it a bit boring.
Line Length: Short / **FastPass+:** Yes

Echo Lake

This land is a bit of a hodge-podge of themes from George Lucas films like Star Wars and Indiana Jones, with the addition of theatres that recreate the palm-tree crowded Southern California feel from just outside of Hollywood.

Theme: Mock studios around a central lake.

Rides

For the First Time in Forever: A *Frozen* Sing-Along Celebration
Best for: Young Kids, Kids, Tweens, Adults 50+
Description: A 30-minute theatre show at the Hyperion Theatre starring Elsa, Anna, and their Frozen friends with music and more from the massively popular film.
Level: Family
Recommendation: Bring every *Frozen* fan that you know.
Line Length: Short / **FastPass+:** Yes

Star Tours – The Adventures Continue
Best for: Kids, Tweens, Teens, Young Adults, Thrill Seekers
Description: A Star Wars themed 3D motion simulator hosted by C-3PO. Visit two of nine planets from the films, but they mix them up, so nearly every ride is excitingly different!
Level: Thrill Seekers
Recommendation: A perfect ride for *Star Wars* fans. If you get motion sickness, you may want to skip this ride.
Line Length: Medium / **FastPass+:** Yes
★ Magic Tip ★
> During the ride, you visit two of nine planets from the films, but they mix them up. Ride multiple times and get a different experience each time!

Shows and Attractions

Indiana Jones Epic Stunt Spectacular!
Best for: Everyone
Description: A 25-minute live stunt show starring Indiana Jones. See the action of *Raiders of the Lost Ark* in this epic attraction.
Level: Everyone

Recommendation: Great for everyone, though Young Kids who have a hard time sitting still for long or don't enjoy loud noises may want to skip this attraction.
Line Length: Short / **FastPass+:** Yes

Jedi Training: Trials of the Temple
Best for: Young Kids, Kids
Description: A 20-minute kid-friendly interactive *Star Wars*-themed show right outside of the Star Tours ride.
Level: Kids
Recommendation: Kids of all ages love this show and can even be lucky enough to participate!
Line Length: Short / **FastPass+:** No
★ Magic Tip ★

1. They usually pick around sixteen kid volunteers ages 4 to 12 years old. To register to participate in the show, volunteers must go with a parent or guardian to the Indiana Jones Adventure Outpost (between the Indiana Jones Epic Stunt Spectacular! and 50's Prime Time Café). We recommend going as soon as the Park opens as the registration is first come, first served.
2. Rain will likely result in this outdoor show's cancellation.

Muppets Courtyard

A zany Muppet-themed land with several references to the movie and television series. And, of course, your favorite Muppets await, dying to meet you!

Theme: Jim Henson's Muppets

Shows and Attractions

Muppet*Vision 3D
Best for: Young Kids, Kids, Tweens, Adults 50+
Description: A hilarious 15-minute 4D show with special effects and silly surprises starring Kermit the Frog and nearly every other character from *The Muppet Show.*
Level: Family
Recommendation: Perfect for families with Kids and fans of *The Muppet Show.*
Line Length: Very Short / **FastPass+:** Yes

Pixar Place

A small boulevard with buildings inspired by Pixar films.

Theme: Pixar

Rides

Toy Story Mania!®
Best for: Everyone
Description: A 4D game where riders attempt to score the most points by shooting at animated targets with a plunger canon.
Level: Everyone
Recommendation: All ages will enjoy this ride from Young Kids to Thrill Riders. Not recommended if you have trouble seeing with 3D glasses.
Line Length: Very Long
FastPass+: Yes
★ **Magic Tips** ★
   1. We've been to Hollywood Studios before where Toy Story Mania! was *only* allowing guests with FastPass+

selections on that day. The ride is one of the most popular in all of Walt Disney World, and we can't stress enough that it should top your FastPass selection choice for this day.

2. How to score BIG:
   - Many "pro" riders hold the plunger between two fingers with their palm facing them (be careful not to pull too hard of course!)
   - Shoot the higher-point targets at the bottom of the screens.
   - Scene #1 (Hamm and Eggs) – Hitting the pigs on the fence will make a cat show that can be hit multiple times for big points.
   - Scene #2 (Rex and Trixie) – Pop the lava balloons on the volcano to make it erupt with 500-point balloons.
   - Scene #3 (Green Army Men) – Look for the yellow-tinted plates that are worth 2,000 points.
   - Scene #4 (Alien Ring Game) – On the far sides are rocket ships and aliens worth big points.
   - Scene #5 (Woody's Western Theme) – Aim for the doors of the saloon to reveal higher point targets. At the end of this scene there are mine carts that roll toward you. Look for the bats above the mine carts that are worth some major points.

Animation Courtyard

Immerse yourself in a studio lot dedicated to the art of Walt Disney Animation Studios. See live shows as well as meet characters in this unique land.

Theme: Walt Disney Animation Studios

Shows and Attractions

Voyage of the Little Mermaid
Best for: Young Kids, Kids, Tweens
Description: A family-friendly live show that brings to life the characters, adventure, and music of Disney's *The Little Mermaid*. The entire show is 17 minutes in length.
Level: Family
Recommendation: Great for families with Young Kids and fans of Disney's *The Little Mermaid*. Others might want to check out the Indiana Jones show or Beauty and the Beast.
Line Length: Short / **FastPass+:** Yes

Disney Junior – Live on Stage!
Best for: Young Kids
Description: A live action stage show designed for preschool aged children who love Disney Junior.
Level: Young Kids
Recommendation: Families with young children.
Line Length: Short / **FastPass+:** Yes

Mickey Avenue

Theme: Mickey Mouse and Walt Disney's Vision

Shows and Attractions

Walt Disney: One Man's Dream

Best for: Adults 30+

Description: An interactive exhibit displaying Walt Disney's dream to bring entertainment to the world.

Level: Everyone

Recommendation: Many Kids, Teens, and Young Adults will likely find this exhibit boring. It's interactive, yet meant to be informative.

Line Length: Short / **FastPass+:** None

Sunset Boulevard

Another classic piece of California set right in the middle of the Walt Disney World Resort. Stroll down a fictionalized version of the famous Sunset Boulevard and see the harrowing Hollywood Hotel in the distance. There are also iconic shows and fantastic shops in this area.

Theme: Hollywood Street

Rides

The Twilight Zone Tower of Terror

Best for: Tweens, Teens, Adults, Thrill Riders

Description: Plummet down 13 treacherous stories in this Twilight Zone themed thrill ride.

Level: Thrill Riders (must be 40"/ 102cm or taller)

Recommendation: Only those looking to be scared!
Line Length: Long
FastPass+: Yes
★ **Magic Tips** ★

1. If you decide to skip the FastPass, we recommend riding Tower of Terror in the evening. The line for this ride tends to get shorter later in the day once everyone has already ridden it.
2. Once you enter the library with the black and white TV, move to the back of the room where you'll see a closed door. That'll be the quickest way to the next line once the screening finishes.
3. Sitting front row can make a slight difference for the view of the ride. If you want to sit in the front, ask a cast member at the end of the queue.

Rock 'n' Roller Coaster Starring Aerosmith

Best for: Teens, Adults, Thrill Seekers
Description: Similar to Space Mountain, this coaster is indoors and fairly dark. Only, you are launched into loops, corkscrews, and inversions to get your blood flowing! Aerosmith sets the tone and music to this epic attraction.
Level: Thrill Seekers
Recommendation:
Line Length: Very Long
FastPass+: Yes
★ **Magic Tips** ★

1. We notice that the lines can be quite long for this ride as there aren't many options for Thrill Riders in Hollywood Studios. If you are looking forward to riding this attraction, make sure that you book a FastPass+ reservation.
2. To avoid much of the line, move to the far left near the doors when you enter the recording studio room with

Aerosmith. You'll bypass the crowd when entering the final line.

Shows and Attractions

Beauty and the Beast – Live on Stage
Best for: Young Kids, Kids, Tweens, Adults 50+
Description: A 25-minute live Broadway-style musical starring the cast of Disney's animated film, *Beauty and the Beast.*
Level: Everyone
Recommendation: Perfect for fans of Broadway musicals and the animated film *Beauty and the Beast.*
Line Length: Short
FastPass+: Yes

Fantasmic!
Best for: Everyone
Description: The stunning Hollywood Hills Amphitheater brings to life the 26-minute Disney spectacular, *Fantasmic!* See Mickey and more in this epic show of light, music, and special

effects all on the water. But be careful because the Disney Villains are out to ruin it all!

Level: Everyone

Recommendation: Everyone should see this show at least once!

Line Length: Medium

FastPass+: Yes

★ **Magic Tips** ★

1. If you opt for the FastPass, you will be placed in a special section in the front and near the center.

2. Get a Dining Package and receive a voucher for seating in the center. Here are the participating restaurants (you may also eat in your seat if you get a to-go option at select locations):

    • Hollywood Brown Derby – Lunch or Dinner with appetizer, entrée, dessert, and non-alcoholic beverage. Adults are $62.99 and Kids under 10 are $21.99.

    • Mama Melrose's Ristorante Italiano – Lunch or Dinner with appetizer, entrée, dessert, and non-alcoholic beverage. Adults are $44.99 and Kids under 10 are $17.99.

    • Hollywood & Vine – Lunch or Dinner with appetizer, entrée, dessert, and non-alcoholic beverage. Adults are $53.99 and Kids under 10 are $32.99.

    Make sure you reserve your dining before you head to the park as these vouchers can sell out.

3. If you miss the FastPass+ option, get to the Amphitheater at least 30 minutes beforehand and sit as close to the center of the seating for the best views.

4. After *Fantasmic!*, you'll either want to leave or head to the Star Wars Fireworks show. Either way, head near the entrance to watch the fireworks or to the fireworks shortly after.

132

Star Wars Launch Bay
Best for: Kids, Tweens, Teens, Adults
Description: Meet Chewbacca, Darth Vader, and Jawas while seeing replicas of props used in the Star Wars films.
Level: Everyone
Recommendation: Best for Star Wars fans as the lines to meet character can get a bit long.
Line Length: Very Short / **FastPass+:** No

Star Wars: A Galactic Spectacular fireworks
Best for: Everyone
Description: The music and images from the Star Wars films come to life on the *Chinese Theatre* with an epic fireworks display.
Level: Everyone
Recommendation: For every fireworks and *Star Wars* fan.
★ **Magic Tip** ★

> To avoid the exiting crowds, you may want to leave before the end of the show, or situate yourself near the exit before the bus, boat, and parking lines grow.

Chapter Ten
Disney's Animal Kingdom

Introduction

Completed in 1998, Disney's Animal Kingdom is a unique theme park dedicated to both the classic Walt Disney World attractions as well as being a place for animal conservation. With lions, tigers, elephants living in the Park, it would seem that Animal Kingdom is Disney's version of a zoo. However, that couldn't be further from the truth. The Park is breathtaking in its seamless foliage between specialized lands and perfect environments for its animals. As you travel through the jungle, you'll meet Disney favorites like meerkats and warthogs as well as critically endangered species. Disney takes this park seriously and works its hardest to bring the best for its animal inhabitants.

Set on more than 500 acres of land, Animal Kingdom is not only the largest park in WDW, it's the largest theme park in the world! The centerpiece is the famous Tree of Life, a 14-story replica of the same tree from Disney's *The Lion King*. Animal Kingdom perfectly ties together fun and information in 6 distinct lands: Oasis (the lush main entrance), Discovery Island (a central hub with The Tree of Life), Africa (an African village with safaris), Rafiki's Planet Watch (a family-friendly outpost), Asia (excursions of the Orient and home of the towering Expedition Everest ride), and DinoLand U.S.A (where dinosaurs roam the Earth once again). Coming in late 2017 is the 7th land, Pandora–The World of Avatar, an alien planet inspired by the James Cameron film, *Avatar*.

While some informative attractions in Epcot and Hollywood Studios can seem a bit boring and dated, Animal Kingdom feels new and exciting in all of its exhibits. Perhaps it's that you are seeing the actual animals roam as you ride on an African-style safari while you learn about the many habits of the spectacular creatures before you. Or maybe it's that Animal Kingdom feels perfectly nestled in the Floridian weather, bringing you a sense that you are climbing the steps of Asian countryside or deep in the heart of the jungle. Then again, it could be the blend of family-friendly attractions, beautiful animals, and expansive thrill rides that gives something to everyone at this unique Park. Whatever the reason, Animal Kingdom is flawless and perhaps the best park in all of Walt Disney World.

In this section, we review each of the lands as well as give you an index of animal locations throughout the park.

Pandora–The World of Avatar

Disney hasn't released much about this amazing new land coming to Animal Kingdom. Though the release date hasn't been set, we expect Summer or Fall 2017 for the grand opening. However, we are leaning toward Fall as we expect details about the addition to be released in at Disney's Expo in California, D23, July 14-16.
Pandora will contain two new rides: a flight simulator and a river boat dark ride. There will also be new dining experiences,

animatronic creatures, and the popular blue Na'vi aliens of Pandora.

We will have free updates available to our readers about Pandora once it opens. To receive these updates, sign up for our free e-mail list on our website: www.magicguidebooks.com/waltdisneyworld

Animal Kingdom Rope Drop

We recommend getting to the Animal Kingdom park 30-minutes before opening. This will allow you to get through security, head through the Oasis and to Discovery Island where guests crowd in front of the Tree of Life. There's also a special surprise for those who get to the Park early. About 10 minutes from opening time, you'll hear an announcement. A pleasant voice will welcome you to the Animal Kingdom, and a small showing of beautiful parrots will glide overhead. It's a stunning display and not to be missed!

The Oasis

The lush entrance to Disney's Animal Kingdom. Here you will find several walkways through bush and along rivers filled with exotic plants and animals that find their home here. The Rainforest Café® also is located here. There are no rides in the Oasis, so this land feels a lot like a well-designed animal sanctuary.

Theme: A Tropical Oasis

Animals

Mammals:
Barbirusa
Giant Anteater
Swamp Wallaby

Reptiles:
Florida Cooter
Rhinoceros Iguanas

Birds:
African Spoonbill

Bufflehead
Chiloe Wigeon
Exotic Ducks
Hooded Merganser
Indian Spotbill
Macaws
Medium Sulpher-crested Cockatoo
Reeves' Muntjac
Teals

Discovery Island

The centerpiece or "Hub" of Animal Kingdom. It's home to several animals, shops, and the Park's signature Tree of Life. Discovery Island is surrounded by the Discover River and connects to nearly every land in the Park.

Theme: An Animal-Inhabited Island

Shows and Attractions

It's Tough to be a Bug!®
Best for: Everyone
Description: A 9-minute family-friendly 4D show starring characters from Pixar's *A Bug's Life*. With special lighting effects and a large 3D screen, you'll feel as small as a bug as you laugh along to this hilarious attraction.
Level: Everyone

Recommendation: Though Disney originally planned this attraction to please families with Kids, everyone appears to get a kick out of this attraction.

Line Length: Short / **FastPass+:** Yes

★ **Magic Tips** ★

1. The theatre is large, so if there ever is a wait, it's usually just until the next show loads.
2. We recommend sitting as central as possible in the 4th-7th rows.

Tree of Life at Night

Best for: Everyone

Description: See the Tree of Life come to life with four different animations that magically project on the tree.

Level: Family

Recommendation: A short, animated feature on the Tree of Life.

Line Length: None / **FastPass:** No

Rivers of Light – Coming Spring 2017

Best for: Everyone

Description: An all-new nighttime spectacular set along the Discovery River. See the light, hear the music, and watch the amazing special effects in this one-of-a-kind show.

Level: Everyone

Recommendation: The Rivers of Light will be a perfect way to conclude the night.

Line Length: Long / **FastPass+:** Yes

★ **Magic Tips** ★

As with all shows, we recommend lining up 1-2 hours in advance for the best standing spaces.

Wilderness Explorers

Best for: Young Kids, Kids

Description: Inspired by Pixar's *Up*, kids can earn up to 30 Wilderness Explorer badges by completing challenges.

Level: Kids

Recommendation: A playground for kids of all ages.

Line Length: Very Short / **FastPass:** No

Discovery Island Trails

Best for: Everyone

Description: Follow pathways around the Tree of Life to see waterfalls, unique animals, and meet Tarzan.

Level: Everyone

Recommendation: Great for animal lovers. Check out the many carvings in the Tree of Life and watch them magically come to life at night!

Line Length: None / **FastPass+:** No

Animals

Mammals:
African Crested Porcupine
Asian Small-Clawed Otter
Axis Deer
Cotton-top Tamarin
Lemurs
Kangaroos

Birds:
Black Neck Swan
Cockatoos
Exotic Ducks
Teals
West African Crowned Crane
White Stork

Reptiles:
Galapagos Tortoise
Lappet Face Vulture
Flamingoes
Macaw
Saddle-Billed Stork

Africa

A popular land for safari excursions, African animals, and eateries, *Africa* in centered around Harambe, a fictional Kenyan village. This area has, by far, the most animals spread throughout its unique attractions.

Theme: African Village and Safari.

Rides

Kilimanjaro Safaris®

Best for: Everyone

Description: Hop aboard a guided caravan tour of Africa. From the jungles to the savanna, you'll see everything from wildebeest to giraffes to rhinos and even lions. The animals are in "cage-less" enclosure (except for the carnivores, of course), so watch them roaming free before your eyes.

Level: Everyone

Recommendation: The Kilimanjaro Safaris are one of the guest attractions in Animal Kingdom for everyone of all ages. This ride does get a bit bumpy, so beware in case you have issues with that. Disney also just opened the ride for nighttime safaris. Sadly, most of the animals almost impossible to see, and portions of the ride are closed.

Line Length: Medium / **FastPass+:** Yes

Animals

Mammals:

Addax
African Elephant
African Wild Dog
Antelope
Ankole-Watusi
Bongo
Bontebok
Cheetah
Duiker
Eland
Giraffe

Greater Kudu
Hippopotamus
Hyena
Impala
Okapi
Oryx
Ostrich
Mandrill
Nyala
Rhinoceros
Waterbuck
Warthog
Wildebeest
Zebra

Birds:
African Ducks
African Geese
African Pelicans
African Pintails
African Storks
Blue Crane
Flamingo
Helmeted Guineafowl
Teals
White-breasted Cormorant

Reptiles:
Nile Crocodile

★ **Magic Tips** ★

1. The Florida sun can be scorching, so if you're looking for a cooler experience, we recommend selecting one of the later FastPass+ times. The animals seem to pick up their energy around then as well!

2. Check out the island with the flamingoes… it's shaped like a very familiar character!

Shows and Attractions

Festival of the Lion King

Best for: Young Kids, Kids, Tweens, Adults 30+

Description: An interactive 30-minute stage show set to the characters and music of Disney's *The Lion King*. Easily one of WDW's best live shows, the Festival of the Lion King entertains guests with dancing, puppetry, and fantastic costumes.

Level: Family

Recommendation: Perfect for families with Kids and fans of *The Muppet Show*.

Line Length: Very Short / **FastPass+:** Yes

★ **Magic Tip** ★

> The theatre is divided into four sections, so depending where you sit, you'll have a slightly different experience. Each section is represented by an animal and the show's four hosts interact with their respective section.

Pangani Forest Exploration Trail

Best for: Everyone

Description: Walk along the Kilimanjaro Safaris to see animals you can't explore from the caravan. There are more primates, reptiles, and even insects on this trail. There's also a large aviary filled with African birds.

Level: Everyone

Recommendation: We recommend this to anyone craving to see more African animals. The walk is short at little over a 1/3 of a mile, so kids will love this one.

Line Length: Very Short / **FastPass+:** No

Animals

Mammals:
Colobus Monkeys
Duiker
Gerenuk
Gorilla
Hippopotamus
Lion
Meerkat
Naked Mole Rat
Okapi
Oryx
Zebra

Birds:
African Ducks
African Geese
African Parrots
African Pigeons
African Pelicans
African Pintails
African Starlings
African Storks

Blake Crake
Brimstone Canary
Blue Crane
Collared Kingfisher
Hamerkop
Hoopoe
Kori Bustard
Shrikes
Taveta Weaver
Teals

White-bellied Go-Away-Bird

Reptiles:
Boa Constrictor
Shield-tailed Agama
Spiny-tailed Lizard

Arachnids and Fish:
Lake Victoria Cichlid
Tarantula

Wild Africa Trek – VIP Experience

Best for: Teens, Adults

Description: If you're looking for an expanded safari experience, we highly recommend this experience. Get closer to the animals, move across rope bridges through the jungle, and ride on a specialized caravan safari during the second half. This is a 3-hour tour with a separate cost.

Pricing: $189-$249

Level: Adults

Recommendation: Because this VIP excursion is so long, we don't recommend it for kids or those who have trouble walking. Guests must be 18 or older or 8 years old with an adult. You must be able to wear harness gear and weigh under 300lbs.

Line Length: None – Reservation

FastPass+: No

Booking: (407) 939-8687 /
https://disneyworld.disney.go.com/events-tours/animal-kingdom/wild-africa-trek

★ **Magic Tip** ★

Due to the summer heat, the Wild Africa Trek will often offer an additional discount.

Rafiki's Planet Watch

A section connected to Africa that highlights how to practice conservation to save the Earth's animals from harm and extinction. This area is hosted by Rafiki from *The Lion* King. It's fun to travel by the Wildlife Express Train, however, it's a bit of a bore for many. Young Kids will enjoy the petting corral known as the Affection Section.

Theme: Africa / Global Conservation

Rides

Wildlife Express Train
Best for: Young Kids, Adults 50+
Description: A slow-paced steam railroad to Rifiki's Planet Watch. The 7-minute ride (5-minute return) takes guests behind the scenes of the habitats before emptying onto the Planet Watch.
Level: Family
Recommendation: If you have curiosity about Rafiki's Planet Watch and want to see some behind the scenes areas where the animals live, we recommend this ride.
Line Length: Short / **FastPass+:** None

Shows and Attractions

Affection Section
Best for: Young Kids, Kids, Tweens
Description: Pet and feed cows, donkeys, goats, pigs, and sheep in this petting corral.
Level: Family
Recommendation: Perfect for young kids and for taking photos with animals.
Line Length: Short / **FastPass+:** No

★ **Magic Tip** ★

> There is a handwashing station near this attraction for after you interact with the animals.

Conservation Station

Best for: Young Kids, Kids

Description: A special care facility designed to help animals from the park. You can interact with some of them as well as watch a 3D movie about the rainforest, see backstage cameras, see cases with crawling insects, and watch the veterinarians care for animals.

Level: Family

Recommendation: Perfect for Kids

Line Length: None / **FastPass+:** No

Habitat Habit!

Best for: Young Kids, Kids

Description: Walk along trails to discover cotton-top tamarin monkeys playing.

Level: Kids

Recommendation: Perfect for kids.

Line Length: Very short / **FastPass+:** No

Asia

Discover the fictional Asian land of Anandapur (Sanskrit for "Place of Many Delights") as you journey along a river village and deep into the Himalayan mountains. Asia is home to unique animals from beautiful tigers to stunning birds, as well as unique rides that can thrill the whole family.

Theme: Asian villages and the Himalayas

Rides

Expedition Everest–Legends of the Forbidden Mountain
Best for: Tweens, Teens, Adults

Description: Animal Kingdom's most sought-after thrill ride. Costing $100 million to make, Everest is the world's most expensive rollercoaster–and it was worth it! Lift high into the peaks of the Earth's most famous mountain deep in the Himalayas, cruise at high speeds, and end up rolling backward when attacked by the mountain's terrifying yeti!

Level: Thrill Riders

Recommendation: Perfect for those who enjoy high-speed rollercoasters.

Line Length: Long / **FastPass+:** Yes

★ **Magic Tip** ★

> Expedition Everest also offers a Single Rider Line. This is an option for those who don't want to wait in the long queues and are okay riding by themselves. There is a very small chance that you'll end up riding with another person in your party, but if you don't snag a FastPass+ reservation and the line is long, this might be a great option. To access the Single Rider line, look for the sign next to the regular line queue entrance.

Kali River Rapids
Best for: Kids, Tweens, Teens, Adults

Description: A family-friendly raft ride through the Asian jungle. You will likely get soaked on this 12-person water ride!

Level: Families, Thrill Riders

Recommendation: Great for hot days. There are dips and spills, so if you're not looking to get wet, you might want to avoid this one.

Line Length: Long / **FastPass+:** Yes

★ Magic Tip ★

Kali River Rapids has shorter lines in the morning when it's cooler and very long lines in the hot afternoons. We always recommend getting a FastPass for this ride, but if you don't and still want to ride, go near the park's closing time to avoid long lines.

Shows and Attractions:

Maharajah Jungle Trek
Best for: Everyone
Description: A walking trail slightly over 1/3 of a mile, showcasing some of the most exotic animals in all of Asia. From tigers to komodo dragons, the Maharajah Jungle Trek is both informative and delightful for all.
Level: Everyone
Recommendation: Not to be missed for those looking to see spectacular and rare animals.
Line Length: Very Short / **FastPass+:** No

Animals

Mammals:
Banteng
Bengal Tiger
Gibbons
Malayan Flying Fox
Sumatran Tiger
Water Buffalo

Reptiles:
Komodo Dragon

Birds:
More than 50 Species of Asian birds like starlings, ducks, parrots, peafowls, pheasants, barbets, and kingfishers.

Flights of Wonder
Best for: Young Kids, Kids, Adults 50+

Description: A 25-minute stage show where live birds take flight. Also learn how you can protect many of these magnificent birds from extinction in the wild.
Level: Family
Recommendation: Families with young children.
Line Length: Short / **FastPass+:** No

DinoLand U.S.A

Disney's Dino Institute takes you on a journey to the past when magnificent dinosaurs roamed the Earth. There are dino-themed rides, fossil replicas, and a carnival-themed area.

Theme: Dinosaur Lab and Carnival

Rides

DINOSAUR
Best for: Kids, Tweens, Teens, Adults, Thrill Riders
Description: Get sent back to the age of the dinosaurs in a special SUV time machine. Themed after Disney's *Dinosaur* film, there's rocky terrain in this unique dark ride similar to Disneyland's Indiana Jones Adventure.
Level: Thrill Riders (must be 40"/ 102cm or taller)
Recommendation: Perfect for Thriller Riders though some Kids may become frightened of the scarier dinosaurs.
Line Length: Long / **FastPass+:** Yes

Primeval Whirl
Best for: Kids, Tweens, Teens
Description: Twist and turn over a zany rollercoaster track.
Level: Family

Recommendation: Designed for the Kids and Tweens, this ride is also enjoyed by many Thrill Seekers.
Line Length: Medium / **FastPass+:** Yes

TriceraTop Spin

Best for: Young Kids, Kids
Description: Similar to Dumbo's Flight at the Magic Kingdom, riders control brightly colored triceratops as they soar through the air.
Level: Kids
Recommendation: A perfect ride for Young Kids.
Line Length: Medium / **FastPass+:** No

Shows and Attractions

Finding Nemo–The Musical

Best for: Young Kids, Kids, Tweens, Adults 50+
Description: A 40-minute live Broadway-style musical starring the cast of Pixar's *Finding Nemo*–and yes, Dory is there, too! Puppetry, lighting, and special effects bring to life this stunning show.
Level: Family
Recommendation: Perfect for fans of Broadway musicals and the animated film *Finding Nemo*.
Line Length: Medium / **FastPass+:** Yes
★ Magic Tips ★

> Get there about 30 minutes ahead for the best seating. On less crowded day, this may not be necessary.

Dino-Sue

Best for: Young Kids, Kids, Tweens, Adults 50+
Description: A replica of one of the largest Tyrannosaurus Rex fossils ever found.
Level: Everyone

Recommendation: A great walkthrough attraction for lovers of fossils. It's impressive to stand next to Sue, the massive T-Rex!
Line Length: Low / **FastPass+:** No

Fossil Fun Games
Best for: Young Kids, Kids, Tweens
Description: Additional cost carnival games to win stuffed animal prizes.
Level: Family
Recommendation: Fun for Kids who love carnival games.

The Boneyard
Best for: Young Kids, Kids
Description: A playground where Kids can dig up dinosaur fossils.
Level: Kids
Recommendation: A great place to sit with a kid while the family rides a Dinosaur.

Chapter Eleven

Disney's Water Parks

Introduction

Walt Disney World opened its original water park, Disney's River Country, in 1976. This Park has been since closed (as of 2001), as the massive popularity of its newer parks, Typhoon Lagoon (1989) and Blizzard Beach (1995) conquered the scene. Combined, the Disney Water Parks bring in nearly 5 million visitors annually–with Typhoon Lagoon being slightly more popular.

Each Water Park is set in a different location in the Walt Disney World Resort. Typhoon Lagoon is near Disney Springs, and Blizzard Beach is on the other end near Animal Kingdom and between the All-Star Sports Resort and Disney's Coronado Springs Resort hotels.

Typhoon Lagoon is themed after a paradise bay–shortly after a storm has hit! There are pirate ships, streams, waterfalls, palm trees, and dozens of attractions. Blizzard Beach pulls its theme from ski lodges where the snow melts in the summer heat. It's an interesting hodge-podge of idea with log cabins and snowy slopes only without the cold! Each park has a similar layout with a mountain peak in the center, wave pool below, and a lazy river around the perimeter.

For families with kids visiting during the summer, the Walt Disney World waterparks have become essential attractions. There are two of them, each with different, captivating themes. These parks contain lazy rivers where guests float around in rafts, water slides from small to daring, wave pools that simulate the ocean, and plenty of lounging spaces.

Many adults who visit without children may want to skip the water park and just lounge at the pools in their Resort hotel. Remember, most of the hotels have their own waterslides. In fact, if you are staying less than five nights, it may be difficult to fit a full day in at the water parks and see all of the theme parks. It's tricky to choose, so we give you concise information on which slides and attractions will benefit your vacation.

Notes:

1. The water parks sometimes have Extra Magic Hours for Disney Resort hotel guests. Check the calendar during your stay to see when these are.

2. During severe weather, the Water Parks can close. Lightning, as you can imagine, doesn't mix well with water.

3. The Water Parks have extended hours during the summer (sometimes as late as 8pm), and they cut back in the fall. During the winter, they can be under refurbishment.

4. Speaking of refurbishment, Disney's Typhoon Lagoon Water Park is scheduled to be closed until March 11th, 2017.

5. These may be the only parks that don't need a set of outlined plans. The line lengths can change frequently (but expect up to 30-minute wait times during the summer peak season for the most popular slides). Since everyone can go at their own pace, the water parks are a perfect time to find relaxation during your stay.

6. If you are feeling adventurous, you can do both water parks in one day. We recommend spacing these out by going at opening to one and heading over to the next in the afternoon when the crowds have lessened. Just remember that you might not get your choice of lounging area at the second park you choose.

7. There are no FastPass+ selections for Typhoon Lagoon, as the average wait time is usually only 10-15 minutes (with some of the more popular attractions having 30-minute waits).

What to Bring

The water parks have nearly everything you'll need for poolside-fun–but with a cost. That's why we recommend bringing these items with you into the parks:

1. Sunscreen – You'll be out in the sun all day, after all.
2. Beach towels – Rentals are available
3. Change of clothing – It's not vital, but we recommend it if you plan to go somewhere afterward.

Note:
You *can* bring the towels from your hotel if you really want, though WDW doesn't recommend this (and we're not saying that you should). However, people do it from time to time.

★ **Magic Tips** ★
1. Get there at opening to reserve the best lounge chairs for your family.
2. Prime spots are near the wave pool or just outside of it near the lazy rivers.
3. Keep your belongings safe. There's a general safe feeling all around the park, so you can leave some items like sunscreen and visors unattended (or under your towel). However, we would recommend storing away your cellphone and car keys in a rental locker.

Rentals

1. Lockers – We highly recommend keeping your things here. There are two locker rental stations in each park near the entrance. Pricing is $10/day for a regular (12.5 inches by 17 inches) and $15/day for a large ($15.5 inches by 17 inches). Lockers take credit cards and cash and your items are kept safe with a 4-digit code that you set. Lockers can sell out, so make sure you get to the park early to reserve one.

2. Cabanas – called Beachcomber Shacks at Typhoon Lagoon and Polar Patios at Blizzard Beach, these reserved areas come with lounge chairs, chairs, a personal locker, and a cooler for up to 6 guests (though you can pay more for 7-10 guests). Prices vary (usually $200-$350), and spaces are limited, so reserve yours as early as possible before your visit by calling: (407) 939-7529.

3. Umbrella and Lounge Chairs – If you don't want to fork out the money for a cabana, you can always reserve an umbrella. These come with two loungers, two chairs, and towels for up to 4 guests. Pricing varies from $40-$50 per reservation. Like the cabanas these are limited, so call ahead to reserve: (407) 939-7529.

4. All of the shops sell quality sunscreen, sunglasses, visors for a premium price.

★ Magic Tip ★

If you have two adults, we recommend splitting up at the start of the day to reserve a locker and lounge chairs. Sometimes the "rope drop" at the start of the day can get crowded. Have one person reserve the chairs in your desired section and the other rent a locker. You don't want to miss out on either! If we had to pick one over the other, we'd pick a lounging space and take our chances that the lockers will still be available.

Disney's Typhoon Lagoon

Escape to the wild tropics in this water park built around Caribbean beach, complete with a sunken ship perched high on a mountain!

Theme: Post-Typhoon Caribbean Beach

Rides and Attractions

Typhoon Lagoon Surf Pool
Best for: Tweens, Teens, and Adults
Description: A wave pool with waves that reach up to 6 feet.
Level: Everyone
Recommendation: This massive pool is wildly popular. Kids, Tweens, Teens, and Adults will love this area to splash in the blue waves. The waves aren't constant, as they come every couple of minutes.
★ **Magic Tip** ★
> Young Kids should be kept near the beach part where the waves are just a couple of inches and fun to splash.

Castaway Creek
Best for: Family, Adults
Description: An expansive, 2000-foot long lazy river that slowly travels around the perimeter of Typhoon Saloon. The entire journey takes about 20 minutes. Hop aboard one of the many floating rafts as you cruise down this gentle river.
Level: Everyone
Recommendation: Best for adults looking to relax, though Young Kids and Kids enjoy splashing around this area as well.
★ **Magic Tip** ★

You can stay in Castaway Creek for as long as you'd like. There are several entry points for all to enjoy.

Ketchakiddee Creek
Best for: Young Kids, Kids
Description: A water play area perfect for Young Kids under 48 inches.
Level: Young Kids and Kids
Recommendation: A great space to take your kids who want to ride water slides and splash in an area designed for them.

Keelhaul Falls
Best for: Kids, Tweens, Teens, Adults, Thrill Riders
Description: A beautiful waterslide with an inner tube.
Level: Family
Recommendation: Perfect for kids to adults, but Young Kids may want to sit this one out.

Mayday Falls
Best for: Kids, Tweens, Teens, Adults, Thrill Riders
Description: A rapids-themed waterslide on a tube. Go over bumps and small drops as you adventure quickly down a river.
Level: Family
Recommendation: Perfect for kids to adults, but Young Kids may want to sit this one out. This one can be a bit rough!

Gangplank Falls
Best for: Kids, Tweens, Teens, Adults, Thrill Riders
Description: A giant inner tube that seats four takes you down a wide waterslide.
Level: Family
Recommendation: Perfect for kids to adults, but Young Kids may want to sit this one out.

Humunga Kowabunga

Best for: Tweens, Teens, Adults

Description: One of the Park's steepest slides–and it's in the dark. Travel alone through a treacherous path that leads to a plunge.

Level: Thrill Riders (must be 48" or taller)

Recommendation: Best for those looking for a thrill.

Storm Slides

Best for: Tweens, Teens, Adults, Thrill Riders

Description: A set of three waterslides that plummet from the ship-wrecked mountain top. Each of them dunk into a pool.

Level: Family

Recommendation: Best for those looking for a family-fun thrill.

Shark Reef

Best for: Kids, Tweens, Teens, Adults, Thrill Riders

Description: Snorkel in a massive, saltwater tank filled with fish and sharks (yes, actually sharks, though they are the harmless leopard and bonnethead species). The tank holds over 350,000 gallons of water!

Level: Family

Recommendation: We recommend this for great swimmers. The water is chilly (68 degrees), so if you can handle it, we highly recommend this experience!

★ **Magic Tip** ★

> Life vests are available to borrow for those who need them.

Bay Slides

Best for: Young Kids, Kids

Description: A water play area perfect for Young Kids under 60 inches.

Level: Young Kids and Kids

Recommendation: A great space to take your kids who want to ride water slides and splash in an area designed for them.

Mountain Trail

Best for: Young Kids and Adults 30+

Description: Green, tree-filled walkways beneath Typhoon Lagoon's famous mountain. There are palm trees, beautiful Caribbean structures, and rope bridges.

Level: Everyone

Recommendation: Perfect for those looking for a stroll, though we recommend this part mostly for Adults, as Kids and Teens may find it boring.

Crush 'n' Gusher

Best for: Tweens, Tween, Adults, Thrill Riders

Description: A high-speed "water coaster" on a raft that holds 2-3 people. This ride is a lot of fun with its bobsled-like experience.

Level: Thrill Riders

Recommendation: A great thrill ride for those looking for high-speed fun.

Miss Fortune Falls – *Coming Spring 2017*

Best for: Kids, Tweens, Tween, Adults, Thrill Riders

Description: The newest slide at Disney's Typhoon Lagoon! Discover the legend of Captain Mary Oceaneer as you discover her fabled lost fortune in this unique attraction. Disney designed Miss Fortune Falls with the entire family in mind. Hop aboard a family-sized raft and climb to the top before descending into a raging river.

Level: Family / Thrill Riders

Recommendation: Great for those wanting to board with their entire family.

Disney's Blizzard Beach

Enter a ski resort on the brink of summer as the snow melts into a stunning water park! Disney's Blizzard Beach is as fun as it sounds–but without the cold! And what's ice and Disney without a little *Frozen*? Yep, there's even areas designed after one of the world's most beloved animated films. The park is built around a snowy summit with three color-coded sections: the Green Slopes, the Purple Slopes, and the Red Slopes.

Theme: Snowy Ski Resort Water Park

Main Rides and Attractions

Melt-Away Bay
Best for: Kids, Tweens, Teens, and Adults
Description: A wave pool filled with rafts and small waves along rocks.
Level: Family
Recommendation: This a big pool is wildly popular for families. The waves are constant, but are small and easy to ride.
★ **Magic Tip** ★
> Young Kids will like it better near the shore where the waves are just a couple of inches and fun to splash.

Cross Country Creek
Best for: Family, Adults
Description: A calm, winding river journey that expands for 3000 feet around the perimeter of Blizzard Beach. Hop aboard one of the many floating rafts as you cruise down this gentle river near waterfalls, by lush foliage, and near some of the thrill rides.
Level: Everyone

Recommendation: Best for adults looking to relax, though Young Kids and Kids enjoy splashing around this area as well.
★ **Magic Tip** ★
> You can stay in Cross Country Creek for as long as you'd like. There are 7 points around the creek to enter.

Ski Patrol Training Camp
Best for: Kids, Tweens
Description: A water play area, short slides, and an obstacle course that's perfect for Kids and Tweens under 60 inches.
Level: Kids
Recommendation: A great space to take your kids who want to ride water slides and splash in an area designed for them.

Tike's Peak
Best for: Young Kids, Kids
Description: A water play area perfect for Young Kids under 48 inches.
Level: Young Kids and Kids
Recommendation: A great space to take your kids who want to ride water slides and splash in an area designed for them.

Green Slope Rides and Attractions
Designed mostly for Thrill Riders.

Summit Plummet
Best for: Thrill Riders
Description: A single body slide that takes thrill riders through a high-speed plunge from the Park's centerpiece, Mt. Gushmore.
Level: Thrill Riders (must be 48 inches or taller)
Recommendation: Thrill Riders only.

Slush Gusher
Best for: Thrill Riders
Description: A body slide that takes thrill riders through a high-speed plunge from this 90-foot tall slide.
Level: Thrill Riders (must be 48 inches or taller)
Recommendation: Thrill Riders only.

Teamboat Springs
Best for: Kids, Tweens, Teens, Adults, Thrill Riders
Description: A massive inner tube that seats 6 as it takes you down a long, wide waterslide.
Level: Family
Recommendation: Perfect for the family, but you might want to leave the Young Kids out of it as it does get a bit scary.

Chairlift
Best for: Kids, Tweens, Teens, Adults, Thrill Riders
Description: What's a ski resort without a ski lift? Take the Chairlift to the top of Mt. Gushmore to ride the Green Slope Rides.
Level: Family (must be 32" or taller)
Recommendation: A fun way to the top, but we don't recommend heading up there if you have a fear of heights.

Purple Slope Rides and Attractions
Family-friendly water slides with toboggan mats and tubes. The general feel is like being on a snow-covered ski slope in the mountains.

Toboggan Racers
Best for: Kids, Tweens, Teens, Adults, Thrill Riders
Description: Fly down wavy slopes on slick mats – a family favorite!
Level: Family and Thrill Seekers

Recommendation: Perfect for Kids and older. The hills are steep, so if someone has an issue with heights, this might not be the ride for them.

Snow Stormers
Best for: Kids, Tweens, Teens, Adults
Description: Built to look like sledding slopes in the snow, the Snow Stormers is another fun mat slide.
Level: Everyone
Recommendation: Great for those who want to try a mat slide without the scary heights. We don't recommend this ride for Young Kids.

Downhill Double Dipper
Best for: Tweens, Teens, Adults, Thrill Seekers
Description: Race against friends and family in these side-by-side, snow-covered tubes in the wilderness.
Level: Thrill Riders (must be 48 inches or taller)
Recommendation: These are short slides with drops, and are very fun to race. The height requirement won't allow many Kids to ride though they may want to.

Red Slope Rides and Attractions
Family-friendly tube slide fun.

Runoff Rapids
Best for: Kids, Tweens, Tween, Adults, Thrill Riders
Description: Three different slides change up the thrills as you travel on inner-tubes over and through the lush wilderness of Disney's Blizzard Beach. Each slide carries you in fun swirls down Mt. Gushmore.
Level: Family
Recommendation: Each slide is different, but all empty into a large pool:

Center: A completely enclosed (and dark) waterslide made to look like stars come through from the outside light.

Outer: Open slides with different paths down the mountain.

★ **Magic Tip** ★

This ride allows you to travel alone or with a companion in a double tube.

Chapter Twelve

Hotel Reviews

Introduction

Booking the right place to stay on your vacation is important. You likely have a list of "must-haves" and whether or not you've been to the Walt Disney World Resort before, you may not know which is the best one for you. In fact, we believe that booking the hotel is the hardest part! After all, there are so many choices.

Some of the WDW Resort Hotels are within walking distance of a Park or two while others might be a bit far away. Generally, the closer you are to a Park, the more expensive your room might be.

In this section, we outline the pros and cons of every hotel in the WDW Resort. We give you our recommendations and hotel details to help you make your decision with ease.

WDW Resort Properties

There are several hotel properties on the resort, each with their own unique sense of themed magic from a wilderness lodge to a New England beachside hotel. There's something for everyone here, but sometimes it's hard to decide since each has its perks, whether it's the amenities, the views, or the overcall cost.

Benefits of Staying at a WDW Resort Hotel:

1. MagicBand for hotel room access, park tickets, easy payment and more
2. Disney's Magical Express*
3. "Extra Magic Hours" get hotel guests in the park earlier (or later) than anyone else on select dates.
4. Disney-themed Rooms
5. Wide variety of affordable rooms
6. Complimentary Parking*
7. Closer proximity to the parks.
8. Free merchandise delivery to your hotel from any of the Disney shops in the parks. The following day you can pick them up from the bell services in your hotel.
9. Gorgeous pools with waterslides.
10. Free Wi-Fi.

Walt Disney World Dolphin and Swan not included.

Resort Types

Value – The least expensive per night. These Resort hotels are typically further away from the parks, only include bus transport, and have fewer amenities. Value Resorts make up for fewer features with heavy Disney themes. Many of these properties well suit families on a budget.

Moderate – More amenities, closer theme park locations, and landscaped resort properties than that of the Value Resorts. Moderate properties often cater to convention crowds, so the rooms aren't as detailed with Disney extras, but many of them have upgrade options. Moderate hotels often have fantastic pool areas and many amenities of the Deluxe Resorts without the high price.

Deluxe – The Walt Disney World Resort's best properties. These are located in prime locations with several travel choices to the Parks from the monorail system, boats, or even the ability to walk. Deluxe Resorts usually have full amenities from gyms to spas and options for leisure. All of these can come with a premium price tag.

Room Types

The Walt Disney World Resort doesn't just have an abundance of hotels to choose from, but there are even more room options. You might have finally picked your hotel, but when you get the room selection, you face another line of questioning: what will you need? What's the difference between the standard and the pool view? Is the extra money worth it? We often hear the phrase "we'll barely be spending time in our room." In a way, this is correct, but after a long day at the Parks, you'll want somewhere comfortable to crash. While we believe that all of the Disney Resort Hotels are comfortable, some of them are worth getting the upgrade– while others are not. Here we detail the variety of room types that the Hotels have to offer.

1. **Standard Room** – These are "run-of-the-house" meaning that you'll get the regular floor plan without any special views or extra space. Standard rooms can come with two beds or one. Sometimes they'll even come with a convertible day bed or bunk bed like at the Animal Kingdom Lodge. The views in the standard rooms slightly vary from hotel to hotel. Often these will have views of the parking areas, rooftops, or parking lot. Sometimes it's as good as a view of the pool. Keep in mind that standard rooms aren't the highest picks when it comes to location. Sometimes they will require more walking than others.

2. **Preferred Room** – These are usually similar to the Standard Room in size and with views and bed options. However, you'll be closer to the lobby and transport stops in these rooms.

3. **Studio** – A slightly different set up than a standard room. These feel more like apartments with their layouts than hotel rooms. There are also often couches and extra seating in these spaces.

4. **Suites** – Larger spaces with extra furniture like couches and small dining tables with chairs.

5. **Club Level** – These rooms grant you access to a special area with food and drink in your hotel. Club levels have free bottles of water, breakfast, lunch, and dinner. Adults 21 and older can also have wine and various other alcoholic beverages depending on the night. Club hours can vary, but they typically open at 7am and close around 10pm. We recommend the Club Level for those with four or more in your party. You can save a lot of money on

food with these options. The food is more like munchies from muffins and cereal to finger food appetizers. However, eat enough of them and you'll be full for the morning or evening.

6. **Family Suites** – Rooms that can sleep up to 6 guests. Family Suites are perfect for large families and have a kitchenette and pull-out sofa.

7. **Villa** – These will be 1 or 2 bedrooms with condo-like appliances. There is a kitchenette with a stove and refrigerator in the villas. There are also cabinets with dining plates, utensils, and drinking glasses.

8. **Views** – Depending on the description, you might get a room with a view of the theme park, pool, garden, or water. Rooms with views aren't always in the best spots, but they are much prettier to look at than a parking lot or rooftop. The spaces of these rooms are typically not any larger than the standard rooms.

★ Magic Tips ★

1. When booking a standard room, always specify your choice of room. Disney is happy to assist you in any way that they can. If you prefer 2 beds or a view of the pool rather than the parking lot, just write it in the preferences section when booking.

2. Sometimes your top room choice isn't available. That's okay! It *might* become available on a different date. Check back daily to see if the options have changed– but don't wait too long, you might miss booking your choice hotel if it sells out.

3. If you want two rooms linked, you can call to specifically ask for this. Many of the rooms have doors between them that can be linked for a larger space.

Things to Know

Hotel AAA Ratings

The AAA Automobile Club ranks hotels based on their amenities, features, and value. These can be very helpful ratings to you as they will speak on the overall quality of the Hotel. AAA takes these rankings very seriously and so does Disney. Most of their Resort Hotels have a ranking in these categories of either 4-Diamond or 3-Diamond. These ranking suggest that the hotels will have a prominent elegance and several amenities for guests to enjoy. The 4-Diamond ranking is given to even more stylish hotels with a bump in service and refineries not found in 3-Diamond. AAA is a bit vague on how they determine these ranking, but the differences in a 3-Diamond and 4-Diamond are noticeable, as each are very nice, yet the 4-Diamond excels. With Disney, these rules are no exception.

Dolphin and Swan Hotels

Keep in mind that these hotels do not have all of the amenities of the other WDW Resort Hotels. We've reviewed these differences in their section of this chapter.

Refurbishment

Like the attractions in the Parks, the hotel also undergo refurbishment from time to time. This process may seem unsavory, but these can often work in your favor! In fact, some of the nicer hotels will go on sale during refurbished periods—and you may never notice that they are! If you see that refurbishment is occurring during your travel period at a hotel, contact WDW to ask specifics about these refurbishments.

Disney's Animal Kingdom Lodge and Villas

Best for: Everyone (especially animal lovers)
Theme: African Savanah Lodge
AAA Rating: 4-Diamond
Cost: Deluxe
Location: Furthest west, close to Disney's Animal Kingdom Park. However, you have to take a bus or drive to get to all of the Parks, including Animal Kingdom.
Pool: Yes, with Waterslide
Transport to Parks: Bus only
Amenities: Savannah views, Magical Express, Wi-Fi, Paid Laundry, 2 Pools, Waterslides, Jogging Trails, Movie Nights at the pool, Playground, Club Access for certain rooms, Spa and Fitness center, Childcare at Simba's Cubhouse, and Arcade.

Our Review: The Animal Kingdom Lodge really is a gorgeous Resort Hotel. You'll feel transported to Africa where over 30 species of wildlife live right outside of your hotel room window! The Savanah view rooms are breathtaking and an unforgettable experience. The animals range from zebras and giraffes to warthogs and exotic birds. The animals are in a "fenceless"

savannah that comes right up to your room (the animals aren't able to come next to your room, just very close to it. There is a sort of fence that keeps them inside, but it's very difficult to see in the grass).

The Lodge feels like a standard wilderness hotel with a breathtaking entrance, authentic African art, views of the Savannah, a massive pool with a waterslide that are next to flamingoes, and well-decorated rooms. The shower part of the bathrooms could use a bit better lighting and the rooms aren't as big as some of the other Deluxe Resorts.

The Villas are like condos with kitchen areas and are great for larger groups. It has a smaller pool with its own waterslide, but an even bigger space for the Savannah. The hotel is beautiful, but if you don't have a Savannah-facing room, we don't think it's worth the cost. We wish that the Lodge and Villas were walking distance to Animal Kingdom, however, we found that this Resort has the most efficient bussing system in all of WDW.

Bottom Line: If you can afford it, we highly recommend staying in a savannah-facing room at the Animal Kingdom Lodge or Villas. If you aren't facing the Savannah, you might want to look into another property as this one is far away from the Parks and only offers busses as transport.

Pros:
- Stunning Savannah views with over 30 African animals.
- 2 pools with waterslides.
- Delicious dining from buffets to the exquisite Jiko. There's also a quick service restaurant for those not interested in African-inspired cuisine.
- Gorgeous lobby and rooms.
- The Villas sleep larger families.

Cons:
- ° Far away from the Parks.
- ° Only transport option are the busses.
- ° Poor room lighting.
- ° Not worth it if you don't get a Savannah view.

★ Magic Tips ★

1. Ask for a room close to the lobby. It'll mean less walking!
2. The animals likely won't be in viewing when you wake up to go to the Parks. They tend to roam in the afternoons and evenings. We recommend taking a break from the Parks in the afternoon to come back to your room and see the dozens of beautiful animals right outside of your room.

Disney's Beach Club Resort and Villas

Best for: Teens, Adults (especially beach lovers)
Theme: Beach Resort
AAA Rating: 4-Diamond
Cost: Deluxe
Location: Central, walking distance to Epcot and Hollywood Studios.
Pool: Yes, with Waterslide and lazy river. Our favorite in all of WDW!
Transport to Parks: Boat, Walk, Busses.
Amenities: Magical Express, Wi-Fi, Paid Laundry and Dry Cleaning, 2 Pools, Waterslides, Jogging Paths, Movie Nights, Playground, Volleyball and Tennis Courts, Bike Rentals, Boat Rentals, Fishing, Club Access for certain rooms, Spa and Fitness center, Child Care, Mini Golf, and Arcade.

Our Review: Disney's Beach Club blew us away. It's a seemingly quaint feel along a massive lake. There is timeless beach feel to the building that will be appreciated by adults and teens alike. Kids will appreciate the pool with pirate ship waterslide and sandy-bottom pool. Adults will love the spacious beach chairs, comfortable rooms, and fine dining in the area.

The boardwalk is right across the way for nightlife and Epcot is just a 5-minute walk straight into the back entrance with the World Showcase for drinking and dining. You'll find some of the finer service here and a leisurely boat ride to Hollywood Studios isn't to be missed.

Bottom Line: Gorgeous property with stunning pool and service. Walking distance to Epcot and several great restaurants. Better recommended for an older crowd because of the mature feel of the property.

Pros:

- 3 acres of pool area at Stormalong Bay with sandy bottom, waterslide, beach loungers, bars, and lazy river with inner tubes.
- Fine dining.
- Gorgeous lobby and rooms.
- 5-minute walk or boat ride to Epcot
- 15-minute walk or boat ride to Hollywood Studios.
- The Villas sleep larger families.
- See the Epcot Illuminations fireworks from the beach.

Cons:

- Longer bus wait times.
- Often difficult to book in advance.

★ **Magic Tips** ★

1. The Beach Club books up fast. If you don't see it available, you can always check back at another time as room options open.

2. There are a few pools on the Yacht Club property with less children. In the middle of the day, you might be able to get one all to yourself.

Disney's Boardwalk Inn and Villas

Best for: Kids, Teens, Adults
Theme: Boardwalk Hotel
AAA Rating: 4-Diamond
Cost: Deluxe
Location: Central, walking distance to Epcot and Hollywood Studios.
Pool: Yes, with Waterslide.
Transport to Parks: Boat, Walk, Busses.
Amenities: Magical Express, Wi-Fi, Paid Laundry and Dry Cleaning, 2 Pools, Waterslides, Jogging Paths, Movie Nights, Playground, Tennis Courts, Bike Rentals, Boat Rentals, Fishing, Club Access for certain rooms, Spa and Fitness center, Valet, Child Care, Mini Golf, and Arcade.

Our Review: The Boardwalk Inn and Villas are directly across the water from the Beach Club and Yacht Club. This makes the Boardwalk Inn in a prime spot for transport to the Parks. Like the Yacht and Beach Clubs, there is a timeless feel the Boardwalk Inn, but the pool is a little weird. Cartoon statue elephants spray water and the waterslide looks like a roller coaster with a massive clown face at the end.

Kids will mostly love this pool, but adults might want to stick to some of the side pools without the carnival feel. Being able to walk or boat to Epcot or Hollywood Studios is a huge benefit, and the boardwalk-facing rooms are stunning if you don't mind a little noise.

Bottom Line: Fun, central property that appeals to Families with Kids more than the Yacht Club or Beach Resort.

Pros:
- Rooms have balconies.
- Carnival-themed pool with waterslide.
- Fun Boardwalk arcades, dining, and dancing.
- Gorgeous lobby and rooms.
- 5-minute walk or boat ride to Epcot
- 10-minute walk or boat ride to Hollywood Studios.
- The Villas sleep larger families.
- See the Epcot Illuminations fireworks from the beach.

Cons:
- Longer bus wait times.
- Spread out with longer walks from the lobby to certain rooms and villas.
- The pool is large, but has a strange carnival theme with a massive clown face slide that might turn off certain guests.

★ Magic Tip ★

> Boating to Epcot isn't necessary. The walk is just a few minutes and puts you on a path right between England and France.

Disney's Contemporary Resort and Bay Lake Tower

Best for: Teens, Adults
Theme: Contemporary Hotel
AAA Rating: 4-Diamond
Cost: Deluxe
Location: Next to the Magic Kingdom Park.
Pool: Yes, with Waterslide.
Transport to Parks: Monorail to Magic Kingdom and Epcot, Boat, Busses, Walk to Magic Kingdom.
Amenities: Magical Express, Wi-Fi, Paid Laundry and Dry Cleaning, 2 Pools, Waterslides, Jogging Trails, Movie Nights, Playground, Volleyball and Tennis Courts, Cabana Rentals, Fishing, Club Access for certain rooms, Spa and Fitness center, Salon, Child Care, and Arcade.

Our Review: The Contemporary Resort opened the same year as the Magic Kingdom Park in 1971. It was designed after Walt Disney's idea to have a state-of-the-art deluxe hotel with a monorail station. The hotel has kept its charm over the years, even when something contemporary could feel dated, it doesn't. The room décor is clean and bright and everything feels streamlined. The Bay Lake Tower opened in 2009, so it's our priority choice to stay even though the rooms aren't as large. However, Chef Mickey's can be a bit noisy around this Hotel Resort, it's a fun atmosphere to dine and meet characters. Something about this Resort feels like a high-end condo building or Las Vegas Hotel (without the casino or cigarette smoke) that's walking distance to the Magic Kingdom Park. It has a more adult feel though Kids will enjoy being close to the Park. Though there are options for Park views, we don't recommend them as they are pricey and much of it is just a view of the parking lot area. However, you still get a great view of the fireworks at night. If this doesn't interest you, book a bay view.

Bottom Line: Beautifully designed modern Resort with a monorail system to Epcot and the Magic Kingdom.

Pros:
- Pools with Waterslides.
- See the Electric Water Pageant from the Bay
- Fine and character dining.
- Gorgeous lobby and rooms.
- 5-10-minute walk to the Magic Kingdom Park.
- Monorail to Epcot.
- Boat to Polynesian, Fort Wilderness, or Grand Floridian.
- See the Magic Kingdom fireworks from this Resort.

Cons:
- Doesn't feel as Disney themed as some of the other hotels.
- Not as close to the other Parks (other than Magic Kingdom).
- Can be a bit noisy at times.
- Smaller rooms in the Bay Lake Tower.
- May not be ideal for larger groups and families.

★ Magic Tip ★

The Bay Lake Tower was set up for Disney Vacation Club members, but you can book it without being part of it. If you need a kitchenette, book the Deluxe studio in the Bay Lake Tower.

Disney's Grand Floridian Resort and Spa

Best for: Tweens, Teens, Adults
Theme: Sophisticated Southern Resort
AAA Rating: 4-Diamond
Cost: Deluxe
Location: Next to the Magic Kingdom Park.
Pool: Yes, with Waterslide.
Transport to Parks: Monorail to Magic Kingdom and Epcot,
Boat, and Busses.
Amenities: Magical Express, Wi-Fi, Turn down service, Paid
Laundry and Dry Cleaning, 2 Large Pools, Waterslides, Jogging
Trails, Movie Nights, Playground, Volleyball and Tennis Courts,
Private Cabana Rentals, Boat Rentals, Club Access for certain
rooms, Spa and Fitness center, and Arcade.

Our Review: Easily the WDW Resort's most stunning Hotel. With
a magnificent southern theme, you'll feel swept away by the
magic and pristine styles of the Grand Floridian. Typically, this
Hotel is the most expensive, so we only recommend it if you are
looking for a more romantic feel to your stay. Some of the best
dining in WDW is located in this Hotel. The Grand Floridian
comes with a certain prestige from Disney World fans, and
sometimes that adds to its appeal. However, the Resort isn't close
to any of the Parks other than the Magic Kingdom, and can feel a
bit isolated. Kids tend to like Animal Kingdom Lodge for the
animals or the Beach Club because of the pool more than they'd
like the Grand Floridian.

Bottom Line: If you're looking for the finest Resort Hotel that
WDW has to offer without the heavy Disney theming, this is your
place. Otherwise, look elsewhere.

Pros:

- Exquisite décor
- Pools with Waterslide at the Beach Pool.
- See the Electric Water Pageant from the Bay
- Fine and character dining.
- Gorgeous lobby and rooms.
- Monorail to Magic Kingdom and Epcot.
- Boat to Magic Kingdom.
- See the Magic Kingdom fireworks from this Resort.
- Villas ideal for larger groups and families.

Cons:

º Not as Kid-friendly.
º Not as close to the other Parks (other than Magic Kingdom).
º No walking to Parks.

★ **Magic Tip** ★

> When you get the Resort, ask for a room upgrade. Sometimes if they have availability, you can get a great deal!

Disney's Polynesian Village Resort

Best for: Everyone (especially Hawaii lovers)
Theme: Island-themed Resort
AAA Rating: 4-Diamond
Cost: Deluxe
Location: Close to the Magic Kingdom Park.
Pool: Yes, with Waterslides.
Transport to Parks: Monorail to Magic Kingdom and Epcot, Boat, and Busses.
Amenities: Magical Express, Wi-Fi, 2 Large Pools, Waterslides, Jogging Trail, Movie Nights, Playground, Volleyball Court, Boat

Rentals, Fishing, Club Access for certain rooms, Spa and Fitness center, and Child Care.

Our Review: The Polynesian Village is stunning. The tropical plants and island smells in the lobby instantly transport you to the Pacific islands. In fact, with Florida's humidity, you might actually feel that you're in Hawaii and not on the main land. The Polynesian Village Resort is well laid out, though it is a bit spread. The rooms are spacious and there are several options from bungalows on the water to villas. The price tag is high on this Resort Hotel because of its many amenities. From Disney themed spaces to large pools and a view of the lake with the Magic Kingdom Park in the distance, the Polynesian Village Resort is nearly impossible to beat in style and fun.

If your group needs more space, the Bora Bora Bungalows sleep up to 8 guests, have 2 bedrooms, 2 full baths, and a washer and dryer. The bungalows also have stunning views of the Magic Kingdom Park from the water and a unique, island feel. However, these are a bit difficult to book since their priority goes to the Disney Vacation Club members.

Bottom Line: If you love the idea of staying in Hawaii with the appeal of Disney, this is the place for you.

Pros:
- Island Resort feel.
- Pools with Waterslide at the Lava Pool.
- See the Electric Water Pageant from the Bay.
- Fine and character dining.
- Gorgeous lobby and rooms.
- Monorail to Magic Kingdom and Epcot.
- Boat to Magic Kingdom.
- See the Magic Kingdom fireworks from this Resort.

- Villas ideal for larger groups and families. They have kitchenettes and balconies.
- Trader Sam's Grog Grotto bar is 21 and up after 8pm.

Cons:

° Not as close to the other Parks (other than Magic Kingdom).

° No walking to Parks.

° May have to walk far from the pool and lobby to your room.

★ **Magic Tip** ★

The Bora Bora Bungalows are set up for Disney Vacation Club members, but they can sometimes have availability for nonmembers. These bungalows are pricey but are well worth the price if you have a large group to accommodate.

Disney's Wilderness Lodge

Best for: Everyone (especially Wilderness lovers)
Theme: Forest Lodge
AAA Rating: 4-Diamond
Cost: Deluxe (more affordable than others in this category)
Location: Close to the Magic Kingdom Park.
Pool: Yes, with Waterslides.
Transport to Parks: Monorail to Magic Kingdom and Epcot, Boat, and Busses.
Amenities: Magical Express, Wi-Fi, 2 Large Pools, Paid Laundry and Dry Cleaning, Valet, Waterslides, Jogging Trail, Movie Nights, Water Playground, Volleyball Court, Bike and Boat Rentals, Fishing, Club Access for certain rooms, Spa and Fitness center.

Our Review: The Wilderness Lodge is a beautifully set Resort near the Magic Kingdom Park. It's on a massive piece of land with campgrounds and forests in its background and a bay lake in the foreground. Sadly, the monorail doesn't travel to the Wilderness Lodge, but its other amenities bring it up to the Deluxe Resort status. However, it doesn't have the same appeal as the Grand Floridian and Polynesian or the central placement of the Beach and Yacht Club. Because of this, the Wilderness Lodge can be hundreds of dollars a night less than the other Resort Hotels. A popular time for the Wilderness Lodge is during the holiday season where the many fir trees come to life with Christmas lights and spirit. It's also a lot of fun to take a boat ride to the Magic Kingdom Park, though the busses can feel a little sluggish to the other Parks. Families with Kids may like the Wilderness Lodge better because of the affordable cost and Kiddie pool area.

Bottom Line: Affordable Deluxe Resort in the Wilderness.

Pros:
- See the Electric Water Pageant from the Bay.
- Pools with Waterslide at the Silver Creek Pools.
- Fine and character dining.
- Gorgeous lobby and rooms.
- Boat to Magic Kingdom.
- Stunning at Christmas time.
- Most rooms aren't far from lobby or amenities.

Cons:
- Not as close to the other Parks (other than Magic Kingdom).
- No walking to Parks.
- No larger rooms for big groups.
- Longer bus wait times.

★ Magic Tip ★

The Wilderness Lodge refurbishment continues into 2017 and may cause some parts like the pool and playground to be unavailable. There may also be extra noise from this between 9am and the evening.

Disney's Yacht Club Resort

Best for: Teens, Adults (especially beach lovers)
Theme: New England Beach Resort
AAA Rating: 4-Diamond
Cost: Deluxe
Location: Central, walking distance to Epcot and Hollywood Studios.
Pool: Yes, with Waterslide and lazy river.
Transport to Parks: Boat, Walk, Busses.
Amenities: Magical Express, Wi-Fi, Paid Laundry and Dry Cleaning, 2 Pools, Valet, Waterslides, Jogging Paths, Movie Nights, Playground, Volleyball and Tennis Courts, Bike Rentals, Boat Rentals, Fishing, Club Access for certain rooms, Spa and Fitness center, Child Care, Mini Golf, and Arcade.

Our Review: If you can't get a room at Disney's Beach Club, stay at the Yacht Club. They were built in the same year and have many of the same features, layout, and amenities. In fact, these properties share the stunning Stormalong Bay pool, but the Yacht Club also has its own quiet pool near the back. This property is a bit spread out and walking to the rooms from the lobby, pool, or busses can be a bit of a journey. Still, the rooms are beautifully decorated with several Hidden Mickeys in the décor. You'll find spacious rooms and quiet at the Yacht Club all while being centrally located to Epcot and Disney's Hollywood Studios. Since the Resort is spread out and the vibe is more adult, Young Kids and Kids may not enjoy this property other than its pool.

Bottom Line: Ideal for an adult experience at WDW while keeping the fun of the Beach Club.

Pros:
- 3 acres of pool area at Stormalong Bay with sandy bottom, waterslide, beach loungers, bars, and lazy river with inner tubes.
- Character and fine dining.
- Gorgeous lobby and rooms.
- 5-minute walk or boat ride to Epcot
- 15-minute walk or boat ride to Hollywood Studios.
- See the Epcot Illuminations fireworks from the beach.
- Rooms have balconies.

Cons:
- Longer bus wait times.
- No quick-service restaurants (have to go to Beach Club or Boardwalk Inn).
- Often difficult to book in advance.

★ Magic Tip ★

> There's not much of a difference between a Lagoon or Pool View room and a Garden View room. The Pool View tends to be more expensive and can just be of the Admiral Pool on the far end of the property. We suggest that you save the money and select a Garden or Woods view.

Disney's Fort Wilderness – Cabins and Campgrounds

Best for: Large Groups and Families (especially Wilderness lovers)
Theme: Camping in the Woods
AAA Rating: N/A
Cost: Deluxe (more affordable than others in this category)
Location: Close to the Magic Kingdom Park.
Pool: Yes, with Waterslides.
Transport to Parks: Boats to Magic Kingdom and Busses to others.
Amenities: Magical Express, Wi-Fi, Pool with Waterslide, Paid Laundry and Dry Cleaning, Animals at Tri-Circle-D Ranch, Jogging Trail, Holiday Sleigh Rides (seasonal), Archery, Wagon Rides, Movies in an Outdoor Theater, Campfire sing-a-longs, Fishing, Volleyball and Basketball Courts, Playgrounds, and Arcades.

Our Review:
Cabins: If you've ever heard of "glamping" (glamorous camping), this is the Disney version. Stay in a 750-acre forest with your family in a specially designed cabin. You'll have access to several beds (each cabin sleeps up to 6) and even outdoor seating. There is also a country music show called Hoop-Dee-Doo, a pool with waterslide, and a kitchen. Bring your own groceries or order your own on DisneyWorld.com and have them waiting in the fridge for your arrival. Keep in mind, this is still a camping feeling so insects and other critters could be sneaking around.

Campgrounds: If you're not looking to glamp, and would rather pitch your own tent or bring an RV, you might want to check out the Fort Wilderness campgrounds. With all of the same perks of the Cabins, just without the housing, you'll be able to pitch a tent, plug in your RV, or stay inside a pop-up tent deep in woods of Walt Disney World. Campsites include picnic bench, grill, and television, electrical, water, and sewage hookups for RVs. The surrounding foliage is placed to give you extra privacy while you stay.

Bottom Line: Affordable spacious cabins and campgrounds for those who like roughing it.

Pros:
- Pool with Waterslide.
- Quick-Service dining and BBQ available.
- Spacious cabins sleep up to 6.
- Several Christmas-themed events during the Holiday season including Sleigh Rides.
- Boat to Magic Kingdom or bus to the other Parks.
- Cook your own meals to save cash on your trip.
- Each cabin has its own driveway for cars.
- Unique activities from pony rides to archery.
- See the Electric Water Pageant from the Water.
- Dogs are allowed in some of the campgrounds.

Cons:
- Longer bus wait times and you have to travel to the stops.
- Smaller bed sizes in the cabins.

Disney's Caribbean Beach Resort

Best for: Kids, Adults (especially pirate lovers)
Theme: Caribbean Resort
AAA Rating: 3-Diamond

Cost: Moderate
Location: Isolated, to the South of Epcot.
Pool: Several, one with waterslides.
Transport to Parks: Busses
Amenities: Magical Express, Wi-Fi, Paid Laundry and Dry Cleaning, Several Pools, Jogging Trail, Bike Rentals, Volleyball Courts, Playgrounds, Fishing, Outdoor Movies, Caribbean Beach Campfires, and Arcade.

Our Review: The Caribbean Beach Resort is an iconic Moderately priced set of Hotels to the southeast of Epcot. Set on a stunning lake, there are several Caribbean-inspired lots with rooms throughout. It's one of the more popular of the Moderate Resorts because of its beautiful design, but the rooms aren't anything special. They are just standard painted walls, a bathroom, and a bed or two. Nothing about them feels like Disney unless you get a Pirate room. Kids will love the pirate theme with ship beds, but adults will likely find it cheesy. It may be tempting to stay at the Caribbean Beach Resort for the price, but as it's a bit far from the Parks and Disney Springs, you may want to consider a Value Resort to save money or upgrade to the Wilderness Lodge and get better amenities. If you don't mind the distance, don't need the Disney theme, and get a great price, this Resort might work well.

Bottom Line: A beautiful moderately priced Resort with simple rooms and a spread out feel.

Pros:
- 45-acres of beautiful Caribbean vibes.
- Island with playgrounds.
- Several pools and beach areas.
- Caribbean Pirate Adventure for Kids.

Cons:

- º Standard rooms feel flat with a sparse theme.
- ° Longer bus wait times.
- º Larger, spread out area that may require a lot of walking.
- º Not very close to any of the Parks or Disney Springs, so you have to take the bussing system.

★ **Magic Tip** ★

Preferred Rooms are closer to the lobby and pool, but busses drop off at each of the different village around.

Disney's Coronado Springs Resort

Best for: Adults (especially Latin America enthusiasts)
Theme: Latin American Resort
AAA Rating: 3-Diamond
Cost: Moderate
Location: Isolated, to the East of Animal Kingdom.
Pool: Yes, one with a waterslide.
Transport to Parks: Busses
Amenities: Magical Express, Wi-Fi, Paid Laundry and Dry Cleaning, Several Pools, Jogging Trail, Volleyball Courts, Playgrounds, Outdoor Movies, Caribbean Beach Campfires, Spa and Fitness Center and Arcade.

Our Review: Our favorite feature of Disney's Coronado Springs Resort is the Lost City of Cibola pool. There is a Mayan-style Pyramid with a waterfall next to a long waterslide and a large, beach-like swimming area. The rest of the Resort is very spread out. In fact, it can feel impossible to walk the entire thing in an afternoon. With several buildings located around a large lake, Coronado Springs brings a Latin flare to WDW. Unfortunately, we feel that this Resort doesn't work as well as the other moderate price Resorts. The rooms are lackluster with almost nonexistent Disney flare and if you don't stay near the lobby, you'll be making long treks to its signature pool. The Maya Grill and Café Rix are Mexican inspired food, but they often lack the flavor and pizzazz of the other parts of the Resort. This Resort appears to fill up more for its Convention Center rather than housing Park guests. The better reason to stay at Coronado Springs is for its pool and an inexpensive moderate hotel room.

Bottom Line: A moderate Resort with a great pool, but that's about it.

Pros:
- Fantastic pools.
- Spa and Fitness Center at a moderate resort.

Cons:
º Standard rooms feel flat with a sparse theme.
° Longer bus wait times for both leaving and returning.
º Larger, spread out area that may require a lot of walking.
º Not very close to any of the Parks or Disney Springs, so you have to take the bussing system.

★ Magic Tips ★
1. We recommend the Club or Preferred rooms. They are in prime spots near the lobby, pool, and bus stops. You will also get food and drinks as part of the Club access.
2. If you need more room, book a Casita or Junior Suite that sleep up to 6 people.

Disney's Port Orleans Resort (Riverside and French Quarter)

Best for: Everyone
Theme: New Orleans Hotel and Resort
AAA Rating: 3-Diamond
Cost: Moderate
Location: Isolated, to the north of Disney Springs.
Pool: Several, 2 with waterslides.
Transport to Parks: Busses, Boat to Disney Springs
Amenities: Magical Express, Wi-Fi, Paid Laundry and Dry Cleaning, Several Pools, Jogging Paths, Playgrounds, Fishing, Bike Rentals, Horse-Drawn Carriage Rides, and Arcades.

Our Review (Riverside): Out of all of the WDW Moderate hotels, we recommend the Port Orleans Riverside. It's a gorgeous property with a charming Louisiana theme. The price is usually perfect to stay in this spacious ground with several pools and dining areas. The busses also take you straight to the Parks from several parts of the Riverside. Kids will love the Royal Guest rooms that are spilling over with Disney-themed magic. The standard rooms are slightly less thrilling, but better for vacationing adults who may find the Royal Guest rooms a bit too themed. However, the touches on the standard room moldings and bathroom sink area are very charming in the standard. Its pool is located on an island in the middle of the river.

Our Review (French Quarter): This part of the Port Orleans Resort is central to the lobby and multi-story. It's smaller than the Riverside and has just one large pool. Many guests prefer the garden view over the river view because of the stunning foliage. The rooms are similar to the standard ones at Riverside.

Bottom Line: Riverside is our favorite moderate Resort with its stunning landscapes and well-designed rooms. However, French Quarter comes in a close second with its great food, and easy access to the bus stops to the Parks. There is also a river boat ride for both parts of the Resort that takes guests to Disney Springs.

Pros:
- Stunning landscapes and rivers.
- Riverboat cruise to Disney Springs with a port in both Riverside and the French Quarter.
- French Quarter requires less walking than Riverside.
- Bussing system feels faster than other moderate resorts.
- Several restaurants and the YeHaa Bob show.

Cons:
- Standard rooms feel flat with a sparse theme.
- Larger, spread out area that may require a lot of walking (Riverside).
- Not very close to any of the Parks, so you have to take the bussing system.

Disney's All-Star Resorts

Best for: Families with Young Kids and Kids
Themes: 3 Hotels with specially designed themed rooms and buildings:
1. Music – Calypso, Jazz, Country Fair, Broadway, and Rock
2. Sports – Surfing, Baseball, Football, Tennis, and Basketball
3. Disney Movies – Toy Story, Fantasia, Love Bug, Mighty Ducks, and and 101 Dalmatians.

AAA Rating: 3-Diamond
Cost: Value

Location: Furthest south. Animal Kingdom is the nearest Park, but it's nowhere walkable. These Resort Hotels are also close to the ESPN Wide World of Sports Complex and Disney's Blizzard Beach.

Pool: Yes / No Waterslides

Transport to Parks: Bus only

Amenities: Magical Express, Wi-Fi, Paid Laundry, 2 Pools, Jogging Trail, Movie Nights, Playground, and Arcade.

Our Review: These three Resort Hotels are clustered together at the very southern part of the WDW Resort. While its guests stay the furthest from the Magic Kingdom and the other 3 Parks, they still receive the promised Disney magic. The All-Star Resorts have the appeal of eye-popping Disney-themed buildings with bright, character paintings on the walls. We recommend families on a tight budget who with Young Kids to stay here. There are 2 pools in each Hotel and plenty of busses traveling to the Theme Parks. The hotels are broken up into themed hotel towers that spread around two pools.

Bottom Line: These are a great place to stay if you want all of Disney's amenities for a much lower price. If you aren't traveling with children or can afford a deluxe hotel, we'd recommend that more because you don't have to travel as far and the pools and dining tend to be much better. Of the three hotels, we'd likely go with Music or Movies for the décor.

Pros:
- Inexpensive rooms.
- 2 Pools in each Hotel.
- Food Court and Pizza Delivery options.
- Disney themes with large statues and decorative spaces that are perfect for Kids.
- Family Suites sleep up to 6 at the All-Star Music Hotel.

Cons:
- ° Far away from the Parks.
- ° Only transport option are the busses and every All-Star Resort Hotel shares the same bus line, so they can feel crowded.
- º Adults may find these rooms cheesy.
- º The Resorts cover a large area and may require some walking to your room from the bus stop, lobby, pools, and dining.

★ Magic Tip ★

> If you have a specific theme you'd like for your room, write it in the preferences section. You can select a type of music, sport, or Disney movie.

Disney's Art of Animation and Pop Century Resorts

Best for: Families with Young Kids, Kids, and Tweens
Themes: Disney and Pixar Animated Movies (Finding Nemo, Cars, and The Little Mermaid). 20th Century Pop Culture (50's, 60's, 70's, 80's, and 90's).
AAA Rating: 3-Diamond
Cost: Value
Location: South of Hollywood Studios and north of ESPN Wide World of Sports Complex.
Pool: One in each themed area (except 70's in Pop Century), no waterslides.
Transport to Parks: Bus only.
Amenities: Magical Express, Wi-Fi, Paid Laundry and Dry Cleaning Several Pools, Jogging Trail, Movie Nights by the Pool, Bike Rentals, Playground, and Arcades.

Our Review: Disney's Art of Animation and Pop Century Resorts face one another over the Hourglass Lake–named for its shape. Depending on the room type you choose, you can stay in that themed part of the Resort. Most of the building have their own pool and unique theme. Most of the rooms in the Art of Animation are Family Suites and sleep up to 6 people. Pop Century has standard rooms with minimal décor. Of the two, we recommend the Art of Animation because of the unique Disney statues and the larger rooms. That is, if you can get a great price. The Art of Animation is popular and sometimes the prices can skyrocket beyond what they are worth. However, if you're a family with 3-4 Kids, this might be your best and cheapest option to stay at the WDW Resort. Keep in mind that these are both family resorts and therefore the noise level can be high.

Bottom Line: Perfect for families on a budget. Tons of Disney décor and statues, but we recommend Art of Animation for its larger rooms and theming.

Pros:
- Inexpensive rooms.
- Several pools.
- Food Court and Pizza Delivery options.
- Disney themes with large statues and decorative spaces that are perfect for Kids.
- Family Suites sleep up to 6 at the Art of Animation.
- Closer to the Parks than the All-Star Resorts.

Cons:
- Far away from the Parks.
- Busses can become crowded quickly.
- Adults may find the themed rooms in the Art of Animation cheesy.

º The Resorts cover a large area and may require some walking to your room from the bus stop, lobby, pools, and dining areas.

º Often noisy with kids.

★ **Magic Tip** ★

> Pop Century: If you have a specific decade theme you'd like for your room, write it in the preferences section. We also recommend the preferred rooms so that you'll be closer to the busses and amenities.

Disney's Old Key West Resort

Best for: Teens, Adults
Theme: Florida's Key West
Cost: Moderate
Location: Isolated, to the South of Epcot and West of Disney Springs.
Pool: Several, no waterslides.
Transport to Parks: Busses to Parks, Boat to Disney Springs.
Amenities: Magical Express, Wi-Fi, Paid Laundry and Dry Cleaning, Several Pools, Jogging Trail along a golf course and canals, Tennis, Volleyball, Basketball, Fishing, Bike Rentals, Playgrounds, Outdoor Movies by the pool, Old Key West Campfires, Fitness Center and Arcade.

Our Review: Disney's Old Key West Resort feels like a country club with a tranquil atmosphere. Guests who stay here are looking to get away from the bustle and noise of the Parks for a relaxing stay. While there are amenities for Kids, Old Key West has several well-placed tennis courts and serene pools that appeal mostly to an older crowd. The rooms are large and typically inexpensive for their size. There are even 2-bedroom villas with a full-sized kitchen that sleeps up to 9. This Resort is home to many DVC members so it may be difficult to get a reservation at times. There are also several choice restaurants in Old Key West and a Riverboat to Disney Springs.

Bottom Line: A tranquil Resort with a country club feel. Has some of the largest rooms in WDW.

Pros:
- Quiet atmosphere.
- Huge rooms.
- Beautiful scenery.
- Several Basketball, Tennis, and Volleyball courts.
- Gym
- Boat to Disney Springs.

Cons:
° Longer bus wait times for both leaving and returning.
º Larger, spread out area that may require a lot of walking.
º Not very close to any of the Parks, so you have to take the bussing system.

★ Magic Tip ★

If Old Key West sounds like your ideal Resort, but you can't get a timeslot, keep checking daily. Last-minute changes and cancellations could free up before your planned vacation.

Disney's Saratoga Springs Resort and Spa

Best for: Teens, Adults
Theme: 19th-Century Upstate New York
Location: Near Disney Springs
Pool: A few, no waterslides.
Transport to Parks: Busses to Parks, Boat or Walking to Disney Springs.
Amenities: Magical Express, Wi-Fi, Paid Laundry and Dry Cleaning, Several Pools, Jogging Trail along a golf course and canals, Tennis, Basketball, Fishing, Bike Rentals, Playgrounds, Outdoor Movies by the pool, Campfires, Full-service Spa, Fitness Center and Arcade.

Our Review: Disney's Saratoga Springs Resort and Spa is similar to the Old Key West Resort as it feels like a country club with a peaceful environment. Older crowds will enjoy the lax pools, scenery, golf courses, spas, and quiet away from the Parks. The Resort is large and very spread out which can be both a good and a bad thing. Shopping is also just a short walk or boat ride at Disney Springs. The rooms are large and typically inexpensive for their size. Saratoga Springs is home to many DVC members so it may be difficult to get a reservation at times. There are also several choice restaurants in Old Key West at the neighboring Disney Springs.

Bottom Line: A peaceful Resort with an old country club feel. It's very spread out and often difficult to book rooms.

Pros:
- Quiet atmosphere.
- Walking distance or boat ride to Disney Springs
- Beautiful scenery.
- Full-service Spa
- Gym
- Easier to book than Old Key West

Cons:
- Longer bus wait times for both leaving and returning.
- Larger, spread out area that may require a lot of walking.
- Not very close to any of the Parks, so you have to take the bussing system.
- Not as up-to-date as Old Key West.

★ **Magic Tips** ★

1. The Treehouse Villas house up to 9 guests.
2. The Congress Park area of Saratoga Springs is the closest to Disney Springs.

Walt Disney World Swan and Dolphin

Best for: Tweens, Teens, Adults
Theme: Premium Hotel
AAA Rating: 4-Diamond
Location: Central, walking distance to Epcot and Hollywood Studios.
Pool: Yes, with waterslide.
Transport to Parks: Boat, Walk, Busses.
Amenities: Magical Express, Wi-Fi, Paid Laundry and Dry Cleaning, Pools with waterslides and waterfall, Jogging Paths, Movie Nights, Playground, Volleyball, Basketball, Tennis, Bike

Rentals, Boat Rentals, Fishing, Club Access for certain rooms, Spa and Fitness center, Child Care at Camp Dolphin, Mini Golf, and Arcade.

Amenities Not Included: Magical Express and MagicBands can't charge to Hotel room (but they can with a credit card).

Our Review: The Swan and Dolphin are several-story tall hotel buildings designed by Disney to compete with the neighboring hotels. Located in prime spots between Epcot and Disney's Hollywood Studios, the Swan and Dolphin are beautiful sister hotels with their own subtle character. These hotels, however, are not run by Disney. Instead, they are leased to another corporation and run by Starwood Hotels (using the Westin brand). While you may not receive the complete magic of staying at other Walt Disney World properties, you still get most of the benefits. Staying at this hotel can be perfect for those who love Epcot and can find great deals on the Swan or Dolphin. If we had to pick between the two, we'd go with the Swan because of the better amenities (though you can use them at both hotels). Just keep in mind, if you are driving you will have to pay a daily parking fee beginning at $18. Also the convention centers can pack these hotels and make them quite loud.

Bottom Line: Two beautiful Resort hotels on the outside with slightly dated interiors. They are leased out by Disney to other companies so guests will not have access to the Magical Express, free parking, or the ability to charge to the room using their MagicBand.

Pros:

- Walking distance or boat ride to Hollywood Studios and Epcot.
- Beautiful exterior
- 3-acre pool area
- Full-service spa (in Dolphin)
- Gym
- Great dining in the hotel and nearby hotels.

Cons:

- No Magical Express
- Typically booked 3rd party, so Magic Bands wait for you at hotel and sometimes you can't choose your design.
- Very little Disney theming.
- Rooms feel a little dated.
- Parking costs $18/day or $26/day for valet.

★ Magic Tips ★

1. To book at the Dolphin or Swan, you'll likely have to do it through a 3rd party site. The bonus is that you can get great deals on rooms, however, you won't receive all of the Disney perks like Magical Express and full use of the MagicBands.

2. Ask for a high-level room with a view of Epcot or Hollywood Studios.

3. If you are a Starwood Preferred Guest, you can gain and use points as well as program perks.

Shades of Green

Best for: Military Families
Theme: Golf Resort
Location: West of Magic Kingdom Park, near the golf courses.
Pool: Yes, no waterslide.

Our Review: Shades of Green is a nice resort with Tennis courts, a pool, a Mickey-shaped pond, and central to the golf courses. It's set up to give discounted vacations to the men and women who serve for the United States. Meals tend to be very inexpensive and the rooms are nice and big for the price. However, you might also want to use your military discount to stay closer to the Parks.

Pros:
• Beautiful landscaping
• Large rooms for the price
• Inexpensive dining in the hotel
• Golfing
• Exclusive busses to the Parks and Disney Springs.

Cons:
° Far away from the Parks
° Very little Disney theming.

To book at Shades of Green, visit their website:
http://www.shadesofgreen.org

Chapter Thirteen
Disney Springs

Introduction

Like many shopping locations in America, Disney Springs has gone through radical transformations. Originally known as Lake Buena Vista Shopping Village when it opened in 1975, this section of the Walt Disney World Resort has always focused heavily on dining and shopping experiences. Soon after its inception, the shopping area transformed into Walt Disney World Village, Disney Village Marketplace, and Downtown Disney before coming to its latest name in 2015.

Disney Springs is a place for both vacationers and Florida residents to find premium restaurants, unique stores, and dazzling entertainment. Whether you're looking for a Disney-themed gift, a romantic dinner, or an unforgettable show, Disney Springs has it all. The area is still under construction with many new shops set to open throughout 2017. However, no matter the date of your visit, Disney Springs is a grand place to check out.

For the most part, Disney Springs is a beautiful outdoor mall with chains as well as unique boutiques. Restaurants fill much of the area that's covered in waterways, bridges, and stunning Floridian scenes. The scene comes to life beautifully paved walkways filled with music, glowing ponds, and spectacular banners. Whether you're in the mood for shopping, a restaurant, a food truck, or even a show, Disney Springs has it all. Here, we explore some of Disney Springs' unique shopping and dining experiences based on our top recommendations.

Getting to Disney Springs

The new Disney Springs has even more parking than ever before. Whether you are traveling by car for within the Disney World Resort, there are a few things you should know before you visit:

1. Parking at Disney Springs is free in any of their lots or guest garages.
2. There are a few ways to travel without a car:

    • Boat – There is free water transport from the Disney's Port Orleans Resort (French Quarter and Riverside), Disney's Old Key West Resort, and Disney's Saratoga Springs Resort.

    • Bus – Perhaps the least glamorous way, but it's efficient. Travel to Disney Springs from any of the Resort Parks or Hotels for free with the Disney Bus system.

    • Walk – From Disney's Saratoga Springs Resort, you can walk directly to Disney Springs.

Unique Shops

There are dozens of shops (and growing) at Disney Springs. However, there are a few favorites that shouldn't be missed:

1. The Art of Disney – Looking for unique Disney-themed gifts? This is the place to get them! It has everything from art to fineries. You won't find anything like these pieces of art anywhere else!
2. Bibbidi Bobbidi Boutique – Perfect for Kids looking to get a makeover to look like their favorite Disney Princess. It's a replica of the one also offered in the Magic Kingdom Park.
3. Build a Dino® – The makers of Build-A-Bear Workshop® bring you a prehistoric version of the same concept. Make your own dinosaur toy or plush or build one as a gift. Kids will go crazy for this experience.
4. Coca-Cola Store – Everything Coca-Cola from clothing to unique flavors in this impressive store.

5. Disney Design-A-Tee – Looking for that perfect Disney gift but haven't quite found it? Design your own shirt instead here at this store. It's becoming even more popular now that families are getting their matching shirts created for their stay in the Parks.

6. Disney's Candy Cauldron – Discover an array of delicious Disney desserts–including their famous hand-designed caramel apples.

7. Disney's Days of Christmas – A magic emporium where the holidays never end. Relive your Christmas spirit any day of the year in this stunning shop.

8. Disney's Photopass Studio – Looking for the perfect Disney photo experience? Search no further because you can have everything from classic Disney backdrops to *Frozen* wonderlands created in this professional photo studio.

9. Disney's Pin Traders – Search through a seemingly endless supply of pins to buy and trade with people all over the Resort.

10. Disney's Wonderful World of Memories – If scrapbooking is your thing, then there is no better place in all of Walt Disney World. Commemorate your vacation with unique Disney-style stickers, pages, and more to complete your beautiful scrapbook.

11. Goofy's Candy Company – Love candy? This is where to get it! We highly recommend Goofy's Sour Gummy Worms as a perfect gift (or even just for you).

12. The LEGO® Store – We can't think of a better way to bribe kids to go shopping than with the magic of LEGO! This store has it all from individual pieces to unique sets. You can even design your own figurines to buy. Even adults will be stunned by the amazing LEGO collections.

13. Star Wars Galactic Outpost – "Star Wars Land" might not be here for 2-3 years, but this store might just hold the

biggest *Star Wars* fan over until then. Buy everything from artwork to t-shirts and toys that range in theme from every *Star Wars* movie ever made.

14. Super Hero Headquarters – Power up with loads of Marvel merchandise in this specially themed store.

15. World of Disney® – This may be the most popular store in all of the Walt Disney World Resort–and for a good reason. Pick from an overabundance of Disney merchandise from pins to toys to clothing and even kitchenware. There's something for every Disney-lover in here and we highly recommend that you pay the World of Disney a visit.

Note:
Again, there are dozens of more shops in Disney Springs. Many of them are often found in malls across the world, so we just opted to list the more unique locations.

La Nouba by Cirque du Soleil

One of Disney Spring's most popular destinations is La Nouba, a Cirque du Soleil acrobatics show that's perfect for the entire family. Set with an additional cost, this breathtaking show is sure to wow everyone in your party. Music, lights, sets, costumes, and amazing acrobatics create an atmosphere that might easily become one of your favorite experiences at the WDW Resort.

Tickets start at $59.00/person and shows are typically twice a night, 5 days a week, with Sundays and Mondays being dark. Performance times are 6pm and 9pm with pricing being the same at each time.

For Tickets, visit:

https://disneyworld.disney.go.com/entertainment/disney-springs/cirque-du-soleil-la-nouba

★ Magic Tips ★

1. La Nouba offers seasonal discount tickets to this show. Always check the Walt Disney World website for discounted tickets.
2. Sometimes you can get discounted tickets through Cirque du Soleil's website. These can be for any Cirque show and can have a discounted rate for the better seating.

Chapter Fourteen

Restaurants

Introduction

You may have come to the WDW Resort for the world-class attractions and themes. However, there's a hidden gem just awaiting you. The WDW Resort is home to some of the best food in the world with cuisine you'll be raving about well after your trip has come to an end. That is, *if* you know where to go.

It's true that there are many quick service stands with bland hamburgers that sound delicious by name and forgettable fries. However, there are places in the Resort with some of the best burgers, fries, and churros. You just need to know where these places are.

In this chapter, we adventure through all of the Walt Disney World eating spots. Whether it's hotel dining or Epcot cuisine, we review it all to tickle your tastebuds.

★ **Magic Tips** ★
1. We also list our favorites from snacks to dining. Just look for the ♥♥♥ next to the item.
2. Don't forget a reservation! The popular places fill up fast, so don't forget to book!

Dining Types

A listing of the different categories of restaurants. WDW keeps it simple by bringing you only three types of eateries. However, it may be difficult to know the pricing based on their recommendations, so we've broken it down here.

Snack Station – Carts, shacks, and huts carrying snacks and drinks.

Bars and Lounges – Calm areas with open seating and typically a full bar.

Quick Service – Meals that you can order and typically seat yourself soon after ordering.

Table Service – Restaurants with a waiter. It is suggested you that you tip based on the service you receive.

Fine Dining – The best that the WDW Resort has to offer with elegant décor and excellent, world-class courses. Fine Dining restaurants come with a premium price and often a dress code.

Note: WDW's soda fountains and bottled waters are Coca-Cola products. The Resort's domestic beer is often Budweiser.

Our Restaurant Pricing

WDW only has 3 tiers of pricing on their website. We don't think it's enough. To the savvy traveler, there is a big difference between something under $10 and something over $10. There's also a big difference between a table-service meal that will cost you $15-$25 versus well-over $25 per person.

$ – Under $10 (typically snack carts)
$$ – $10 - $15 (typically Quick Service Restaurants)
$$$ – $15 - $30 (Table Service Restaurants)
$$$$ – more than $30 (Fine Dining)

Disney Dining

Book your restaurant reservations in advance.
(714) 781-DINE
https://disneyworld.disney.go.com/dining

Parks

The Magic Kingdom

Aloha Isle ♥♥♥
Adventureland
Description: Grab a famous Dole Whip here. One of the best treats in all of WDW.
Type: Snack Cart
Price: $ / **Dining Plan:** Yes
Menu Items: Dole Whip, Juice, Water, Pineapple
Recommendation: Pineapple Float ♥♥♥
★ Magic Tips ★
> Dole Whips are also sold at the Polynesian Resort and Animal Kingdom with a rum option.

Auntie Gravity's Galactic Goodies
Tomorrowland
Description: Ice cream stand
Type: Snack Cart
Price: $ / **Dining Plan:** No
Menu Items: Ice cream, floats, muffins, fruit, smoothies, soda pop
Recommendation: Hot Fudge Sundae
★ Magic Tips ★
> Did a kid spill their cone? WDW has a strict no-sad-faces policy–we're not kidding! Tell a cast member at the ice cream stand and they will happily replace it for free.

Be Our Guest Restaurant ♥♥♥

Fantasyland

Description: Not to be missed! A dazzling restaurant with three main dining areas: the dark west wing, the ballroom, and the rose gallery. It has some of the best food in the Magic Kingdom.

Type: Casual Dining – breakfast and lunch, Table Service – dinner

Price: $$$ / **Dining Plan:** Yes

Menu Items:

> **Breakfast:** eggs, bacon, croissant doughnut, ham, breakfast sandwiches, vegetable quiche, fries, soda pop, coffee, milk – *Kids*: crepes, French toast, eggs, cereal
>
> **Lunch:** soups, braised pork, sandwiches, salads, vegetable quiche, soda pop, coffee, milk, iced tea, various dessert – *Kids*: meatloaf, turkey sandwich, macaroni, shrimp, pork, soup, fries
>
> **Dinner:** steak, shrimp and scallops, chicken, lamb, braised pork, ratatouille, vegetables, fries, various desserts – *Kids*: Meatloaf, steak, chicken, seafood

Recommendation: Braised Pork, the "Grey Stuff" Cupcake ♥♥♥

Skip: Lunch French Onion Soup.

★ **Magic Tips** ★

> Eat in the west wing! It's dark and beautifully decorated. Thunder and lightning clash every few minutes near the red rose with the wilting petals.

Casey's Corner ♥♥♥

Main Street, U.S.A.

Description: A quick grab hot dogs and drinks

Type: Quick Service

Price: $$ / **Dining Plan:** Yes

Menu Items: hot dogs, pulled pork, brownie, soda pop, lemonade, juice, hot chocolate, coffee, iced tea

Recommendation: Corn Dog Nuggets ♥♥♥

★ **Magic Tips** ★

> Can't find seating? Eat on the grass near the hub in front of the castle. It's comfortable an easy place to rest.

Cheshire Café

Fantasyland
Description: A quick grab hot dogs and drinks
Type: Snacks
Price: $ / **Dining Plan:** No
Menu Items: cereal, muffin, fruit, soda pop, lemonade, juice, hot chocolate, coffee, iced tea

Cinderella's Royal Table

Fantasyland
Description: A fanciful castle feast with Disney Princesses
Type: Character Dining
Price: $$$ / **Dining Plan:** Yes
Menu Items:

> **Breakfast:** eggs, bacon, ham, beef, French toast, shrimp and grits, quiche, soda pop, coffee, milk, juice – *Kids*: eggs, bacon, waffle
>
> **Lunch and Dinner:** pork, chicken, vegetable couscous, fish, beef and shrimp, salad, desserts, soda pop, coffee, milk, juice, various desserts – *Kids*: salad, turkey pot pie, chicken nuggets, chicken leg, beef tenderloin

Recommendation: Chef's Tasting Platter

Columbia Harbour House ♥♥♥

Liberty Square
Description: The best place for American-style seafood in the Magic Kingdom
Type: Quick Service
Price: $$ / **Dining Plan:** Yes

Menu Items:

> **Lunch and Dinner:** lobster roll, sandwiches, chicken nuggets, fried shrimp, chicken pot pie, salad, battered fish, grilled salmon, clam chowder, French fries, chili, vegetables, various desserts, soda pop, iced tea, juices, coffee – *Kids*: sandwiches, salad, chicken nuggets, fish

Recommendation: Lobster Roll ♥♥♥ and Slushy Lemonade

Cool Ship

Tomorrowland
Description: snack cart
Type: Snacks
Price: $ / **Dining Plan:** No
Menu Items: Mickey pretzel, soda pop, lemonade, juice, hot chocolate, coffee, iced tea

Cosmic Ray's Starlight Café

Tomorrowland
Description: Futuristic hamburger fast-food joint
Type: Quick Service
Price: $$ / **Dining Plan:** Yes
Menu Items:

> **Lunch and Dinner:** burgers, chicken, hot dog, sandwiches, French fries, vegetables, cheese dip, various desserts, soda pop, iced tea, juices, coffee – *Kids*: sandwiches, salad, macaroni and cheese, chicken nuggets

Recommendation: Bland food, try another spot

The Crystal Palace

Main Street, U.S.A.
Description: Beautiful, Victorian-style character buffet with Winnie the Pooh and friends
Type: Character Buffet
Price: $$$ / **Dining Plan:** Yes

Menu Items:

> **Breakfast:** fruit, cereals, pasties, custom scrambled eggs and omelets, potatoes, other changing breakfast choices
> **Lunch and Dinner:** salad, carved meats, shrimp, chicken, beef, fish, vegetable, pastas, various desserts
> *Drinks*: soda pop, lemonade, juice, hot chocolate, coffee, iced tea

The Diamond Horseshoe

Liberty Square
Description: Old West dining and music hall with American eats
Type: Casual Dining
Price: $$ / **Dining Plan:** Yes
Menu Items:

> **Lunch and Dinner:** salad, carved meats, corn on the cob, beans, sausage, pulled pork, macaroni and cheese, braised beef, brownie
> *Drinks*: soda pop, lemonade, juice, hot chocolate, coffee, iced tea, milk

Recommendation: Barbecue Pulled Pork

The Friar's Nook

Fantasyland
Description: Mac and cheese and more American bites to eat
Type: Quick Service
Price: $ / **Dining Plan:** Yes
Menu Items:

> **Lunch and Dinner:** macaroni and cheese, hot dogs, various desserts
> *Drinks*: soda pop, lemonade, juice, hot chocolate, coffee, iced tea, milk

Recommendation: Macaroni and Cheese

Gaston's Tavern
Fantasyland
Description: Beauty and the Beast-inspired tavern where you can meet Gaston and try snacks
Type: Quick Service
Price: $ / **Dining Plan:** No
Menu Items: cinnamon rolls, pretzels, chocolate croissant, specialty drinks, soda pop, lemonade, juice, hot chocolate, coffee, iced tea, milk
Recommendation: Mac and Cheese-stuffed Pretzel and Warm Cinnamon Roll
Skip: The LeFou's Brew unless you *really* like very sweet Apple Juice. If you just want to try it, there's enough to share.

Golden Oak Outpost
Frontierland
Description: Old West quick service with American eats
Type: Quick Service
Price: $ / **Dining Plan:** Yes
Menu Items: chicken nuggets, waffle fries, chocolate chip cookies, soda pop, lemonade, juice, hot chocolate, coffee, iced tea, milk

Jungle Navigation Co. Ltd. Skipper Canteen
Adventureland
Description: Food inspired by Asia, South America, and Africa in a jungle outpost setting
Type: Casual Dining
Price: $$$ / **Dining Plan:** Yes
Menu Items: pot stickers, salad, falafel, soup, beef, fried fish, steak, shrimp, noodle bowls, pasta, fried chicken, vegetable stew, various desserts, specialty drinks, soda pop, lemonade, juice, hot chocolate, coffee, iced tea, milk – *Kids*: fish, chicken noodle soup, steak, salad, macaroni and cheese, crispy chicken
Recommendation: Gyoza pot stickers for an appetizer

Jungle Navigation Co. Ltd. Skipper Canteen
Liberty Square
Description: American Snacks
Type: Snacks
Price: $$$ / **Dining Plan:** No
Menu Items: hot dogs, baked potato, fruit, soda pop, lemonade, juice, hot chocolate, coffee, iced tea, milk

Liberty Square Market
Liberty Square
Description: American Snacks
Type: Snacks
Price: $$$ / **Dining Plan:** No
Menu Items: hot dogs, baked potato, fruit, soda pop, lemonade, juice, hot chocolate, coffee, iced tea, milk

Liberty Tree Tavern
Liberty Square
Description: Colonial style dining area with New England eats
Type: Casual Dining
Price: $$$ / **Dining Plan:** Yes
Menu Items:
Lunch and Dinner: clam chowder, soups, corn fritters, salad, pot roast, cheeseburger, grilled chicken, turkey, pork sandwich, pastas, various desserts, specialty drinks, soda pop, lemonade, juice, hot chocolate, coffee, iced tea, milk – *Kids*: pot roast, turkey, pasta, macaroni and cheese
Recommendation: Crab and Lobster Dip for Two, Tavern-battered Fish and Chips

The Lunching Pad
Tomorrowland
Description: Futuristic fast-food snacks
Type: Quick Service

Price: $$ / **Dining Plan:** Yes
Menu Items:
Lunch and Dinner: hot dog, pretzels, chips, soda pop, lemonade, juice, hot chocolate, coffee, iced tea, milk
Recommendation: Ham and Cheese-Stuffed Pretzel

Main Street Bakery – Starbucks
Main Street, U.S.A.
Description: Starbucks coffee and pastries
Type: Quick Service
Price: $ / **Dining Plan:** Yes
Menu Items: Starbucks brand coffees and specialty drinks, smoothies, Teavana Iced teas, hot chocolate

Pecos Bill Tall Tale Inn and Cafe
Frontierland
Description: Old West saloon with Southwest flavors
Type: Quick Service
Price: $$ / **Dining Plan:** Yes
Menu Items:
Lunch and Dinner: nachos, burgers, fajitas, burrito, salad, various desserts, slushies, soda pop, lemonade, juice, hot chocolate, coffee, iced tea, milk – *Kids*: macaroni and cheese, mini corn dogs, sandwich
Recommendation: Beef nachos

Pinocchio Village Haus
Fantasyland
Description: A cottage inspired by Disney's Pinocchio with Italian eats
Type: Quick Service
Price: $ / **Dining Plan:** Yes

Menu Items:
Lunch and Dinner: flatbreads, chicken parmesan, pasta, chicken nuggets, salad, fries, tomato soup, breadsticks, various desserts, soda pop, lemonade, juice, hot chocolate, coffee, iced tea, milk – *Kids*: macaroni and cheese, pizza, chicken nuggets, sandwich
Recommendation: Sausage and Pepper Flatbread

Plaza Ice Cream Parlor
Main Street, U.S.A.
Description: Classic American ice cream shop
Type: Quick Service
Price: $ / **Dining Plan:** No
Menu Items: various ice cream flavors, sundaes, kids cone, floats, toppings, bottled water

The Plaza Restaurant
Main Street, U.S.A.
Description: Classic American dining
Type: Casual Dining
Price: $$ / **Dining Plan:** Yes
Menu Items: meatloaf, sandwiches, burgers, salad, various desserts, soda pop, lemonade, juice, hot chocolate, coffee, iced tea, milk – *Kids*: macaroni and cheese, cheeseburger, chicken strips, sandwiches
Recommendation: Plaza Club, Caramel-Apple Pie a la Mode

Prince Eric's Village Market
Fantasyland
Description: Fruit cart
Type: Snack Cart
Price: $ / **Dining Plan:** No
Menu Items: fruit, hummus, chips, lemonade, bottled water
Sleepy Hollow
Liberty Square

Description: Waffle sandwich house
Type: Snacks
Price: $ / **Dining Plan:** No
Menu Items: waffle sandwiches, funnel cake, ice cream sandwiches, chocolate chunk cookie, soda pop, lemonade, juice, hot chocolate, coffee, iced tea, milk
Recommendation: Fresh Fruit Waffle Sandwich with Chocolate Hazelnut Spread

Storybook Treats
Fantasyland
Description: Ice cream and floats
Type: Snacks
Price: $ / **Dining Plan:** No
Menu Items: sundaes, floats, soft-serve ice cream, soda pop, hot chocolate, coffee, iced tea, milk

Sunshine Tree Terrace
Adventureland
Description: Ice cream and slushies
Type: Snacks
Price: $ / **Dining Plan:** No
Menu Items: slushies, soft-serve ice cream cup, soda pop, hot chocolate, coffee, iced tea, milk

Tomorrowland Terrace Restaurant
Tomorrowland
Description: Futuristic fast food dining
Type: Quick Service
Price: $$ / **Dining Plan:** Yes
Menu Items: burgers, chicken strips, sandwiches, salads, soda pop, hot chocolate, coffee, iced tea, milk – *Kids*: macaroni and cheese, chicken strips, sandwich

Recommendation: Kids may like it, but adults will likely find the food bland

Tony's Town Square Restaurant
Main Street, U.S.A.
Description: Lady and the Tramp-inspired Italian Restaurant
Type: Casual Dining
Price: $$ / **Dining Plan:** Yes
Menu Items: steak, spaghetti, shrimp scampi, pizza, pasta, salads, soda pop, hot chocolate, coffee, iced tea, milk – *Kids*: macaroni and cheese, chicken strips, sandwich
Recommendation: It's fun for the Lady and the Tramp feel, but the food isn't as great as you'd hope.

Tortuga Tavern
Adventureland
Description: Pirate-themed American eats
Type: Quick Service
Price: $$ / **Dining Plan:** Yes
Menu Items: sandwiches, salads, soda pop, hot chocolate, coffee, iced tea, milk – *Kids*: macaroni and cheese
Recommendation: They have great brisket and a bunch of options with it.

Westward Ho
Frontierland
Description: Snack cart
Type: Snacks
Price: $$ / **Dining Plan:** No
Menu Items: corn dog, chips, chocolate chip cookie, soda pop, hot chocolate, coffee, iced tea, milk – *Kids*: macaroni and cheese
Recommendation: Good if you want a bag of chips or a drink, but the corn dog is forgettable.

Epcot

Akershus Royal Banquet Hall
World Showcase – Norway
Description: Dine while you meet your favorite Disney princesses in this Norwegian castle. The food has a Norway flare.
Type: Character Dining
Price: $$$$ / **Dining Plan:** Yes
Menu Items:
Breakfast: eggs, sausage, bacon, potato casserole, salami, turkey, porn, fish, cheeses, punch
Lunch and Dinner: salmon, chicken, pork, pasta, meatballs, shrimp, assorted desserts, punch, specialty cocktails, wine – *Kids*: macaroni and cheese, meatballs, pizza, chicken, salmon, beef
Recommendation: Traditional Kjottkake
★ **Magic Tips** ★
> If you are looking to meet several Disney princesses without the line, this is the place to do it. The dining options for kids is great and adults can try new flavors. Get a reservation and make sure that you have a spot.

Biergarten Restaurant ♥♥♥
World Showcase – Germany
Description: German feasts in a nighttime village.
Type: Character Dining
Price: $$$$ / **Dining Plan:** Yes
Menu Items: schnitzel, salad, sausage, greens, soup, chicken, potato, macaroni and cheese, cheese platter, meatballs, spätzle, ham, meat loaf, assorted desserts, beer, wine, schnapps
Recommendation: pork schnitzel ♥♥♥

Block and Hans
World Showcase – America
Description: American beer stand

Type: Quick Service
Price: $$ / **Dining Plan:** Yes
Menu Items: beer, pretzels, bottled water
Recommendation: order a beer with a Mickey-shaped Pretzel and cheese sauce

Chefs de France ♥♥♥

World Showcase – France
Description: French cuisine restaurant
Type: Fine Dining
Dress Code: Park attire
Price: $$$ / **Dining Plan:** Yes
Menu Items: French onion soup, escargot, salad, flatbread, lasagna, baked macaroni,
Recommendation: everything here is great, and we recommend the Gratin de Macaroni (Baked Macaroni and Cheese), Boeuf Bourguignon (Beef Short Ribs), or Filet de boeuf grille (Grilled Tenderloin) ♥♥♥

Coral Reef Restaurant

Future World
Description: Restaurant with a massive aquarium wall filled with exotic fish and other sea life
Type: Table Service
Price: $$$ / **Dining Plan:** Yes
Menu Items: salad, octopus, calamari, fondue, soups, pork, chicken, fish, shellfish, steak, assorted desserts, beer, wine, specialty cocktails – *Kids*: macaroni and cheese, steak, fish and chips, pork, chicken tenders
Recommendation: This spot is fantastic for unique dining. We recommend the Crispy Rhode Island Calamari

Crepes des Chefs de France
World Showcase – France
Description: Crepe hut
Type: Quick Service
Price: $ / **Dining Plan:** No
Menu Items: crepes, ice cream, soda pop, bottled water, coffee, beer
Recommendation: Chocolate Crepe

Electric Umbrella
Future World
Description: Futuristic fast food
Type: Quick Service
Price: $ / **Dining Plan:** Yes
Menu Items: burgers, sandwiches, chicken nuggets, flatbread, salad, beer, margarita, slushies, coffee, hot tea, hot chocolate, soda pop, assorted desserts – Kids: flatbread, cheeseburger, macaroni and cheese, chicken wrap
Recommendation: This is typical WDW bland quick service. We recommend skipping it and heading to one of the choices in the World Showcase.

Fife and Drum Tavern
World Showcase – America
Description: American favorite snacks
Type: Snack cart
Price: $ / **Dining Plan:** Yes
Menu Items: turkey leg, popcorn, soft-serve ice cream, soda pop, slushies, beer, wine, hard root beer
Recommendation: Disney has some delicious popcorn! The American Dream slushy is a good one, too

Fountain View

Future World
Description: Starbucks coffee and pastries
Type: Quick Service
Price: $ / **Dining Plan:** Yes
Menu Items: Starbucks brand coffees and specialty drinks, smoothies, Teavana Iced teas, hot chocolate, smoothies

Funnel Cake ♥♥♥

World Showcase – America
Description: American desserts
Type: Snack cart
Price: $ / **Dining Plan:** No
Menu Items: funnel cake, bottled water
Recommendation: Funnel cake with sugar ♥♥♥

The Garden Grill ♥♥♥

Future World
Description: Rotating restaurant serving freshly picked food while overlooking Living with the Land
Type: Character Dining
Price: $$$ / **Dining Plan:** Yes
Menu Items:
Breakfast Buffet: sticky buns, fruit, potatoes, scrambled eggs, bacon, ham, Mickey waffles, juices, coffee, tea
Lunch and Dinner Buffet: salad, turkey, beef, macaroni and cheese, fries, vegetables, stuffing, sausage, short cake, punch, beer, wine
Recommendation: All of the buffets are delicious ♥♥♥

Gelati

World Showcase – Italy
Description: Gelato stand
Type: Snack shack

Price: $ / **Dining Plan:** No
Menu Items: gelato, tiramisu, cannoli, margarita, wine, Italian soda, iced tea, soda pop, sparkling water, bottled water
Recommendation: Gelato sandwich

Joy of Tea

World Showcase – Japan
Description: Tea hut
Type: Snack hut
Price: $ / **Dining Plan:** No
Menu Items: Pork buns, egg rolls, curry chicken pockets, tea, slush, ice cream, wine, beer, mixed drinks
Recommendation: Pork and Vegetable Egg Rolls

Kabuki Cafe

World Showcase – Japan
Description: Japanese sushi and soda bar
Type: Snack hut
Price: $ / **Dining Plan:** No
Menu Items: sushi, edamame, shaved ice, bottled soda, hot chocolate, bottled water
Recommendation: try a shaved ice – adults might like the Sake Mist, an alcoholic shaved ice

Katsura Grill

World Showcase – Japan
Description: Japanese restaurant in a tranquil garden
Type: Quick Service
Price: $ / **Dining Plan:** Yes
Menu Items: sushi, noodles, miso soup, edamame, steamed rice, teriyaki, chicken, shrimp, bottled soda, hot chocolate, bottled water, beer, wine, juice, tea, various desserts – *Kids*: chicken, beef, or shrimp teriyaki
Recommendation: Chicken and Beef Teriyaki

Kringla Bakeri Og Kafe
World Showcase – Norway
Description: Norwegian cafeteria-style cuisine
Type: Quick Service
Price: $$ / **Dining Plan:** Yes
Menu Items: sandwiches, meatballs, biscuit, pastries, salad, fish, soda pop, hot chocolate, bottled water, beer, wine, juice, tea, various desserts – *Kids*: sandwich
Recommendation: Norwegian Club

La Cantina de San Angel
World Showcase – Mexico
Description: Mexican cafeteria-style cuisine
Type: Quick Service
Price: $$ / **Dining Plan:** Yes
Menu Items: tacos, salad, nachos, chips and guacamole, queso, beans, rice, churro, juices, coffee, various desserts, beer, margarita – *Kids*: empanadas, chicken tenders
Recommendation: Tacos de Barbacoa, Churros with Caramel Sauce ♥♥♥

La Cava del Tequila
World Showcase – Mexico
Description: Underground tequila bar
Type: Lounge
Price: $$ / **Dining Plan:** No
Menu Items: tequila
Recommendation: Hibiscus

La Hacienda de San Angel
World Showcase – Mexico
Description: Mexican restaurant
Type: Table Service

Price: $$ / **Dining Plan:** Yes
Menu Items: gorditas, empanada, steak, short ribs, fried shrimp, chicken, pork confit, tacos, fish, margaritas, tequila, beer, wine, various desserts – *Kids*: salad, fruit cup, grilled chicken, tacos, quesadilla, fish, churros, ice cream
Recommendation: Taquiza taco sampler

The Land Cart
Future World
Description: Fruit cart
Type: Snack Cart
Price: $ / **Dining Plan:** No
Menu Items: fruit, cheese plate, vegetable plate, pretzels, hummus, soda pop, juice, beer

L'Artisan des Glaces
World Showcase – France
Description: Ice cream parlor
Type: Ice Cream Shop
Price: $ / **Dining Plan:** No
Menu Items: ice cream, macaron, bottled water

Le Cellier Steakhouse ♥♥♥
World Showcase – Canada
Description: French Canadian restaurant
Type: Fine Dining
Dress Code: business causal, though the dress code is not always enforced, don't wear a tank top, hats, cut off clothes, or sports clothing
Price: $$$$ / **Dining Plan:** Yes
Menu Items: cheeses, steak, pork rib, chicken breast, tofu, halibut, fries, mashed potatoes, macaroni and cheese, scallops, poutine, various desserts, wine, teas – *Kids*: cheddar soup, salad, grilled

chicken, salmon, pasta, sirloin with French fries, chocolate "moose" ice cream

Recommendation: Le Cellier is known for its poutine and steaks. We highly recommend the Signature Poutine ♥♥♥ is French fries with cheese, truffles, and a red wine sauce and Le Cellier Filet Mignon ♥♥♥

Les Halles Boulangerie-Patisserie

World Showcase – France

Description: Fast French Favorites

Type: Quick Service

Price: $$ / **Dining Plan:** Yes

Menu Items: French sandwiches, salad, croissant, quiche, lobster bisque, pastries, various desserts, soda pop, champagne, mimosa, beer, wine, coffees, milk, smoothies, teas

Recommendation: Croque Monsieur, crème brulee

Liberty Inn

World Showcase – America

Description: Fast American Favorites

Type: Quick Service

Price: $$ / **Dining Plan:** Yes

Menu Items: Burger, steak, fried shrimp, hot dog, chicken, sandwiches, salad, croissant, clam chowder, various desserts, soda pop, beer, coffees, milk, hot chocolate – *Kids*: pasta with marinara, grilled chicken, macaroni and cheese, fried shrimp, cheeseburger, chicken nuggets

Recommendation: New York Strip, Warm Peach Cobbler

Lotus Blossom Café

World Showcase – China

Description: American takes on Chinese Favorites

Type: Quick Service

Price: $$ / **Dining Plan:** Yes

Menu Items: egg rolls, pot stickers, orange chicken, shrimp fried rice, salad, ice cream, soda pop, beer, coffees, milk, hot chocolate – *Kids*: pot stickers and spring rolls, sweet-and-sour chicken
Recommendation: Pork and Vegetable Egg Rolls
Skip: The Orange Chicken, especially if you like the one at Panda Express. You'll be disappointed.

Nine Dragons Restaurant
World Showcase – China
Description: Chinese Dining
Type: Table Service
Price: $$$ / **Dining Plan:** Yes
Menu Items: spring rolls, pot stickers, dumplings, Asian chicken, fried rice, Asian beef, lo mein, tofu stir fry, salad, various desserts, soda pop, specialty cocktails, smoothie, beer, wine, teas
Recommendation: Great atmosphere, but the food likely won't impress if you've had very good Chinese food in your hometown. Still, it's fairly good. We do enjoy the General Tso's Chicken Buns though!

Popcorn in Canada
World Showcase – Canada
Description: Popcorn cart / **Type:** Snack cart
Price: $ / **Dining Plan:** No
Menu Items: popcorn, beer, whisky, bottled water
Recommendation: WDW has great popcorn!

Promenade Refreshments
World Showcase – Canada
Description: Snack House / **Type:** Snack cart
Price: $ / **Dining Plan:** Yes
Menu Items: hot dogs, chips, ice cream, beer, soda pop, bottled water
Recommendation: Chili Hot Dog

Refreshment Cool Post
World Showcase – China
Description: Snack Cart / **Type:** Snack Cart
Price: $ / **Dining Plan:** Yes
Menu Items: hot dogs, chips, ice cream, beer, soda pop, slushy, hot chocolate, bottled water

Refreshment Port
World Showcase – Canada
Description: Snack House / **Type:** Snack Shack
Price: $ / **Dining Plan:** Yes
Menu Items: Croissant Doughnut, chicken nuggets, ice cream, French fries, beer, soda pop, slushy, hot chocolate, bottled water
Recommendation: Croissant Doughnut ♥♥♥

Restaurant Marrakesh
World Showcase – Morocco
Description: Moroccan dining experience with belly dancers / **Type:** Table Service
Price: $$$ / **Dining Plan:** Yes
Menu Items: chicken skewers, beef rolls, salad, roast lamb, lemon chicken, couscous, kebab, beer, mixed drinks, soda pop, various desserts – *Kids*: chicken tenders, hamburger, pasta
Skip: The food here isn't very impressive, though it does feel healthier than a lot of other choices in Epcot. Also the promised belly dancing is short-lived and unimpressive.

Rose and Crown Dining Room ♥♥♥
World Showcase – United Kingdom
Description: Authentic British restaurant with excellent food and beer / **Type:** Table Service
Price: $$$ / **Dining Plan:** Yes
Menu Items: soup, salad, fish and chips, shepherd's pie, burger, corn beef and cabbage, bangers and mash, beer, mixed drinks,

soda pop, various desserts – *Kids*: fish and chips, bangers and mash, steak and chips, turkey meatballs, grilled chicken, baked fish

Recommendation: Fish and Chips, Bangers and Mash

★ **Magic Tip** ★

Get a late reservation for the patio and see the Illuminations fireworks.

Rose and Crown Pub

World Showcase – United Kingdom

Description: Authentic British pub with a wide variety of beers / **Type:** Lounge

Price: $$ / **Dining Plan:** No

Menu Items: scotch egg, fish and chips, crisps, beer, mixed drinks, soda pop, wine, whiskey

Recommendation: Fish and Chips

San Angel Inn Restaurante

World Showcase – Mexico

Description: Indoor Mexican dining / **Type:** Table Service

Price: $$$ / **Dining Plan:** Yes

Menu Items: soup, queso, quesadilla, steak, tacos, chicken, various desserts, margarita, soda pop – *Kids*: tacos, grilled tilapia, cheese quesadilla

Skip: The atmosphere is very cool but the food is bland and inauthentic. You can walk inside here to check out the scenery and shops without dining.

Sommerfest

World Showcase – Germany

Description: Fast German Favorites / **Type:** Quick Service

Price: $$ / **Dining Plan:** Yes

Menu Items: bratwurst, frankfurter, potato salad, pretzel, baked macaroni, various German desserts, beer, wine, soda pop, bottled water

Spice Road Table
World Showcase – Morocco
Description: Mediterranean Restaurant / **Type:** Table Service
Price: $$$ / **Dining Plan:** Yes
Menu Items: calamari, shrimp, skewers, fondue, lamb, chicken, vegetable platter, fish, various desserts, cappuccino, espresso, soda pop, sparkling water, beer, specialty drinks
Recommendations: Lamb Slider

Sunshine Seasons
Future World
Description: Indoor fresh, yet fast food / **Type:** Quick Service
Price: $$ / **Dining Plan:** Yes
Menu Items: chicken, fish, soups, salad, fish tacos, flatbread, stir-fry, various desserts, cappuccino, espresso, soda pop, bottled beer – Kids: Mongolian beef, salmon, chicken, macaroni and cheese, cheese panini, sandwich
Recommendation: Fish tacos – fresh and delicious

Tangierine Café
World Showcase – Morocco
Description: Mediterranean Restaurant / **Type:** Quick Service
Price: $$$ / **Dining Plan:** Yes
Menu Items: salad, falafel, shawarma, hummus, pastries, soda pop – Kids: hamburger, chicken tenders
Recommendation: Mediterranean Falafel Wrap

Taste Track
Future World
Description: Dessert station / **Type:** Snack Station

Price: $ / **Dining Plan:** Yes
Menu Items: ice cream, floats, sundae, alcoholic floats

Teppan Edo ♥♥♥
World Showcase – Japan
Description: Authentic Japanese cuisine with amazing chefs that perform before you / **Type:** Table Service
Price: $$$ / **Dining Plan:** Yes
Menu Items: chicken, sushi, steak, seafood, sake, beer, various desserts, soda pop, tea, milk – *Kids*: shrimp, steak, chicken
Recommendation: Teppan Edo is a must if you've never done Teppan-style Japanese dining before. These authentic Japanese chefs are incredible and put on a show like no other. Try the Filet Mignon and lobster tail. The green tea ice cream is also incredible.

Test Track Cool Wash
Future World
Description: Slushy Station / **Type:** Snack Station
Price: $ / **Dining Plan:** No
Menu Items: slushies, chips, alcoholic floats, soda pop, bottled water

Tutto Gusto Wine Cellar
World Showcase – Italy
Description: Impressive Italian wine cellar that showcases over 200 bottles / **Type:** Lounge
Price: $$ / **Dining Plan:** No
Menu Items: wine, cheeses, bread, small plates, pasta, sliders, paninis, various desserts
Recommendation: Meatball sliders

Tutto Italia Ristorante
World Showcase – Italy
Description: Authentic Italian Restaurant / **Type:** Table Service

Price: $$$ / **Dining Plan:** Yes
Menu Items: salad, calamari, chicken, pasta, seafood, various desserts, beer, cocktails, soda pop – Kids: spaghetti, pizza, mozzarella sticks, chicken tenders
Recommendation: Meatball sliders

UK Beer Cart
World Showcase – United Kingdom
Description: Beer Cart / **Type:** Snack Cart
Price: $ / **Dining Plan:** Yes
Menu Items: beer, pear cider, bottled water

Via Napoli Ristorante e Pizzeria ♥♥♥
World Showcase – Italy
Description: Authentic Italian Pizzeria / **Type:** Table Service
Price: $$$ / **Dining Plan:** Yes
Menu Items: pizza, calamari, small plates, pasta, various desserts, beer, cocktails, soda pop – Kids: spaghetti, pizza, salad
Recommendation: Their pizzas are amazing and authentic. We love creating our own Margherita pizza with meatball ♥♥♥

Yorkshire County Fish Shop
World Showcase – United Kingdom
Description: British quick service / **Type:** Quick Service
Price: $ / **Dining Plan:** Yes
Menu Items: fish and chips, sponge cake, soda pop, beer, bottled water
Recommendation: Fish and chips

Hollywood Studios

50's Prime Time Café ♥♥♥
Echo Lake
Description: Swanky 1950's inspired American dining
Type: Table Service
Price: $$$ / **Dining Plan:** Yes
Menu Items: pot pie, pork chops, lasagna, pot roast, salad, fried chicken, fish, meatloaf, fries, onion rings, shakes, ice cream, various desserts, soda pop, hot chocolate, coffee, iced tea, milk, wine, beer, specialty cocktails – *Kids*: salad, soup, salmon, spaghetti, meatloaf, chicken
Recommendations: Onion Rings, Aunt Liz's Golden Fried Chicken ♥♥♥, Peanut Butter and Jelly Milk Shake

ABC Commissary
Commissary Lane
Description: Studio-style Art Deco dining
Type: Quick Service
Price: $$ / **Dining Plan:** Yes
Menu Items: burgers, salad, sandwiches, steak, chicken nuggets, various desserts, soda pop, hot chocolate, coffee, iced tea, milk – *Kids*: cheeseburger, sandwich
Recommendations: Another one of WDW's typical fast food. It's not very flavorful so we recommend trying another spot.

Anaheim Produce
Sunset Boulevard
Description: Snacks
Type: Snack cart
Price: $ / **Dining Plan:** No
Menu Items: fruit, chips, snack bars, pretzels, granola, lemonade, soda pop, beer, margarita, hard cider, bottled water

Backlot Express
Echo Lake
Description: *Star Wars*-themed fast food
Type: Quick Service
Price: $$ / **Dining Plan:** Yes
Menu Items: burgers, chicken and waffles, chicken nuggets, salad, sandwiches, steak, chicken nuggets, various desserts, soda pop, hot chocolate, coffee, iced tea, milk, beer, wine, margarita – *Kids*: chicken and waffles, sandwiches
Recommendations: The food here is impressively decorative. Though much of the flavor is fairly bland, even, sadly, the chicken and waffles with Darth Vader printed on them

Catalina Eddie's
Sunset Boulevard
Description: Pizza shack
Type: Quick Service
Price: $$ / **Dining Plan:** Yes
Menu Items: pizza, Caesar salad, various desserts, soda pop, hot chocolate, coffee, iced tea, milk, beer, sangria – *Kids*: cheese pizza, sandwiches
Recommendations: Any of the pizzas

Fairfax Fare
Sunset Boulevard
Description: American favorites shack
Type: Quick Service
Price: $$ / **Dining Plan:** Yes
Menu Items: ribs, sandwiches, salads, chicken, chili-cheese dog, baked potatoes, various desserts, soda pop, hot chocolate, coffee, iced tea, milk, beer – *Kids*: sandwiches
Recommendations: ½ Slab of Spareribs

The Hollywood Brown Derby

Hollywood Boulevard

Description: Replica of the Brown Derby restaurant in the Golden Age of Hollywood

Type: Fine Dining

Dress Code: Park attire

Price: $$$$ / **Dining Plan:** Yes

Menu Items: steak, lamb, pork chops, pho, salmon, chicken, salad, fish, burger, lobster, various desserts, soda pop, hot chocolate, coffee, iced tea, milk, beer, wine – *Kids*: sandwiches, chicken noodle soup, chicken, fish, penne pasta

Recommendations: Premium American Kobe Beef and Double Vanilla Bean Crème Brulee.

Why We Skip It: The Hollywood Brown Derby is a top-choice for many fine-diners at WDW. However, the food isn't that remarkable for the price you're paying. We'd much rather recommend the 50's Prime Time Café.

The Hollywood Brown Derby Lounge

Hollywood Boulevard

Description: Lounge in the iconic Brown Derby

Type: Lounge Dining

Dress Code: Park attire

Price: $$ / **Dining Plan:** Yes

Menu Items: shrimp, corn bisque, cheese boards, sliders, salad, various desserts, soda pop, hot chocolate, coffee, iced tea, milk, beer, extensive wine list, specialty cocktails

Recommendations: Artisanal Cheeses and Charcuterie Board

Hollywood Scoops

Sunset Boulevard

Description: Ice Cream Parlor

Type: Lounge Dining

Price: $ / **Dining Plan:** No

Menu Items: ice cream, sundaes, apple crisp, root beer float, bottled water

Recommendations: Brownie Sundae, Hard Root Beer Float

Hollywood and Vine

Echo Lake

Description: Buffet with Disney Junior Characters

Type: Character Dining

Price: $$$ / **Dining Plan:** Yes

Menu Items:

Breakfast Buffet: Mickey waffles, pancakes, potato tots, custom omelets, fruit, cereal, pastries, scrambled eggs, bacon, sausage, ham

Lunch and Dinner Buffet: salad, baked chicken, pork, pasta, lobster and shrimp macaroni and cheese, vegetables, desserts, ice cream

Mama Melrose's Ristorante Italiano

Muppet Courtyard

Description: Italian Restaurant

Type: Table Service

Price: $$$ / **Dining Plan:** Yes

Menu Items: steak, calamari, mussels, salad, flatbread, pasta, chicken, fish, lasagna, gelato, various desserts, soda pop, hot chocolate, coffee, iced tea, milk, beer, wine – *Kids*: sandwiches, spaghetti, chicken, fish, penne pasta

Recommendations: Flatbreads

Min and Bill's Dockside Diner

Echo Lake

Description: Fast food from a boat

Type: Quick Service

Price: $$ / **Dining Plan:** Yes

Menu Items: wraps, chili-cheese hot dog, macaroni and cheese, various desserts, soda pop, hot chocolate, coffee, iced tea, beer, wine – *Kids*: turkey sandwich

Recommendations: Seasonal Milkshake

Oasis Canteen

Echo Lake

Description: Indiana Jones-themed dining outpost

Type: Quick Service

Price: $ / **Dining Plan:** No

Menu Items: chicken nuggets, brownie, soda pop, bottled water, beer

Recommendations: Sweet Chili-Glazed Chicken Breast Nuggets

Rosie's All-American Café

Sunset Boulevard

Description: American favorites shack

Type: Quick Service

Price: $$ / **Dining Plan:** Yes

Menu Items: burgers, chicken nuggets, sandwiches, various desserts, soda pop, hot chocolate, coffee, iced tea, beer, sangria – *Kids*: chicken nuggets, sandwich

Recommendations: Sweet Chili-Glazed Chicken Breast Nuggets

Sci-Fi Dine-In Theater Restaurant ♥♥♥

Commissary Lane

Description: Drive-in theater

Type: Table Service

Price: $$ / **Dining Plan:** Yes

Menu Items: steak, pasta, shepherd's pie, burgers, chicken nuggets, sandwiches, ribs, salad, various desserts, soda pop, hot chocolate, coffee, iced tea, beer, sangria – *Kids*: penne pasta, chicken breast, salmon, salad, chicken noodle soup

Recommendations: The food is just okay, but the dining experience is awesome. Sit in cars while you watch classic sci-fi film clips

Starring Rolls Café
Sunset Boulevard
Description: Studio sandwich shack
Type: Snacks
Price: $ / **Dining Plan:** Yes
Menu Items:
Breakfast: croissants, muffins, pastries, various desserts, soda pop, beer, coffee, milk, hot chocolate, bottled water
Lunch: sandwiches, salad, yogurt, parfait, pastries, various desserts, soda pop, beer, coffee, milk hot chocolate, bottled water – Kids: peanut butter and jelly sandwich

The Trolley Car Café – Starbucks
Description: Starbucks coffee and pastries
Type: Quick Service
Price: $ / **Dining Plan:** Yes
Menu Items: Starbucks brand coffees and specialty drinks, smoothies, Teavana Iced teas, hot chocolate

Tune-In Lounge ♥♥♥
Echo Lake
Description: Swanky 50's lounge
Type: Snacks
Price: $$ / **Dining Plan:** No
Menu Items:
Menu Items: pot pie, pork chops, lasagna, pot roast, salad, fried chicken, fish, meatloaf, fries, onion rings, shakes, ice cream, various desserts, soda pop, hot chocolate, coffee, iced tea, milk, wine, beer, specialty cocktails – *Kids*: salad, soup, salmon, spaghetti, meatloaf, chicken

Recommendations: Beer-battered Onion Rings, Aunt Liz's Golden Fried Chicken ♥♥♥, Dad's Electric Lemonade ♥♥♥

Animal Kingdom

Anandapur Ice Cream Truck
Asia
Description: Decorative Ice Cream Truck
Type: Snack Truck
Price: $ / **Dining Plan:** No
Menu Items: ice cream, float, bottled water, soda pop
Recommendations: Float

Creature Comforts – Starbucks
Discovery Island
Description: Starbucks coffee and pastries
Type: Quick Service
Price: $ / **Dining Plan:** Yes
Menu Items: Starbucks brand coffees and specialty drinks, smoothies, Teavana Iced teas, hot chocolate

Dawa Bar ♥♥♥
Africa
Description: African outdoor wine bar
Type: Lounge
Price: $ / **Dining Plan:** No
Menu Items: margarita, mojito, alcoholic punch, domestic and specialty beer, wines
Recommendations: Lost on Safari ♥♥♥

Dino-Bite Snacks
DinoLand U.S.A.
Description: Dinosaur-themed Ice Cream Parlor

Type: Ice Cream Shack
Price: $ / **Dining Plan:** No
Menu Items: ice cream, floats, sundaes, pretzels, cheese dip, chips, cookies, beer, coffee, hot chocolate
Recommendations: Bugs Sundae

Eight Spoon Café
Discovery Island
Description: Snack shack
Type: Quick Service
Price: $ / **Dining Plan:** Yes
Menu Items: pasta, Mickey pretzel, cheese dip, chips, soda pop, bottled water
Recommendation: Bugs Sundae

Flame Tree Barbecue
Discovery Island
Description: Barbecue
Type: Quick Service
Price: $$ / **Dining Plan:** Yes
Menu Items: ribs, chicken, sandwiches, salad, French fries, mousse desserts, soda pop, coffee, hot chocolate, hot tea, iced tea, beer, wine – *Kids*: hot dog, drumstick, sandwiches
Recommendations: Ribs and Chicken Combo, French Fries with Pulled Pork and Cheese

Harambe Fruit Market
Africa
Description: Fruit Cart
Type: Quick Service
Price: $ / **Dining Plan:** No
Menu Items: fruit, yogurt, crackers, chips, soda pop, coffee, bottled water

Harambe Market
Africa
Description: African themed worldly cuisine
Type: Quick Service
Price: $$ / **Dining Plan:** Yes
Menu Items: ribs, skewers, sausage, soda pop, coffee, hot chocolate, iced tea, beer, wine, sangria, bottled water
Recommendation: Grilled Chicken Skewer

Isle of Java
Discovery Island
Description: Coffee shack
Type: Quick Service
Price: $ / **Dining Plan:** No
Menu Items: cappuccino, espresso, pastries, coffee, hot chocolate, iced tea, beer, rum and Coke
Recommendation: Island Cappuccino

Kusafiri Coffee Shop and Bakery
Africa
Description: Coffee shack
Type: Quick Service
Price: $ / **Dining Plan:** No
Menu Items:
Breakfast: breakfast wrap, cinnamon roll, pastries, yogurt, fruit, cappuccino, espresso, pastries, coffee, iced coffee, hot chocolate, iced tea
Lunch: panini, sandwiches, cinnamon roll, pastries, yogurt, fruit, cappuccino, espresso, pastries, coffee, iced coffee, hot chocolate, iced tea
Recommendation: Ham and Cheese Panini

Mahindi
Africa
Description: Popcorn Hut
Type: Quick Service
Price: $ / **Dining Plan:** No
Menu Items: popcorn, nuts, chips, slushy, soda pop, beer, bottled water
Recommendation: Jungle Juice Slushy

Nomad Lounge ♥♥♥
Africa
Description: African Safari lounge
Type: Lounge
Price: $$ / **Dining Plan:** No
Menu Items: chicken wings, tapas, ribs, specialty non-alcoholic and alcoholic drinks, domestic and specialty beer, wines
Recommendations: Indian Butter Chicken Wings ♥♥♥

Pizzafari
Africa
Description: Pizza Restaurant
Type: Quick Service
Price: $$ / **Dining Plan:** Yes
Menu Items: flatbread, pizza, salad, subs, pasta, soups, various desserts, hot tea, cold tea, coffee, hot chocolate, beer, vodka lemonade – *Kids*: cheese pizza, macaroni and cheese, sandwich, pasta with marinara
Recommendations: Mediterranean Flatbread

Rainforest Cafe
Main Entrance
Description: Jungle-themed restaurant
Type: Table Service
Price: $$ / **Dining Plan:** Yes

Menu Items:
Breakfast: omelets, bacon, sausage, eggs benedict, French toast, waffle, breakfast pizza, breakfast slider, specialty drinks – Kids: waffle, oatmeal, toast, cereal
Lunch and Dinner: burgers, sandwiches, soup, salad, steak, chicken, shrimp, pasta, French fries, onion rings, various desserts, beer, wine, hard cider, specialty cocktails – *Kids*: chicken, popcorn shrimp, cheese pizza, macaroni and cheese, sandwich, grilled cheese
Recommendations: The Rainforest Cafe is great for families because of the wide variety of options for Kids. However, adults will likely find the food forgettable–though not bad. Still, the theme is so well done, especially with the décor, that it's worth a stop with Kids.

Restaurantosaurus
DinoLand U.S.A.
Description: Archeological dig restaurant
Type: Quick Service
Price: $$ / **Dining Plan:** Yes
Menu Items: burgers, salad, sandwiches, soups, chicken nuggets, various desserts, soda pop, hot chocolate, coffee, iced tea, beer – *Kids*: cheeseburger, sandwich, corn dog nuggets
Recommendations: Another one of WDW's typical fast food. It's not very flavorful so we recommend trying another spot.

The Smiling Crocodile
Asia
Description: Snack Shack
Type: Quick Service
Price: $$ / **Dining Plan:** No
Menu Items: grits, drumstick, soda pop, beer, bottled water

Tamu Tamu Refreshments ♥♥♥
Africa
Description: Dessert Hut serving Dole Whips
Type: Quick Service
Price: $$ / **Dining Plan:** No
Menu Items: Dole whip, sundae, chocolate waffle, ice cream sandwich, soda pop, bottled water
Recommendation: Dole Whip ♥♥♥, Dole Whip Cup with Coconut Rum ♥♥♥

Terra Treats
Discovery Island
Description: Healthy Snack Shack
Type: Quick Service
Price: $ / **Dining Plan:** No
Menu Items: Hummus, gluten-free snacks and desserts, soda pop, bottled water, soy milk, gluten-free beer

Thirsty River Bar and Trek Snacks
Asia
Description: Specialty Drink Hut
Type: Quick Service
Price: $$ / **Dining Plan:** No
Menu Items: pastries, juice, fruit, chocolate twist, soda pop, bottled water, milk, hot chocolate, iced coffee

Tiffins ♥♥♥
Discovery Island
Description: International cuisine fine dining
Type: Fine Dining
Dress Code: Park attire
Price: $$$$ / **Dining Plan:** Yes
Menu Items: chicken, lamb chop, pork tenderloin, prawns, fish, short rib, vegetable curry, duck, seafood, salad, various desserts,

specialty cocktails, soda pop, beer, iced tea – Kids: salad, soup, chicken, fish, pasta, short ribs

Recommendation: Just about everything you get at Tiffins is absolutely delicious. We recommend the Wagyu Strip Loin and Braised Short Rib ♥♥♥

Trilo-Bites

Discovery Island
Description: Dinosaur outpost shack
Type: Snacks
Price: $ / **Dining Plan:** Yes
Menu Items: chicken and waffles, waffle sundae, float, soda pop, beer, bottled water
Recommendation: Buffalo Chicken Waffle Slider

Tusker House Restaurant

Africa
Description: American Buffet in Africa with Donald Duck and friends
Type: Character Dining
Price: $$$ / **Dining Plan:** Yes
Menu Items:
Breakfast Buffet: Mickey waffles, pancakes, potato tots, custom omelets, fruit, cereal, pastries, scrambled eggs, bacon, sausage, ham, apple turnovers
Lunch and Dinner Buffet: BBQ pork loin, chutney, salad, spit-roasted chicken, pork, pasta, lobster and shrimp macaroni and cheese, vegetables, corn dog nuggets, desserts, ice cream, mojito, beer, margarita

Warung Outpost

Asia
Description: Asian outdoor bar
Type: Walk-up Bar

Price: $ / **Dining Plan:** No
Menu Items: margaritas, beer, Mickey pretzel, chips, smoothie, bottled water

Yak and Yeti ♥♥♥
Asia
Description: Asian-style eatery at the base of the Himalayas
Type: Bar, Quick Service, and Table Service Restaurant
Price: $ – $$$ / **Dining Plan:** Yes – but not for Quality Beverages bar
Menu Items:
Local Food Cafes: beef bowl, cheeseburger, chicken, sandwich, hot dog, wrap, salad, egg rolls, various desserts, soda pop, juice, milk, beer – *Kids*: cheeseburger, sandwich, chicken strips
Quality Beverages: chicken sandwich, salad, turkey leg, egg rolls, frozen lemonade, soda pop, juice, bottled water, draft beer, sangria, margarita
Restaurant: chicken wings, egg rolls, pot stickers, lettuce cups, lo mein noodles, seafood curry, tempura shrimp, Mahi Mahi, fish, salad, tikka masala, wok dishes, BBQ ribs, kabobs, fried ride, bok choy, various desserts, specialty drinks, beer, wine, sake – Kids: cheeseburger, sandwich, egg roll, macaroni and cheese, chicken tenders, mini corn dogs, teriyaki chicken breast
Recommendation: Pork Pot Stickers, Pork Egg Rolls ♥♥♥, Tempura Shrimp ♥♥♥, Chicken Tikka Masala

Disney's Typhoon Lagoon

Happy Landings Ice Cream
Snack Shack
Price: $ / **Dining Plan:** No
Menu Items: ice cream, sundae, bottled water, soda pop, all-day refillable mug for soda pop

Leaning Palms
American dining beach house / Quick Service
Price: $$ / **Dining Plan:** Yes
Menu Items: burgers, chicken nuggets, wraps, sandwiches, pizzas, hot dogs, assorted desserts, soda pop, beer, wine, sangria, hot chocolate, coffee, milk, frozen lemonade – *Kids*: chicken nuggets, turkey sandwich

Let's Go Slurpin'
Beach bar / Lounge Bar
Price: $$ / **Dining Plan:** No
Menu Items: margarita, mai tai, rum, specialty cocktails, beer, wine

Lowtide Lou'd
Beach Sandwich Bar / Snacks and drinks
Price: $ / **Dining Plan:** Yes
Menu Items: turkey pesto, sandwiches, wraps, nachos, soda pop, bottled water, margarita, pina colada, vodka mixed drinks, beer, wine, sangria – *Kids*: sandwiches

Snack Shack
Dining Hut / Quick Service
Price: $$ / **Dining Plan:** Yes
Menu Items: turkey pesto, sandwiches, wraps, salads, soda pop, bottled water, margarita, pina colada, refillable fountain beverage mug – *Kids*: sandwiches

Typhoon Tilly's
Barbecue Shack / Quick Service
Price: $$ / **Dining Plan:** Yes
Menu Items: sandwiches, wraps, salads, shrimp, fish, soda pop, bottled water, beer, wine, sangria – *Kids*: turkey sandwich, corn dog nuggets

Disney's Blizzard Beach

Arctic Expeditions
Food Truck / Snacks
Price: $$ / **Dining Plan:** No
Menu Items: gyro, cheese steak, salad, turkey leg, various desserts, beer, lemonade, bottled water

Avalunch
Dining Hut / Quick Service
Price: $$ / **Dining Plan:** Yes
Menu Items: brisket, specialty hot dogs, pretzels, various desserts, beer, sangria, soda pop, bottled water

Cooling Hut
Dining Hut / Quick Service
Price: $ / **Dining Plan:** Yes
Menu Items: tuna sandwich, chicken wrap, popcorn, hummus, fruit cup, pretzels, chips, yogurt, various desserts, beer, hard cider, soda pop, bottled water

Cooling Hut ♥♥♥
Snack Shack / Snacks and Frozen Drinks
Price: $ / **Dining Plan:** Yes

Menu Items: Dole whip soft-serve, fruits, vegetables, churro bites, various desserts, soda pop, lemonade, frozen cappuccino, bottled water

Recommendation: Dole Whip Soft-serve Cone or Cup ♥♥♥, Frozen Cappuccino ♥♥♥

I.C. Expeditions
Ice Cream Truck / Snacks
Price: $ / **Dining Plan:** No
Menu Items: sundaes, floats, ice cream bars, bottled water

Lottawatta Lodge
Ski Lodge Restaurant / Quick Service
Price: $$ / **Dining Plan:** Yes
Menu Items: burgers, fries, wraps, rolls, hot dog, flatbread, various desserts, ice cream, sundaes, all-day refillable mug, frozen lemonade, hot chocolate, coffee, beer, sangria, wine – *Kids*: chicken nuggets, sandwiches

Blizzard Beach Mini Donuts ♥♥♥
Donut Cart / Snacks
Price: $ / **Dining Plan:** No
Menu Items: mini donuts and dipping sauces, coffee, hot chocolate, hot tea, frozen lemonade – *Kids*: chicken nuggets, sandwiches
Recommendation: Mini Donuts ♥♥♥

Polar Pub
Outdoor Bar / Lounge
Price: $$ / **Dining Plan:** No
Menu Items: margarita, daiquiri, specialty drinks, beer, wine, bottled water, chips

Warming Hut
International Food Hut / Quick Service
Price: $$ / **Dining Plan:** Yes
Menu Items: teriyaki rice bowl, egg roll, empanada, chicken wrap, various desserts, soda pop, beer, all-day refillable mug, hard cider

Hotel Dining

The WDW hotels have some of the best dining choices around. If you're not staying at that particular Resort hotel, you can still wander in and dine at a restaurant. The Quick Service locations are often just hamburgers, sandwiches, hot dogs, and soda. These aren't that special, unfortunately, so we haven't detailed them much in this section.

All-Star Resorts

These Resorts have their own themed quick service restaurants. The breakfasts here are pretty good!

All-Star Movie Resort
Silver Screen Spirits Pool Bar – $$ / Dining: Yes / Quick Service
World Premiere Food Court – $$ / Dining: Yes / Quick Service
Breakfast, Lunch, and Dinner

All-Star Music Resort
Intermission Food Court – $$ / Dining: Yes / Quick Service
Breakfast, Lunch, and Dinner
Singing Spirits Pool Bar – $$ / Dining: Yes / Quick Service

All-Star Sports Resort
End Zone Food Court – $$ / Dining: Yes / Quick Service Breakfast, Lunch, and Dinner
Grandstand Spirits – $$ / Dining: Yes / Quick Service pool bar

Disney's Animal Kingdom Lodge and Villas

Boma – Flavors of Africa
Description: African cuisine in a safari setting / **Type:** Table Service
Price: $$$ / **Dining Plan:** Yes
Menu Items:
Breakfast: fruit, salad, yogurt, salmon, cheeses, omelets, pancakes, bread pudding, oatmeal, ham, turkey, waffles, corned beef hash, potatoes, vegetables, coffee, tea, lemonade, juices, soda pop, milk
Dinner: soups, stews, salads, salmon, pork ribs, chicken, beef sirloin, vegetables, soda pop, coffee, tea, milk
Recommendations: Come for breakfast. The dinner is pricey, so we'd recommend just dining a Jiko instead.

Jiko – The Cooking Place ♥♥♥
Description: African dinner cuisine with an extensive South African wine selection / **Type:** Fine Dining
Dress Code: Business casual / cocktail attire – though we've seen plenty of men in shorts here
Price: $$$$ / **Dining Plan:** Yes
Menu Items: steak, wild boar tenderloin, halibut, vegetables, pork shank, seafood, short rib, macaroni and cheese, ice, lamb shank, assorted desserts, teas, liqueurs, wines, specialty cocktails,

soda pop, coffee, tea, milk – *Kids*: cheese pizza, macaroni and cheese, chicken, steak, fish, scallops

Recommendations: Crispy Bobotie Roll for appetizer ♥♥♥, Grilled Buffalo Rib-Eye or Botswana-style Seswaa Beef Short Rib for entrée ♥♥♥, Braai Macaroni and Cheese enhancement ♥♥♥

Sanaa

Description: American and African dining with an Indian flare overlooking an animal-filled savannah / **Type:** Table Service

Price: $$$ / **Dining Plan:** Yes

Menu Items: lamb sliders, shrimp, salad, tandoori chicken, burger, fish, chicken sandwich, steak, assorted desserts, teas, liqueurs, margarita, specialty cocktails, soda pop, coffee, tea, milk – *Kids*: cheese pizza, macaroni and cheese, chicken, cheeseburger, fish, shrimp

Recommendations: If you want to dine and see the animals at the same time, this is the place to do it. Sanaa is better for those not looking for African flares.

Unique Dining Experiences

Dine with Animal Specialist – $$$$ / Dining: No / Dine with an animal Specialist at Sanaa. You'll learn a lot about the many species of African Animals while dining on a 4-course meal of bread, salad, meat, and a dessert. Reservations are a must!

Wanyama Safari – $$$$ / Dining: No / Board a caravan safari and meet several of the Animal Kingdom Lodge's African animals like giraffe and zebra. Afterward, you'll dine at Jiko. Reserve before you arrive.

Quick Service Spots

Maji Pool Bar – $$ / Dining: Yes / Quick Service

Uzima Springs Pool Bar – $$ / Dining: No / Quick Service Pool Bar

Disney's Art of Animation

This Resort hotel has two quick service dining experiences.

The Drop Off Pool Bar – $$ / Dining: No / Quick Service

Landscape of Flavors – $$ / Dining: Yes / Quick Service Breakfast, Lunch, and Dinner / Recommendation: breakfast or build-your-own-burger for lunch or dinner.

Disney's Beach Club and Yacht Club

The hotels are connected, so it's easy to walk between them to the restaurants. They are also home to some of the best dining and desserts in WDW.

Beaches and Cream Soda Shop ♥♥♥
Description: Premium Ice Cream Parlor / **Type:** Quick Service
Price: $ / **Dining Plan:** Yes
Menu Items: ice cream, soda pop, floats
Recommendations: This ice cream parlous is extremely popular for its delicious desserts. We recommend getting a reservation to avoid the line.

Cape May Café ♥♥♥
Description: New England-style beach buffet / **Type:** Character Dining
Price: $$$ / **Dining Plan:** Yes
Menu Items:
Breakfast:
Lunch and Dinner:
Recommendations: Character breakfast buffet ♥♥♥

Captain's Grille ♥♥♥
Description: New England-style steakhouse / **Type:** Fine Dining
Price: $$$$ / **Dining Plan:** Yes
Menu Items:
Breakfast: fruit, oatmeal, salmon and bagel, pastries, yogurt, cereal, bacon, sausage, eggs, coffee, tea
Lunch and Dinner:
Recommendations: If the Yachtsman Steakhouse is too pricey, the Captain's Grille is a wonderful second choice. Try their Cabernet-braised Short Rib or New York Strip.

Yachtsman Steakhouse ♥♥♥
Description: New England-style steakhouse / **Type:** Fine Dining
Price: $$$$ / **Dining Plan:** Yes
Menu Items: Steaks,
Recommendations: Try any one of their famous steaks ♥♥♥

Disney's Boardwalk Inn and Villas

Most of the Boardwalk Inn's dining experiences are on Disney's Boardwalk. These are listed in the next section of this chapter.

Belle Vue Lounge – $$ / Dining: Yes / Quick Service

Leaping Horse Libations – $$ / Dining: Yes / Quick Service

Disney's Caribbean Beach Resort

Shutters at Old Port Royal
Description: Caribbean restaurant / **Type:** Table Service

Price: $$$ / **Dining Plan:** Yes
Menu Items: crab cakes, shrimp, salad, steak, pork ribs, scallops, fish, pasta, chicken, assorted desserts, specialty drinks, beer, coffee, tea, soda pop – *Kids*: steak, cheese pizza, chicken nuggets, fish, turkey
Recommendations: Char-crusted 10-oz New York Strip Steak

Banana Cabana Pool Bar – $$ / Dining: No / Pool Bar

Old Port Royale Food Court – $$ / Dining: Yes / Quick Service Breakfast, Lunch, and Dinner / Recommendation: breakfast with Mickey waffles

Disney's Contemporary Resort and Bay Lake Tower

California Grill ♥♥♥
Description: American and Seafood Restaurant that overlooks the Magic Kingdom and Seven Seas Lagoon / **Type:** Fine Dining
Dress Code: Business casual / cocktail attire
Price: $$$$ / **Dining Plan:** Yes
Menu Items:
Brunch: pastries, salad, greek yogurt, fish, shrimp tempura, sushi, pancakes, chicken, grits, eggs benedict, assorted desserts, wine, cocktails
Dinner: sausage, flatbread, cheese boards, charcuteries, sushi, soup, salad, steak, pork, fish, chicken, vegetable curry, seafood ramen, various desserts, wine, cocktails, beer, ciders – Kids: chicken breast, salmon, beef tenderloin, cheese pizza, macaroni and cheese
Recommendations: One of WDW's best dining experiences. Go for brunch ♥♥♥

Chef Mickey's
Description: Buffet with Mickey and friends / **Type:** Character Dining
Price: $$$ / **Dining Plan:** Yes
Menu Items:
Breakfast: bagels, croissants, pastries, biscuits and gravy, pancakes, potato casserole, shrimp, frittatas, tofu scramble, oatmeal, fruit, yogurts, soda pop, coffee, tea
Brunch: fruit, salad, yogurts, soup, frittatas, pork ribs, assorted desserts – *Kids*: scrambled eggs, tater tots, macaroni and cheese, chicken nuggets, mini waffles, soda pop
Dinner: mixed fruit, salad, shrimp, seafood, pasta, beef, turkey, soup, salmon, macaroni and cheese, mashed potatoes, vegetables, pastries, assorted desserts, specialty cocktails, lemonade, soda pop – *Kids*: chicken nuggets, mini corn dogs, vegetables, macaroni and cheese
Recommendations: Because of its lively environment and central location near the monorail, Chef Mickey's can get a bit noisy. However, if you're looking for a character dining experience with Mr. Mouse himself, there's no better place! Go for the breakfast buffet.

The Wave... of American Flavors
Description: American Buffet Favorites / **Type:** Buffet
Price: $$$ / **Dining Plan:** Yes
Menu Items:
Breakfast: omelets, French toast, frittata, continental breakfast, pancakes, eggs benedict, juices, soda pop
Brunch: fruit, salad, yogurts, soup, frittatas, pork ribs, assorted desserts, soda pop, breakfast specialty cocktails, teas, coffee – *Kids*: cereals, eggs, waffles, pancakes, fruit

Lunch: salads, soup, burgers, sandwiches, fish, fried rice, assorted desserts – *Kids*: pork tenderloin, penne pasta, chicken strips, grilled fish, cheeseburger, grilled cheese, beef kabob, cheese pizza
Dinner: steak, salads, soup, gnocchi, seafood, pork chop, fried rice, assorted desserts – *Kids*: pork tenderloin, penne pasta, chicken strips, grilled fish, cheeseburger, grilled cheese, beef kabob, cheese pizza
Recommendations: Sweet Potato Pancakes for breakfast, The Wave Bison Burger for lunch

California Grill Lounge – $$ / Dining: No / Lounge
Cotemporary Grounds – $ / Dining: No / Snacks and Coffee
Cove Bar – $$ / Dining: No / Lounge
Outer Rim – $$ / Dining: No / Lounge
The Sand Bar – $ / Dining: Yes / Quick Service
The Wave Lounge – $$ / Dining: No / Lounge

Disney's Coronado Springs Resort

Cafe Rix – $ / Dining: Yes / Dessert Bar

Las Ventanas
Mexican and American Cuisine / **Type:** Table Service
Price: $$$ / **Dining Plan:** Yes
Menu Items:
Breakfast: omelets, eggs, chorizo, French toast, pancakes, continental breakfast, cereal, bacon, sausage, ham, potatoes, coffee, tea, milk, bottled water
Lunch and Dinner: corn chowder, soup, crab cakes, calamari, salads, burger, sandwiches, chicken, fish, assorted desserts, specialty drinks, beer, coffee, tea, soda pop – *Kids*: chicken, grilled cheese
Recommendations: Gourmet Grilled Cheese

Maya Grill
Mexican and American Cuisine / **Type:** Table Service
Price: $$$ / **Dining Plan:** Yes
Menu Items: queso, calamari, tacos, tomatillos, pork, short ribs, fish, Cornish hen, fajita, steak, assorted desserts, specialty drinks, beer, wine, margaritas, coffee, tea, soda pop
Recommendations: Maya Grill's Signature Fajita Skillet

Pepper Market – $$ / Dining: Yes / Quick Service Breakfast, Lunch, and Dinner / Recommendation: breakfast with Mickey waffles, skip the bland lunch and dinner options and head to Las Ventanas or the Maya Grill

Siestas Cantina – $$ / Dining: Yes / Pool bar

Disney's Fort Wilderness Resort

Trail's End Restaurant
Description: American Dining / **Type:** Table Service
Price: $$$ / **Dining Plan:** Yes
Menu Items:
Breakfast and Brunch: fruit, pastries, eggs, breakfast pizza, Mickey waffles, cheese grits, carving station, soup, chili, fried chicken, desserts, bacon, sausage, coffee, tea, milk, juices
Lunch and Dinner: chicken breast, shrimp, salad, flatbread, sandwiches, chicken and waffles, steak, grits, assorted desserts, beer – *Kids*: baked chicken, grilled salmon, cheeseburger, macaroni and cheese, chicken nuggets, grilled cheese
Recommendations: Breakfast or Brunch Buffet, Chicken and Waffles

Hoop-Dee-Doo Musical Revue ♥♥♥ – $$$$ / Dining: Yes / Dinner Show / Recommendation: Show-stopping numbers in a 2-hour show includes a delicious American feast. It's all-you-care-to enjoy fried chicken, BBQ ribs, salad, beans, cornbread, and a dessert. Buy your tickets in advance to reserve your seat.

Mickey's Backyard BBQ – $$$$ / Dining: Yes / Character Dining BBQ Show / Recommendation: Meet Mickey, Minnie, Goofy and Chip n Dale while you eat American BBQ favorites like hamburgers, hot dogs, corn on the cob, macaroni and cheese, BBQ ribs, and grilled chicken. Beer and wine is included for 21+ adults.

Crockett's Tavern – $ / Dining: No / Quick Service pizzas, wings, nachos and Lounge
Meadow Snack Bar – $$ / Dining: Yes / Quick Service salads and sandwiches
P and J's Southern Takeout – $$ / Dining: Yes / Quick Service Western favorites

Disney's Grand Floridian Resort and Spa

1900 Park Fare
Description: American Buffet and Tea Party / **Type:** Character Dining Buffet
Price: $$$ / **Dining Plan:** Yes
Menu Items:
Brunch: salads, bacon, bagels, soup, rice, potato puffs, sausage, eggs, French toast, shrimp, fruit, croissants, Mickey waffles, assorted pastries, tea, coffee, soda pop
Dinner: salad, greens, soup, chicken, salmon, fried catfish, stir fry, shrimp, mashed potatoes, pork, ravioli, assorted desserts, tea, coffee, soda pop – *Kids*: macaroni and cheese, cheese ravioli, hot dog, pizza, chicken tenders, vegetables, taco bar

Recommendations: Dine any time for delicious meals and many characters

Citricos
Description: American and Mediterranean dining / **Type:** Table Service
Price: $$$ / **Dining Plan:** Yes
Menu Items: cheese board, meat board, salad, flatbread, pork, shrimp, soup, short ribs, fish, tofu ratatouille, chicken, beef, vegetables, mashed potatoes, assorted desserts, mixed drinks, wines, beer, soda pop, tea – *Kids*: chicken, pasta with marinara, shrimp, pork tenderloin, macaroni and cheese, cheese pizza, macaroni and meat sauce
Recommendations: Slow-Roasted Pork Belly, Red Wine-braised Beef Short Ribs

Grand Floridian Cafe
Description: American dining / **Type:** Table Service
Price: $$$ / **Dining Plan:** Yes
Menu Items:
Breakfast: omelets, eggs, steak, bacon, sausage, breakfast potatoes, French toast, pancakes, Mickey waffles, salads, yogurt, oatmeal, pastries, morning mixed drinks, wines, beer, soda pop, tea – *Kids*: omelet, eggs, Mickey waffles, pancakes with sprinkles
Lunch: shrimp, soup, salad, sandwiches, fish, chicken, wraps, burgers, assorted desserts, mixed drinks, wines, beer, soda pop, tea – *Kids*: chicken, salmon, chicken wrap, meaty macaroni, cheese pizza, chicken nuggets
Dinner: salad, soup, shrimp, chicken, fish, steak, pork chops, burgers, grits, ravioli, assorted desserts, mixed drinks, wines, beer, soda pop, tea – *Kids*: chicken, salmon, chicken wrap, meaty macaroni, cheese pizza, chicken nuggets
Recommendations: Slow-Roasted Pork Belly, Red Wine-braised Beef Short Ribs

Narcoosee's ♥♥♥

Description: American and Seafood Restaurant / **Type:** Fine Dining

Dress Code: Business Casual

Price: $$$ / **Dining Plan:** Yes

Menu Items: soups, salads, shellfish, fish, cheeses, pasta, steak, chicken, pork, lobster, vegetables, assorted desserts, wines, soda pop, tea – *Kids*: steak, cheeseburger, hamburger, mac and cheese, fried chicken tenders, shrimp, pasta, veggie burger

Recommendations: St. Augustine Soft-shell Crab, Grass Fed Filet Mignon ♥♥♥, Chocolate Crème Brulee ♥♥♥

Victoria and Alberts ♥♥♥

Description: Victorian dining / **Type:** Fine Dining

Dress Code: Men: dinner jackets and slacks with shoes / Women: dress, pant suit, or skirt and blouse – This dress code is strictly enforced.

Price: $$$$ / **Dining Plan:** Yes

Menu Items: caviar, shrimp, fish, scallops, duck, pork, lasagna, lamb, beef, cheeses, various desserts, soda pop, coffee, tea, wines

Recommendations: The finest dining in all of WDW with perfect Victorian décor and service. There are options for Kids, but this is mostly an adult affair. Note that the menu changes from time to time, so we don't provide recommendations other than the food here is exquisite.

Beaches Pool Bar and Grill – $$ / Dining: Yes / Pool Bar

Citricos Lounge – $$ / Dining: No / Lounge

Courtyard Pool Bar – $$ / Dining: No / Pool Bar

Garden View Tea Room – $$ / Dining: No / Tea Lounge

Gasparilla Island Grill – $$ / Dining: Yes / American Quick Service Pool Bar

Mizner's Lounge – $$ / Dining: No / Lounge

Disney's Old Key West Resort

Good's Food to Go – $ / Dining: Yes / Burger and Hot Dog Quick Service

Gurgling Suitcase – $ / Dining: No / Pool bar

Olivia's Cafe
American Cuisine / **Type:** Table Service
Price: $$$ / **Dining Plan:** Yes
Menu Items:
Breakfast: biscuits and gravy, omelets, eggs, chorizo, French toast, pancakes, waffles, cereal, bacon, sausage, ham, potatoes, coffee, tea, milk, morning cocktails, bottled water – *Kids*: mini pancakes, waffles, eggs and breakfast potatoes
Lunch and Dinner: corn fritters, onion rings, crab cakes, soup, salads, burger, pork ribs, chicken, pasta, sandwiches, chicken, fish, assorted desserts, specialty drinks, beer, coffee, tea, soda pop – *Kids*: chicken, grilled cheese
Recommendations: Island Barbecue Pork Ribs, Olivia's Potatoes for a side

Turtle Shack Poolside Snacks – $ / Dining: Yes / Pool bar

Disney's Polynesian Village Resort and Villas

Kona Cafe
Description: American and Seafood Restaurant / **Type:** Table Service
Price: $$ / **Dining Plan:** Yes

Menu Items:

Breakfast: French toast, steak and eggs, ham, bacon, sausage, pancakes, omelets, eggs, fruit, oatmeal, assorted pastries, tea, coffee, soda pop, juices – *Kids*: oatmeal, fruit, eggs, pancakes, French toast, toast

Lunch: crab cakes, beef, pork, pot stickers, salad, soup, tacos, Asian noodles. Sandwiches, burgers, assorted desserts, tea, coffee, soda pop, milk – *Kids*: salad, chicken, shrimp skewers, cheeseburger, cheese tortellini, hot dog

Dinner: crab cakes, beef, pork, pot stickers, sushi, salad, soup, duck, pork, lamb, assorted desserts, tea, coffee, soda pop, milk – *Kids*: salad, chicken, shrimp skewers, cheeseburger, cheese tortellini, hot dog

Recommendations: Big Kahuna for breakfast, fish tacos for lunch, any of the pan noodles for dinner

'Ohana

Description: Polynesian Character Dining / **Type:** Character Dining

Price: $$$ / **Dining Plan:** Yes

Menu Items:

Breakfast Buffet: scrambled eggs, fried potatoes, pork, Mickey-shaped waffles, assorted pastries, tea, coffee, soda pop, juices, milk

Dinner Buffet: breads, salads, dumplings, chicken wings, Asian chickens, steak, shrimp, stir fry, assorted desserts, tea, coffee, soda pop, milk

Recommendations: Great for adventurous eaters and fans of Lilo and Stitch.

Trader Sam's Grog Grotto ♥♥♥

Description: Island Dive Bar / **Type:** Lounge

Price: $$ / **Dining Plan:** No

Menu Items: mixed drinks, wines, beer, sushi, lettuce cups, tacos, fish, sliders, sausages, dumplings, soda pop

Recommendations: We love Trader Sam's! The room is a bit secret and stored away behind a metal door. Open it to discover a hidden gem in the WDW Resort. The room and the waiters react to different ordered drinks. Watch the volcanoes erupt, room storm, and bartenders transform to zombies looking for brains! Okay, it's more funny than scary, but Trader Sam's is not to be missed! Order any of their delicious mixed drinks and Kalua Pork Tacos. After 8pm, it's 21+ only.

Barefoot Pool Bar – $ / Dining: No / Pool Bar
Capt. Cook's – $$ / Dining: Yes / Quick Service Breakfast, Lunch, and Dinner
Kona Island – $ / Dining: No / Quick Service treats and drinks
Oasis Bar and Grill – $$ / Dining: Yes / Quick Service and Pool Bar
Pineapple Lanai ♥♥♥ – $$ / Dining: Yes / Dole Whip Station
Tambu Lounge – $$ / Dining: No / Lounge
Trader Sam's Tiki Terrace – $$ / Dining: No / Lounge / Recommendation: Go to Trader Sam's Grog Grotto instead for a better theme

Disney's Pop Century

This Resort hotel has two quick service dining experiences.

Everything POP Shopping and Dining – $$ / Dining: Yes / Quick Service

Pedals Pool Bar – $$ / Dining: No / Pool Bar

Disney's Port Orleans – French Quarter

Mardi Grogs – $ / Dining: No / Quick Service Bar

Sassagoula Floatworks and Food Factory – $$ / Dining: Yes / Quick Service

Scat Cat's Club – $$ / Dining: No / Lounge

Disney's Port Orleans – Riverside

Boatwright's Dining Hall
Description: Southern American Boat Restaurant / **Type:** Table Service
Price: $$$ / **Dining Plan:** Yes
Menu Items: seafood, salad, fritters, gumbo, meat and cheese board, prime rib, steak, catfish, pork chop, pasta, jambalaya, chicken, vegetables, assorted desserts, tea, coffee, soda pop, juices, beer, mixed drinks, soda pop – *Kids*: turkey, pasta, fish, beef skewers, macaroni and cheese, cheeseburger, cheese pizza, jambalaya
Recommendations: Cajun Bayou Catfish, Crawfish Mac and Cheese, red velvet cheesecake

Muddy Rivers – $ / Dining: No / Bar

River Roost – $$ / Dining: No / Lounge with live entertainment

Riverside Mill Food Court – $$ / Dining: Yes / New Orleans-style Quick Service

Disney's Saratoga Springs Resort and Spa

The Turf Club Bar and Grill
Description: American Dining / **Type:** Table Service
Price: $$$ / **Dining Plan:** Yes
Menu Items: calamari, mussels, soups, onion rings, salad, shrimp, prime rib, lamb chops, pasta, fish, chicken, steak, vegetables, assorted desserts, tea, coffee, soda pop, juices, beer, mixed drinks, soda pop – *Kids*: grilled fish, pasta, chicken breasts, cheeseburger, hot dog, cheese pizza
Recommendations: Onion Rings with dips, Grilled New York Strip

The Artist's Palette – $ / Dining: Yes / Quick Service Sandwiches while painting

Backstretch Pool Bar – $$ / Dining: Yes / Pool bar

On the Rocks – $ / Dining: Yes / Lounge

The Paddock Grill – $ / Dining: Yes / Lounge

The Turf Club Lounge – $ / Dining: No / Lounge

Disney's Wilderness Lodge and Villas

Artist Point
Description: American Dining / **Type:** Fine Dining
Price: $$$ / **Dining Plan:** Yes

Menu Items: artisanal cheeses, meat boards, shrimp, mussels, oysters, duck liver pate, prosciutto, soup, salad, steak, chicken, eggplant panisse, scallops, salmon, assorted desserts, wines, specialty cocktails, craft beers, soda pop – *Kids*: fish, chicken breast, pasta, steak
Recommendations: Cheese board, Aged Buffalo Strip Loin

Whispering Canyon Cafe
Description: American Dining / **Type:** Table Service
Price: $$$ / **Dining Plan:** Yes
Menu Items:
Breakfast: fruit, pastries, breakfast skillet, omelets, eggs, oatmeal, eggs benedict, pancakes, French toast, bacon, sausage, coffee, tea, milk, morning cocktails, smoothies – *Kids*: omelet, egg, waffles, French toast, oatmeal, fruit cup, pancakes, breakfast skillet
Lunch and Dinner: pot stickers, bison burger, grilled cheese, salad, skillet, sandwiches, pork ribs, assorted desserts, specialty drinks, beer, coffee, tea, wine, mixed drinks, beer, soda pop – *Kids*: cheese dipper, fish, chicken breast, cheeseburger, macaroni and cheese, chicken nuggets
Recommendations: All-You-Care-To-Enjoy Skillet

Roaring Fork – $ / Dining: Yes / Quick Service breakfast and sandwiches
Territory Lounge – $$ / Dining: No / Bar and Lounge / Recommendation: Great for adults
Trout Pass Pool Bar – $ / Dining: No / Pool Bar

Disney's Yacht Club
See Disney's Beach Club Resort

WDW Dolphin and Swan Hotels

Dining plans are not accepted at these hotels.

The Fountain
Description: American Dining / **Type:** Table Service
Price: $$$ / **Location:** Dolphin
Menu Items:
Breakfast and Brunch: fruit, pastries, eggs, breakfast pizza, Mickey waffles, cheese grits, carving station, soup, chili, fried chicken, desserts, bacon, sausage, coffee, tea, milk, juices
Lunch and Dinner: chicken breast, shrimp, salad, flatbread, sandwiches, chicken and waffles, steak, grits, assorted desserts, beer – *Kids*: baked chicken, grilled salmon, cheeseburger, macaroni and cheese, chicken nuggets, grilled cheese
Recommendations: We're not very impressed with this menu. For the price, you may as well boat over to Disney's Boardwalk.

Fresh Mediterranean Market
Description: American and Mediterranean Dining / **Type:** Table Service / **Location:** Dolphin
Price: $$$
Menu Items:
Breakfast and Brunch: French toast, grits, eggs, cereal, yogurt, pancakes, omelets, bacon, sausage, coffee, tea, milk, juices, breakfast mixed drinks

Lunch: salads, wine
Recommendations: "Monkey Puzzle" French Toast

Garden Grove
Description: American and Seafood Dining / **Type:** Character Dining
Price: $$$ / **Location:** Swan

Menu Items: clam chowder, soups, salads, meat and seafood buffet, assorted desserts, soda pop, wine, sangria, beer – *Kids*: pasta, fish tacos, chicken fingers, turkey sliders, tuna salad sandwich, Margherita pizza

Recommendations: Dinner Buffet

Il Mulino

Description: Italian Restaurant / **Type:** Table Service
Price: $$$ / **Location:** Swan
Menu Items: shrimp, calamari, steaks, mussels, clams, insalate, beef, soup, pizza, risotto, pasta, fish, assorted desserts, soda pop, wine, sangria, beer – *Kids*: pizzas, fettuccini alfredo
Recommendations: Rustica pizza

Kimonos ♥♥♥

Description: Sushi Bar / **Type:** Table Service
Price: $$$ / **Location:** Swan
Menu Items: sushi, salad, kimchee, tempura, miso soup
Recommendations: The best sushi in Orlando! Get the gyoza or tempura platter to start, Shrimp Tempura Roll for the entrée ♥♥♥

Shula's Steak House

Description: American Steakhouse styled after the Miami Dolphins history / **Type:** Fine Dining
Price: $$$$ / **Location:** Dolphin
Menu Items: steak, seafood, soup, salad, mashed potatoes, vegetables, assorted desserts, wines, soda pop – *Kids*: chicken, cheeseburger
Recommendations: Try any of their savory steaks

Todd English bluezoo

Description: Stylish Seafood Restaurant / **Type:** Fine Dining
Price: $$$$ / **Location:** Dolphin

Menu Items: fish, steak, chicken, lobster, Bolognese, fries, vegetables, assorted desserts, wines, soda pop – *Kids*: beef tenderloin, chicken, fish fillets, spaghetti, cheese pizza, clam chowder, shrimp, cocktails, wines, cider, beer

Recommendations: Maine Lobster pot pie, lobster broccoli stuffed cheddar potato

Cabana Bar and Beach Club – $ / Dolphin / Poolside fish tacos and salads

Il Mulino Lounge – $$$ / Swan / Lounge

Java Bar – $$ / Swan / Lounge

Kimonos Lounge – $$ / Swan / Lounge

Lobby Lounge – $ / Dolphin / Lounge

Picabu – $$ / Dolphin / Cafeteria-style American Favorites

Shula's Lounge – $$ / Dolphin / Lounge

Splash – $$ / Swan / Quick Service wraps, burgers, and pizza

Todd English bluezoo Lounge – $$ / Dolphin / Lounge with burgers and nachos

Dining Out

Disney Springs and Disney's Boardwalk have several delicious dining options. Their spaces are ever-evolving, so we've included the best choices.

Disney Boardwalk

<u>Flying Fish</u> ♥♥♥
Description: American Seafood Dining / **Type:** Fine Dining
Dress Code: Business casual / cocktail attire
Price: $$$$ / **Dining Plan:** Yes
Menu Items: fish, crab, salad, steak, chicken, shellfish, assorted desserts, specialty cocktails, wine, beer, cider – *Kids*: fish, chicken breast, pasta
Recommendations: Easily one of the Walt Disney World Resort's best and well-themed dining experiences. There aren't as many options for Kids, but adults will love this seafood culinary experience. Try the Tour of the Coast for a seafood appetizer and Wagyu Filet Mignon for the savory entrée.

<u>Recommended Bars and Treats:</u>
$ - $$ / These do not accept Disney Dining Plans

Boardwalk Joe's Marvelous Margaritas – delicious margaritas and other tropical drinks.
Funnel Cake Cart – try one of WDW's famous funnel cakes. They are fried and dusted with powdered sugar to perfection.
AbracadaBar – try one of several delicious mixed drinks, beers, or wines. There are also non-alcoholic choices for the kids.

Disney Springs

The BOATHOUSE ♥♥♥
Description: American Seafood Dining / **Type:** Table Service
Price: $$$ / **Dining Plan:** Yes
Menu Items: steak, fish, lobster, shrimp, salad, burger, sandwiches, seafood small plates, fries, macaroni and cheese, cocktails, wines, beer, assorted desserts, soda pop – *Kids*: fish, chicken, popcorn shrimp, pig in a blanket, cheese burger, macaroni and cheese, chicken tenders and fish nuggets
Recommendations: We love the presentation of this restaurant. It's classy but fun and the food is fantastic. Their steaks are great and you can make a surf and turf combo by adding Main Lobster.

D-Luxe Burger ♥♥♥
Description: Burger Joint / **Type:** Quick Service
Price: $ / **Dining Plan:** Yes
Menu Items: Burgers, fries, macaron, soda pop, beer, wine, alcoholic sodas, shakes, floats – *Kids*: cheeseburger, chicken burger
Recommendations: The burgers are the best in all of WDW. The fries are nothing to remember. Try the Barbecue Classic Burger and a Red Velvet Burger Macaron for dessert.

Earl of Sandwich ♥♥♥
Description: Sandwich Shop / **Type:** Quick Service
Price: $ / **Dining Plan:** Yes
Menu Items: hot sandwiches, soups, wraps, mac n cheese, salad, various desserts, soda pop, hot tea, coffee, wine, beer, hot chocolate, milk
Recommendations: The best hot sandwiches in all of WDW – maybe even the world. We love Earl of Sandwich and it's rare that sandwich lovers don't agree. We recommend The Earl's Club ♥♥♥

Morimoto Asia

Description: Modern Asian Cuisine / **Type:** Table Service
Price: $$$ / **Dining Plan:** Yes
Menu Items: shrimp tempura, edamame, miso soup, salad, calamari, dumplings, egg rolls, sushi, kung pao, noodles, fried rice, fish, vegetable dishes, assorted desserts, sake, cocktails, beer, wine – *Kids*: macaroni and cheese, lo mein, orange chicken, menchi katsu, hot dogs, fried chicken
Recommendations: The sushi is great. There is also a Morimoto Asia Street Food next door. You can spend less and still have great flavors.

T-REX

Description: Dinosaur-themed Restaurant / **Type:** Table Service
Price: $$$ / **Dining Plan:** Yes
Menu Items: nachos, quesadilla, salad, soup, burgers, sandwiches, shrimp, fish, fries, pasta, chicken, steak, various desserts, cocktails, beer, wine, soda pop – *Kids*: grilled chicken, corn dog, sliders, popcorn shrimp, chicken nuggets, pork ribs, pasta, pizza, macaroni and cheese
Recommendations: Like the Rainforest Café, T-REX is more about the theme than the food. Kids will love it, but adults will find it okay, but nothing to write home about. Still, it's worth seeing the enormous dinosaurs and prehistoric scenery while you eat. We recommend a burger here.

Recommended Bars and Treats:

$ / These do not accept Disney Dining Plans

Ghirardelli Ice Cream and Chocolate Shop – try some delicious San Francisco chocolates, sundaes, and shakes

Sprinkles – delicious cupcakes! Look for the long line and don't be intimidated. They work fast and it's worth the weight. Get their famous Red Velvet Cupcake.

Not Recommended:

Paradiso 37 – while the outside looks fun and inviting, the Latin American food is less than savory and the seating is very close together.

Wolfgang Puck Grand Café – he's famous, but this restaurant is packaged, delivered, and forgettable. If you're really craving something from there, visit the Wolfgang Puck Express and get much of the same for less.

Disney Dining Plan – Is It Worth It?

Our experience with the Disney Dining Plan have been mixed. There's a possibility that you can save money, that is, if you love to eat – especially at the fancier restaurants. However, if you are planning on just grabbing food when you want, there's a huge chance that you won't save any money. Often, we find ourselves so caught up in the attractions that we go for a snack instead of a meal. Unfortunately, many of our favorite snack carts aren't available on the Disney Dining Plan.

If you want to try it, here are some helpful tips to ensure that you save money:

1. Use this guide to help browse our recommended restaurants.
2. Look at the menu to see the cost of the food you'd like to enjoy.
3. Reserve all of your dining reservations ahead of time.

Chapter Fifteen

Bringing Kids: From Toddlers to Teens

Introduction

If you're planning a vacation to Walt Disney World, there's a huge chance that you'll be visiting with children (if not, you might want to skip this chapter and head straight to the next one). Walt Disney World feels like a haven for families with kids–and, for the most part, it is! There are hundreds of attractions, dozens of Disney-themed places to stay, pools with waterslides, and, of course, the enchanting magic of the Parks.

If your kids know that they're visiting Disney World, they are likely bursting at the seams and counting down the days. After all, it's one of the happiest places they can be! That's not to assume there won't be a snag or two… or *six* on your vacation. Kids have their limitations, even on fun. Unfortunately for adults, the not-so-fun times can be difficult to deal with outside of the home. Fortunately, however, there are ways that you can limit the problems and even cut them short when they arise.

If you're traveling with preteens or teenagers, we have some excellent tips for you, too. Maybe you're looking for the best places to stay, eat, or play, we've got it covered. Now we'll review the best of everything designed for kids of all ages at Walt Disney World.

Note:
If you want a complete listing of all kid-friendly rides, restaurants, and hotels, review the corresponding chapters in this book. We note on every place and ride who they are designed for and why we recommend it.

Tips for Visiting with Kids

1. **Get to the Parks Early** – This may be the most valuable piece of information that we can give you when traveling to the Walt Disney World Theme Parks. Kids aren't fans of long lines (but who is?), and the best way to keep them happy is to avoid waiting. Getting to the Parks early on will help you. We recommend riding an attraction you didn't receive a FastPass+ selection for at the start of your day.

2. **Don't Over-Do It** – Kids get tired. Ride after ride. Show after show. From morning until night. The Young Kids likely won't make it and even the Teens will be groaning for some pool time. Plan for about 4-5 hours on the rides with Kids and Young Kids (Tweens and Teens can generally last longer). After that, take a break and see what everyone is in the mood for afterward. We also recommend spacing out your days. If you know that everyone loves the Magic Kingdom Park and Epcot is not as important, get a Park Hopper and return to the Magic Kingdom later in your trip for more of what they love.

3. **Take Breaks** – In order to not "over-do it" you'll need to take breaks. Plan to head back to the Hotel for lunch or right after. Keep them cool, hydrated, and ready for more one their battery has charged. In fact, both you and the kids might be craving naps!

4. **Have Backup Plans** – Sometimes weather or tantrums can wreck an otherwise perfect day. Plan to have something else fun to do. Maybe bring a board game for the hotel room or change your timeslot for lunch or dinner. Like temper tantrums, Florida showers tend to

last under a half hour, but if you're faced with longer poor-weather or fits, having a backup is a lifesaver.

5. **Consider Giving *Yourself* a Break** – In a perfect world, being around our Kids 24/7 would bring us endless joy. However, this is not a perfect world. We invite you to review our next chapter that's all about adults. It'll give you tips on what to do with your kids while you save some time for the spa, dining out, or just visiting the Parks without them.

Visiting with Babies and Toddlers

We hear a lot of parents ask: "Should I bring my baby to Walt Disney World? Is there a *best* age?" If you're hankering to go to WDW, we highly recommend bringing your kids of any age. Many parents love bringing their babies to the Parks because it brings new enjoyment through the eyes of a child. If you decide to bring your baby to the WDW Resort, here is a list of what to bring, do, and all about the baby care centers.

What to Bring:

Stroller – Rentals start at $15 a day ($13/day for longer stays) or bring your own. Fantasyland has several locations for parking your stroller while you wait in line. Cast members patrol the area for safety.

Protection from the Sun – We recommend sunscreen, hats, blankets, and a covered stroller to keep your little one comfortable.

Blankets and Warm Clothes – These items are essential for cooler days (or at night when the temperatures drop).

Diapers, Wipes, and a Change of Clothes – Just in case of a mess, a change of clothes can be a lifesaver.

Bottles and Formula – Don't forget the liners!

Baby Food – The WDW Resort will allow small glass jars as long as they contain baby food.

Backpack – This is for you to carry your baby's items. Sometimes you can hide these in a stroller, but just in case you leave your stroller for a ride, we recommend carrying your items with you.

The Baby Care Center

Just in case you forget something, the WDW Resort Parks are equipped with nannies that are there to help. They offer nursing rooms, rocking chairs, changing tables, highchairs for feeding, a microwave, and fresh water. You can also purchase items like clothing, medications (over-the-counter), formula, baby food, diapers, and wipes.

Locations

Magic Kingdom Park – Next to First Aid, between Main Street, U.S.A. and Adventureland.

Epcot – In the World Showcase, in the Odyssey Center building, next to the Mexican Pavilion.

Disney's Hollywood Studios –Hollywood Boulevard, the left as you enter through the main gate.

Disney's Animal Kingdom – Discovery Island, near the bridge to Africa.

Changing Rooms – These are found in most restrooms (men and women).

Breast Feeding – Feeding your baby is a top priority and you shouldn't be nervous to do so at WDW. If you want privacy (or quiet), head to the Baby Care Centers in the parks.

First Aid – Located next to the Baby Care Center in the Magic Kingdom on Main Street, U.S.A.

Attraction Tips with Babies and Toddlers

See a Show or Parade – With wonderful music and dancing characters, your baby or toddler will be delighted. Check the map for a schedule of shows and parades.

Space Out Rides – Space out rides and times waiting in line for simple joys like looking at the baby ducks in the many ponds or eat a snack under some shade.

Don't Forget FastPass+ – These reservations save everyone waiting in line. The less time waiting, the happier the kid!

Rider Switch

Do you have a Young Kid with you, but all of the adults in your party want to ride? Many WDW Resort rides give you the option to wait and switch places when finished. This especially helps when a kid turns out not to be tall enough to ride or he/she becomes too scared. To use the Rider Switch, ask a cast member at the start of the queue. You will be assigned a Rider Switch pass and moved to a special area as people from your party ride the attraction.

Rides with Rider Switch:

Magic Kingdom Park
- The Barnstormer
- Big Thunder Mountain Railroad
- Space Mountain
- Splash Mountain

- Stitch's Great Escape
- Tomorrowland Speedway

Epcot
- Frozen Ever After
- Mission: SPACE
- Soarin' Around the World
- Test Track

Disney's Hollywood Studios
- Rock 'n' Roller Coaster Starring Aerosmith
- Star Tours – The Adventures Continue
- Twilight Zone Tower of Terror

Disney's Animal Kingdom Park
- DINOSAUR
- Expedition Everest – Legend of the Forbidden Mountain
- Kali River Rapids
- Primeval Whirl

Kids (Ages 3-9)

Taking Kids this age is fun because their excitement is unparalleled. They will be *itching* to ride attractions, see parades, and meet their favorite characters. You'll be busy keeping them busy, but planning everything ahead is what makes things go a lot smoother. As far as Kids go, you'll want to also take time for these activities:

1. **Make Time for the Pool** – Even though you spend hundreds of dollars on Park tickets, one of the best memories for Kids will likely be the Hotel pool. The

WDW Resort Hotel pools all have waterslides and so do many outside of the Resort. A couple of hours in the pool can be the recharge that everyone needs.

2. **Budget to Shop** – Kids love to buy things at the Parks. Disney knows this so they place gift shops with dazzling trinkets *everywhere*. Kids will likely want to avoid strolling through Disney Springs, but getting a Buzz Lightyear, Elsa, or Stitch toy can be unforgettable. Sometimes getting pre-filled Disney gift cards is the best way to go. Your Kids can manage their own budget without expecting you to fork out more money. This will save you a lot of *no's* and negotiating.

3. **Book Character Dining** – If your kids are going to want to meet characters, there's really no better way. These are buffets where characters hang out, take pictures, sign autographs, and joke around with your family. A dozen characters can show up to a Character breakfast. We recommend booking one of these experiences early in your trip so that the kids are burnt out of attempting to get autographs. This will save you *tons* of time waiting in long lines for character meetups in the Parks.

Tweens (Ages 10-12)

Tweens can be both a very fun and very challenging group to visit WDW with. They call them "Tweens" because they're in between being a Kid and a Teen. Because of this, you might be dealing with an array of emotions. They might want to be a diehard *Frozen* fan with you as well as in a "leave me alone" mood, all at the same time. There are ways to avoid the latter. Here are a few tips to planning a trip with Tweens:

1. **Plan with Them** – You'll need to make the final choices, but ask your Tween what their interests are. Which Parks are most important? What rides are they itching to jump on? Do the water parks sound fun to them? If you're having trouble picking a hotel, you might even narrow it down to a few and have your Tween help you decide. They are often very good at expressing themselves emotionally and logically. That's the perfect combination for planning a trip to Walt Disney World!

2. **Tween-Only Time** – It's completely up to you, but you might opt to let your Tween explore in a group. A group of responsible thirteen year olds can often explore the water parks and even some of the Parks by themselves. You're the adult, so you set the rules. Maybe give them a few hours alone. Check in with them on a phone. Have them meet you promptly at a certain location. They'll be happy they had their independence and extremely excited to share their experiences with you. Also keep in mind that not every Tween will want to go off on his or her own. Sometimes you are their comfort zone. In that case, embrace it, and take turns picking the rides.

3. **Try Something New** – If you've been to the Parks before with your Tweens, maybe it's time for them to try something you like. Have them explore the foods of Epcot with you or sit and watch a fireworks display. They'll appreciate you treating them older, even though you also allow them to be a kid at the Resort.

Teens (Ages 13-17)

We recommend all of the Tween activities for Teens as well. Because Teens are much more decisive and independent, they'll often want more wiggle room to be themselves. There are a few other options that Teens will crave:

1. **Get Some Sleep** – Don't plan early with Teens. Most of the time, they'd rather be at the Parks until closing and not have a bright and early agenda. Book your FastPass+ reservations for the afternoon and mosey into the Parks when everyone is refreshed and comfortable.

2. **Disney Springs** – Shopping at Disney Springs is a blast for Teens. There are so many amazing stores for them to look at, clothes to try on, unique items to buy. Teens will also love the movie theatre with dine-in seating.

3. **The Spa** – Perhaps have a mom/daughter or father/son spa day. Take them out for their first bit of relaxation at the spa. Being pampered came sometimes feel very adult and like a rite of passage. Let them indulge with you!

Chapter Seventeen

Adults, Things to Do

Introduction

The Walt Disney World Resort may have been originally built with families in mind, but that doesn't mean it hasn't also become an adult retreat. After all, Walt Disney himself was an adult when he came up with the idea for the Parks, and he knew that even the kids at heart would come there for enjoyment.

Over the decades, WDW has done a fantastic job catering to adults. With the previous Pleasure Island in the former Downtown Disney, they created an adult playground with sweeping sights and delicious food and beverages. However, they've since revamped with Disney Springs, and the adult-aimed entertainment has never been better. With bountiful places to shop and eat all around the Resort, adults have an abundance of choices. From dive bars to thrill rides to fine-dining and even golf courses, the WDW Resort has something for every grown-up. In this section, we outline adult activities from the best places to drink to avoiding families with children.

Parents' Evening Out

If you're an adult with children, part of your perfect WDW Resort vacation might be a night without them. If you're interested in heading back to the Parks, many are often open until midnight. Our top choice is Epcot for its beautiful views, fine dining, and variety of adult beverages. Then again, you might just feel like hitting the Parks late at night, utilizing those Extra Magic Hours at the Magic Kingdom or Hollywood Studios. At times, some of these Parks are open as late as 2AM!

Whatever you choose to do with your time, there are great options for kids without their parents inside the resort. We recommend planning the night ahead of time to ensure you can have an easy transition into your night alone.

Children's Activity Centers

A place just for kids – without the parents! Kids make arts and crafts, watch movies, and even eat while parents can enjoy an evening at the Resort. This is a perfect time for your kids to make new friends as they enjoy Disney-themed fun under the supervision of Disney's professional caregivers.

Notes:
1. Make a reservation in advance.
2. Your child must be potty trained (without using pull-up diapers)
3. If your child has special dietary needs, check out Lilo's Playhouse at Disney's Polynesian Village Resort.

There are currently 4 Activity Centers and you don't have to stay at that particular Resort to book there:

Disney's Animal Kingdom Lodge
Simba's Cubhouse
Location: On the first floor of the Hotel near the Uzima Pool deck.
Hours: 4:30pm – 11:55pm
Ages: 3 - 12
Cost: $15/hour per child with a 2-hour minimum. Dinner is included with this cost and served at 6PM. Call ahead to ask for that day's meal. They do not allow outside food.
Reservation Number: (407) 939-3463 – Book up to 180 days in advance and call during business hours.

Disney Beach Club Resort
Sandcastle Club
We *love* this one! Kids can dress up like pirates, build volcanoes that erupt, and even learn to make chocolate desserts like Remy from *Ratatouille*!
Location: In the lobby of the Beach Club Resort.

Hours: 4:30pm – 11:55pm

Ages: 3 - 12

Cost: $55 flat rate per child. Dinner is included with this cost and served at 6PM. Call ahead to ask for that day's meal. They do not allow outside food.

Reservation Number: (407) 939-3463 – Book up to 180 days in advance and call during business hours.

Disney's Polynesian Village Resort

Lilo's Playhouse

Another great one! Kids can build volcanoes that erupt, and also learn to make chocolate desserts like Remy from *Ratatouille*!

Location: Next to Tangaroa Terrace in the Polynesian Village Resort.

Hours: 4:30pm – 11:55pm

Ages: 3 - 12

Cost: $55 flat rate per child. Dinner is included with this cost and served at 6PM. Call ahead to ask for that day's meal. They do not allow outside food.

Reservation Number: (407) 939-3463 – Book up to 180 days in advance and call during business hours.

Walt Disney World Dolphin Hotel

Camp Dolphin

This might be our least favorite because of the fewer activities, but older kids might enjoy their Xbox 360. However, for just a couple of hours, it's perfect for any kid.

Location: On the first floor of the Dolphin Hotel.

Hours: 5pm – Midnight

Ages: 4 - 12

Cost: $12/hour per child. You can get 2 hours free if you book a spa package at the Mandara Spa or a dining reservation at Shula's Steak House, Todd English's bluezoo or Mulino New York Trattoria. Dinner is an additional $10 per child.

Reservation Number: (407) 934-4241 – Book up to 180 days in advance and call during business hours.
Note: Reservations are required.

Babysitters
The Walt Disney World works with a third-party service for babysitting. This service is call Kid's Nite Out and it's perfect if you'd rather have a babysitter in the room, rather than take your child to one of the 4 Activity Centers.

Services:
- Professional assistance in-room.
- Professional assistance at the Parks. If you desire, the babysitter will accompany your family around the Resort.
- Provides for Kids ages 6 months to 12 years old.
- Offers arts and crafts, bedtime reading, and even games to play.

Rates
- Per hour: 1 Child - $18 / 2 Children - $21 / 3 Children - $24 / 4 Children - $26
- A $2 per hour charge occurs for every hour after 9PM.
- $10 transportation fee (one-time only).

Reservations: (407) 828-9020

The Best Restaurants and Bars for Adults

If you're looking for an evening out, there are plenty of choices around the Walt Disney World Resort. However, you might have a difficult choice deciding. Should you just stay at your Hotel? Should you go off-property? Maybe you just want to try something different, but don't even know where to begin. In this section, we review all of the best bars, restaurants, and activities that we highly recommend for adults looking for a delicious evening by themselves.

#1 Trader Sam's Grog Grotto – Polynesian Village Hotel
Theme: Island-themed tiki bar inspired by the character in the Jungle Cruise ride.
Price: $$ / **Disney Dining Plan:** No
Why We Recommend It: Dim lighting, air conditioning, and scraggly bartenders serve excellent drinks and bar food in this unique setting. Try a specialty cocktail or order a beer on draft. Certain drinks cause the room's volcanoes to erupt or brew a storm. Trader Sam's is also known for its excellent tacos.
★ Magic Tip ★
After 8pm, Trader Sam's is 21 and older only.

#2 Teppan Edo – Epcot World Showcase, Japan
Theme: Teppanyaki grill with live chefs
Price: $$$ / **Disney Dining Plan:** Yes, but not for alcohol
Why We Recommend It: Very similar to Benihana. Watch talented Japanese chefs make your choice of course right before your eyes! They are like ninjas with their knives and even create delicious masterpieces on a hot grill. If you've never been to a Teppanyaki-style restaurant, you can't miss this one!

#3 Victoria & Albert's – Grand Floridian Hotel
Theme: Elegant, Victorian-style fine dining
Price: $$$$ / **Disney Dining Plan:** Yes, but not for alcohol.
Why We Recommend It: A 5-Diamond culinary experience. If you're craving a perfectly prepared meal for a special occasion, look no further than Victoria & Albert's.

★ Magic Tip ★
This restaurant is only open for dinner and has a strict dress code. It's required for men to wear dinner jackets, slacks, and shoes. Women must wear a dress, pant suit, or skirt and blouse.

#4 **Kimonos** – Swan Hotel
Theme: Freshly made sushi house.
Price: $$ / **Disney Dining Plan:** No
Why We Recommend It: The best sushi in Orlando – and sake

#5 **Jiko - The Cooking Place** – Animal Kingdom Lodge
Theme: African cuisine.
Price: $$$$ / **Disney Dining Plan:** Yes, but not for alcohol.
Why We Recommend It: Get a taste for Africa in a unique, wild setting. Try an African wine or specially marinated chicken or vegetables.
★ Magic Tips ★
1. When you're done eating, you can roam the Hotel and see some of the exotic animals on site.
2. This restaurant is only open for dinner and has a strict dress code. It's required for men to wear collared shirts, slacks or jeans, and shoes. Women may wear a dress, jeans or capris, dress shorts or skirts. Dinner jackets are not required. Hats, tank tops, swimming gear, and cut-off clothing are not permitted.

#6 **Rose and Crown Dining Room** – Epcot World Showcase, United Kingdom
Theme: British Pub
Price: $$$ / **Disney Dining Plan:** Yes, but not for alcohol
Why We Recommend It: A cool environment with great beer, cocktails, and tasty fish and chips.

★ **Magic Tip** ★

> Book a reservation to see the IllumiNations fireworks from the patio.

#7 La Cava del Tequila – Epcot World Showcase, Mexico
Theme: Tequila cellar with authentic Mexican flare.
Price: $$ / **Disney Dining Plan:** No
Why We Recommend It: Dim lighting, air conditioning, and delicious margaritas! Need we say more?

#8 Raglan Road™ Irish Pub and Restaurant – Disney Springs
Theme: Authentic Irish pub.
Price: $$ / **Disney Dining Plan:** Yes, but not for alcohol
Why We Recommend It: Join the boisterous fun in the center of Disney Springs' Irish pub. There is beer, food, dancers, and other nightly entertainment.

#9 River Roost – Port Orleans Riverside
Theme: Southern-style lounge.
Price: $$ / **Disney Dining Plan:** No
Why We Recommend It: If you're craving some zany performances with a Southern feel, this is the place to be! Yehaa Bob performs a wacky, high-energy show here, twice a night, Wednesday through Saturday (8:30pm and 10:30pm).

#10 Yachtsman Steakhouse – Yacht Club Resort
Theme: New England steakhouse
Price: $$$$ / **Disney Dining Plan:** Yes, but not for alcohol.
Why We Recommend It: Savory steaks and wines made better here than anywhere else in the WDW Resort.
★ **Magic Tip** ★

> This restaurant is only open for dinner and has a strict business casual dress code.

#11 <u>Territory Lounge</u> – Wilderness Lodge
Theme: A rustic, woodland bar with an array of craft beers, wine, and specialty drink choices.
Price: $$ / **Disney Dining Plan:** No
Why We Recommend It: A very calm, underrated bar to relax. If you're hungry, try one of their savory flatbreads.

#12 <u>Jellyrolls</u> – Boardwalk Resort
Theme: Boardwalk-style dueling piano bar for those 21+.
Price: $$ / **Disney Dining Plan:** No
Why We Recommend It: If you are into loud, fun piano music this is the place to be. Everyone laughs and sings along to the performers.

How to Avoid Children

It's impossible to absolutely avoid *all* children at the WDW Resort. But you can avoid being around the bulk of them. We've listed some great tips on how to stay clear of families with small children at the Resort.

Resorts with the Fewest Children:

1. Disney's Grand Floridian Resort and Day Spa – It's expensive, so many families won't want to spend their budget on this.
2. Disney Contemporary Resort Bay Lake Tower – The modern edge of this tower and its simple pool appears to deter children.
3. Coronado Springs – Not our favorite hotel, but on a budget, this is a great choice to avoid kids.

Places to Visit or Avoid:

1. Visit Trader Sam's Grog Grotto after 8PM – No one under 21 is allowed in Trader Sam's after 8PM. Jelly Rolls is also 21+ only.
2. Stick to Epcot's World Showcase – You'll have plenty of adult activities that will simply bore children.
3. Ride at Hollywood Studios – 2017 is the perfect opportunity to enjoy Hollywood Studios. With Star Wars Land and Toy Story Land in the distance, the families will likely stick to Magic Kingdom and Animal Kingdom. This will leave the thrill rides like Tower of Terror and Rock 'n' Roller Coaster all to the adults.
4. Avoid the Water Parks – These are often wall-to-wall with families with kids.
5. Stay Away from Pools with Water slides – Even at night the children play in these. The simple pools without water slides have by far the fewest children.
6. Avoid "Kids Lands" – Fantasyland in the Magic Kingdom Park, Pixar Place in Hollywood Studios, and Rafiki's Planet Watch in Animal Kingdom are all spots filled with kid attractions. Avoid them.
7. Look for Height Restrictions – Rides with height requirements will weed out the littlest ones.
8. Go at Night – The Parks are often open late during the peak seasons of Summer and Winter. They even stay open as late as 2am with Extra Magic Hours. It'll be less common to see children at those times.
9. Say *NO* to Parades and Shows – These attractions are like magnets for small children. You've been warned.
10. Ride During a Parade – If you must ride a Fantasyland attraction, these are the best times! The families will flock to the parade route, generally leaving adults behind to

wait for these popular rides. Check your park map for parade times.

11. Dine at a Bar – Pick from one of the places we've mention in the previous section of this chapter.

12. Forget the Characters – You might be *dying* to meet Ariel from *The Little Mermaid*, but if you're looking to avoid those kiddies, you're gonna have to make some sacrifices. Bye, Ariel!

Other Adult Ideas

Get a Massage – Traveling can be stressful. Flying around the parks can be stressful. Dealing with your kids… well, you get it. Take some time for yourself and schedule a message with your Resort Hotel. They are world-class and unforgettable:

- Animal Kingdom Lodge – Zahanati Massage & Fitness Center
- Boardwalk Villas – Muscles & Bustles Health Club
- Contemporary Resort – Olympiad Fitness Center
- Coronado Springs – La Vida Health Club
- Dolphin Hotel – Mandara Spa
- Grand Floridian – Senses*
- Saratoga Springs – Senses*
- Wilderness Lodge Villas – Sturdy Branches
- Yacht Club – Ship Shape Massage Salon

*The Senses Spas are our favorites. We highly recommend them if you are planning an even more relaxing getaway. They offer most Spa treatments from massages to facials, wraps, and steam rooms.

Mandara Spa Reservations: (407) 934-4772
Reservations for all other Spas: (407) 939-7727

See La Nouba– La Nouba by Cirque du Solei is stunning and the exact entertainment you might be searching for!
https://disneyworld.disney.go.com/entertainment/disney-springs/cirque-du-soleil-la-nouba

See a Concert – The House of Blues in Disney Springs offers a wide variety of live music shows. We always recommend pre-booking tickets for these events in case they sell out.
http://www.houseofblues.com/orlando

Watch a Movie – AMC Disney Springs 24 offers a wide selection of movies. They also have an amazing Dine-In experience where you can sit and eat while you watch a movie. Visit www.amctheatres.com for show times.

Golf – Walt Disney World has some world-class golfing.

Go Shopping – Pick up a bag at Kate Spade or a polo at Lacoste.

Hit the Gym – If fitness is your thing, here are the locations:
- Animal Kingdom Lodge – Zahanati Massage & Fitness Center
- Animal Kingdom Villas – Survival of the Fittest Fitness Center
- Boardwalk Villas – Muscles & Bustles Health Club
- Contemporary Resort – Olympiad Fitness Center
- Coronado Springs – La Vida Health Club
- Grand Floridian – Senses
- Old Key West – Old Key West Exercise Room
- Saratoga Springs – Senses
- Wilderness Lodge Villas – Sturdy Branches
- Yacht Club – Ship Shape Massage Salon

Chapter Seventeen
Non-Rider Guide

Introduction

Typically, the first thing that people think about Walt Disney World is Mickey Mouse. The second thought is usually the rides that fill the Resort's Parks. But what if you or your guest don't enjoy the drops, turns, and twists? Are there things for you to do? Would you enjoy yourself? Would it be worth the money to plan a vacation around a set of theme parks? In short, is the Walt Disney World Resort for you?

The answer: *YES*! There are about 150 attractions all around the WDW Resort–and the best part for non-riders is that most of them aren't rides. These attractions are found in every Park, whether you'd like to see exotic tigers in Disney's Animal Kingdom, watch a stunning fireworks display at the Magic Kingdom, see a Broadway-style musical at Disney's Hollywood Studios, sunbathe at the water parks, or sample an array of worldly cuisine at Epcot.

In this chapter, we explore the dozens of options in each park and give non-riders the opportunity to discover the best that Walt Disney World has to offer without the craze of the heart-racing rides.

Top 8 Recommendations:

1. Photograph the Sights: The Walt Disney World Resort is truly a feast for the eyes. The Parks offer intricate architecture, well-planned lands, and lush, meticulously manicured foliage. There are unlimited things to take photos of!

2. Try Gourmet Food – Dazzle your senses with savory meals and sweet treats all around the Parks, Hotels, and

Disney Springs. Epcot offers some of the best samplings from all over the globe!

3. See Stunning Shows – The WDW Resort is known for magnificent shows. Every park has a huge list of attractions.

    Most Recommended Shows to Watch (in order):

    1. Festival of the Lion King (Animal Kingdom)
    2. *Finding Nemo*–The Musical (Animal Kingdom)
    3. *Beauty and the Beast* – Live on Stage (Hollywood Studios)
    4. Indiana Jones Stunt Spectacular! (Hollywood Studios)
    5. Illuminations: Reflections of Earth (Epcot)
    6. Wishes fireworks (Magic Kingdom)
    7. Jedi Training Academy – best for Kids (Hollywood Studios)
    8. La Nouba by Cirque Du Solei (Disney Springs – Additional Cost)

4. Meet Famous Characters – Take a photo with your favorite Disney character. Or watch the many musical bands playing around the park. We recommend watching the barbershop quartet, the Dapper Dans on Main Street in the Magic Kingdom Park.

5. Ride a Slow-Moving Attraction – Some rides don't have drops or move fast, many of them can be perfect for your speed as you experience the magnificent stories these rides have to offer. Epcot has over a dozen slow-moving boat rides perfect for everyone.

Best of the Slow Rides and Attractions (not in order):

> Epcot – We listed these together because Epcot is *filled* with slow-moving rides. Journey into Imagination with Figment is a great start.
>
> Jungle Cruise (Magic Kingdom) – A humorous tour guide takes you on a riverboat through the Amazon and Africa.
>
> Peter Pan's Flight (Magic Kingdom) – See the story of *Peter Pan* while flying in a slow-moving pirate ship.
>
> The Little Mermaid – Ariel's Undersea Adventure (Magic Kingdom) – a slow-moving "dark ride" that explores the story of Disney's *The Little Mermaid*.
>
> Haunted Mansion (Magic Kingdom) – A slow-moving dark ride through a haunted house. Might be too scary for Young Kids.
>
> "it's a small world" (Magic Kingdom) – The classic, slow-paced boat ride around the world.
>
> Tomorrowland Transit Authority PeopleMover (Magic Kingdom) – Another classic WDW attraction that travels slowly through Tomorrowland. It's also a great way to beat the heat!
>
> The Great Movie Ride (Hollywood Studios) – See the history of Hollywood movie making in this slow-moving dark ride.
>
> *Honorable Classic Mention: The Walt Disney World Railroad (Magic Kingdom)*

6. Shop! – There are stores on every corner of the Resort. Disney Springs is loaded with stores for yourself or to bring back souvenirs. We've spent *hours* looking at the unique items in the World of Disney store!

7. Get a Princess Makeover at the Bibbidi Bobbidi Boutique – Perfect for kids who want to dress as their favorite

Disney Princess. The Boutiques are located in Disney Springs and the Magic Kingdom Park.

8. People Watch – This will either sound fun or creepy to you, but WDW has some unique visitors in creative outfits and style. Or just sit by a ride like Splash Mountain in the Magic Kingdom Park and watch them plummet!

9. Look for Hidden Mickeys! We have a list of elusive, Mickey Mouse-shaped hidden marks found all over the Resort.

Even More to Do

1. **The ESPN Wide World of Sports Complex** – Get your game on in this massive 220-acre hub for athletics located in the Walt Disney World Resort, close to Disney's All-Star Resorts. There are baseball fields, softball diamonds, basketball courts, cross country courses, track and field, and so much more. The base fee for entry is $17.50 for Adults and $12.50 for Children ages 3-9. For more information, visit: https://www.espnwwos.com

2. **Disney Mini Golf** – The WDW Resort is home to a few fantastic, Disney-themed mini golf courses. Not only are these inexpensive, but they are stunning. The price is $14.00 for Adults and $12.00 for Children ages 3-9. The golf courses include the magical Fantasia Gardens by the Walt Disney Swan Hotel and the snowy Winter Summerland near Blizzard Beach.

3. **Disney Golf** – Disney has enormous golf fields located just outside the Magic Kingdom near the Grand Floridian and

Disney's Polynesian Resort Village. These lush fields include up to 36 par courses. There are strict dress codes and reservations are a must.

For more information, visit: http://golfwdw.com

4. **Even More Amenities** – Most the hotels will come with volleyball, tennis, or basketball courts to play games. Many of the Resorts based on water have fishing and boat rentals for extra fun. Always check out the Times Guide brochure when arriving to your hotel.

Chapter Eighteen

Hidden Mickey List

Introduction

It's no secret that Walt Disney loved his cartoon mouse, Mickey.
Ever since he created the character in the 1920's, Mickey has
found his way into nearly every piece of Walt Disney's creations
from films to logos to them parks. Now, you might be thinking
Mickey Mouse isn't in Cinderella or Aladdin!– where, in fact, he is–
or, at least, his image is.

You know that famous logo of the Mickey ears? It's just
three circles, a large one for the face and two smaller ones for the
ears. Well, these show up *everywhere* from the bubbles while
Cinderella scrubbed the floors during her labors to a quick scene
where Jasmine's pet tiger, Raja, changes briefly into a Mickey-
like head. Even *Frozen* has a Mickey doll in a bookcase in one of
the scenes.

But like we said, Mickey doesn't just show up in the
films–he's also all over the parks. These often hard-to-spot
images of him are called "Hidden Mickeys" because, well,
they're hidden! Who does this? Is it on purpose? It's hard to say
because Disney rarely confirms any, but our sources point to the
Imagineers. Disney Imagineers are the people responsible for the
creation of the rides and attractions in and out of the Parks. Since
they make every detail from the structure to the paint, they often
ensure that the Mouse leaves his mark.

But why? Think of Hidden Mickeys as a nod to Walt, the
spirit of the Parks, and as a special treat for the guests. Finding
Hidden Mickeys is a fun way to pass the time waiting in the
decorated queues. Discovering the Mickeys is fun for everyone
of all ages–especially tweens and teens. Even if you know where
one is, it's always exciting when you see one for the first time. As
we've discovered, once you find one, you start seeing them
everywhere! In this exciting chapter, we reveal dozens of
Hidden Mickeys in the Parks to the Resort Hotels and Disney
Springs!

The Magic Kingdom

1. Adventureland – Look for the Jungle Cruise sign. There are some bumps on the wood below the curve of the "J" that reveal a small Hidden Mickey.
2. Adventureland – Look for a wooden tiki near the entrance. The paint reveals a mousy shape.
3. Fantasyland – The Be Our Guest Restaurant has a few Hidden Mickeys. The first are along the walls where the corner craftwork twists together to form a Mickey Mouse head (this may be easier to spot in back of the knight armor).
4. Fantasyland – Still in the Be Our Best Restaurant, this Hidden Mickey is located at the top where the axes point between silk banners. Check out the steel on one of the axes to see a shape punctured through the middle of the blade.
5. Fantasyland – Still in the Be Our Best Restaurant, the soap suds of the Mrs. Potts and Chip mural reveal a Mickey-shaped head.
6. Fantasyland – Naturally, the Cinderella Castle has a Hidden Mickey, but it's hard to see. Look near the roof canopy to see a Mickey Mouse head (it's right above a vent-looking piece).
7. Fantasyland – In the pond with the ducks and frogs during The Little Mermaid–Ariel's Undersea Adventure, look for three lily pads in the pond in the shape of Mickey's head.
8. Frontierland – Look inside of the Mercantile store to see the shapes of the ropes on the cashier wall.
9. Frontierland – In the grass near the station in Big Thunder Mountain are three gears covered in rust. They come together to make a Hidden Mickey.

10. Frontierland – Splash Mountain has a clever Hidden Mickey that's very rewarding once you find it. Look for Brer Frog and his fishing pole. The red and white bobber is an unmistakable shape.

11. Liberty Square – Check out the shape of the three charts on a wall in the Harbour House.

12. Liberty Square – Enter the Hall of Presidents to spot George Washington holding a gold sword. You might have to squint for this one, but the Hidden Mickey is located at the tip of his sword.

13. Liberty Square – There's a fancy, rustic Hidden Mickey on the hinges of the Haunted Mansion gates.

14. Main Street, U.S.A – One of our favorite Hidden Mickeys is also one of the loveliest of all. Located in Tony's Town Square restaurant, there's a bouquet of flowers near some book on a high shelf. Three red roses make the shape of a Hidden Mickey.

15. Tomorrowland – Buzz Lightyear's Space Ranger Spin ride has a couple of great Hidden Mickeys. The first is a bit hard to spot. Right after loading onto the ride, look on the glowing wall paint to see a pile of batteries. On the left side is a Mickey Mouse-shaped head with a blue face and orange ears.

16. Tomorrowland – Another great Buzz Lightyear Space Ranger Spin Mickey is in the gift shop where the exit is. One of the monitors in the mural with the aliens has a Mickey.

17. Tomorrowland – This one is a little hard to spot. Look for a sign for the Recreational Rocket Vehicle Show on a dark blue wall. There's a moon on the sign with craters that make a Hidden Mickey.

18. Tomorrowland – The Mickey's Star Traders store naturally has a row of Hidden Mickeys. There are side-

by-side, lining the walls with characters within their portholes.

19. Tomorrowland – Stay inside Mickey's Star Traders to see the murals on the walls. One is an expressway filled with cars. The tracks make up a hidden Mickey.

20. Tomorrowland – There's another one in the same mural! Look at the satellite tower windows!

21. Tomorrowland – Yet another Hidden Mickey in Mickey's Star Traders! Look above to the front of the train painting. You'll see the sideways shape of Mickey's head in the chrome.

Epcot

22. Canada Pavilion – Look for a spotted wooden trout in the décor of the Northwest Mercantile store. Some of its spots form a very familiar shape!

23. China Pavilion – The white posts at the entrance to China have Mickey heads carved into them.

24. France Pavilion – The painting of Vincent Van Gogh has a Hidden Mickey in the sky near his left shoulder (his left, not yours).

25. Germany Pavilion – When roaming this section, look for the clock tower in the Biergarten. There is a bell held onto the stone wall with an iron hoist. Look at the shape of the iron to reveal a Hidden Mickey.

26. Mexico Pavilion – Look for the erupting volcano in the back of the pyramid. The smoke is in a cloudy, familiar shape.

27. Morocco Pavilion – The Moroccan Souk has metal plates on the red store door. Three of them come together for that famous shape.

28. United Kingdom Pavilion – The Sportsman's Shoppe sign just outside of the door has several sports items that make a peculiar shape.

29. United States Pavilion – There's a painting called "Building a Future Together" where construction workers do their job high in the sky. The man in the center is standing on a crane. The metal hooks at his feet appear to make a Mickey Head.

30. Future World – Imagination! the ride has a small, glittery Hidden Mickey just below the dragon's mouth as he blows air. It's hard to spot as it's printed in one of the pink clouds.

31. Future World – Innoventions has a several in the murals in the character meet area. Look for a Hidden Mickey next to a spaceship on a monitor.

32. Future World – There's another one in Innoventions mural by the character meet area. Look at the painted windows for a flying Mickey head.

33. Future World – Test Track has a couple of cool Mickeys. The first is in the queue where a few bolts on the table of tools is in the shape.

34. Future World – The second Test Track Hidden Mickey we've seen is also in the queue. Look for the depiction of the artist drawing on the wall with a dry erase pen. He's recently outlined a small Mickey Head.

35. Future World – Living With the Land has one in the last fish tank on the right. It's made of mesh.

36. Future World – Living With the Land has a second Mickey in the green house. Look for the chocolate vine curling around the familiar shape.

37. Future World – The Land's Soarin' Around the World has a great Hidden Mickey that you'll never miss once you see it. During the ride there is a fireworks display right behind Epcot's Spaceship Earth. Two bursts of

light come behind the globe to reveal a massive Hidden
Mickey.

38. Future World – There's yet another Hidden Mickey in
Soarin' Around the World. Look for three hot air
balloons that come together to make a Hidden Mickey.

Disney's Hollywood Studios

39. Echo Lake – Look for a Mickey Mouse-shaped piece
under the lightsaber builder of the Star Tours gift shop.
It's a bit hard to find, but there are black markings to
make the ears that look like they might have been made
by laser blasts.

40. Muppets Courtyard – During the Muppet*Vision 3D
ride, look for the 3D character changing into Mickey
Mouse.

41. Muppets Courtyard – In the waiting area, look for a set
of pressure gauges in the shape of a Mickey head.

42. Muppets Courtyard – On the fountain with Ms. Piggy as
Lady Liberty, look for a Muppet standing on a rubber
ducky with a Mickey-shaped head.

43. Muppets Courtyard – This is one of the trickiest to find.
In the Company Store, look up to see cables on the
lighting fixtures that form a Hidden Mickey with looped
wire ears.

44. Sunset Boulevard – The Rock 'n' Roller Coaster®
Starring Aerosmith has a couple of Hidden Mickeys. The
first is lead singer Steven Tyler's blouse which is covered
in Mickey print.

45. Sunset Boulevard – The second from the Rock 'n' Roller
Coaster is in the groovy-looking carpet. The warped
swirls make out Mickey heads.

46. Sunset Boulevard – The Hollywood Tower of Terror has
one located in the cobweb-covered office at the ride's

exit. Look for a drawer with a Hidden Mickey popping out of it.

Disney's Animal Kingdom

47. Africa – The flamingo island on the Kilimanjaro Safari is made to look like a Mickey head.
48. Asia – There are three very cool Hidden Mickeys around Expedition Everest. The first is in the queue for the ride where a Mickey-shaped head is behind some wires in the initial supply area.
49. Asia – Expedition Everest's second Hidden Mickey is a rustic Mickey head at the top of pillars in the queue.
50. Asia – The third from Expedition Everest is hard to find and located near the restrooms. The posts have metal wires that look near the top to form a Mickey.
51. DinoLand U.S.A. – A few of the scales on the triceratops head on TriceraTop Spin appear to make a Hidden Mickey.
52. DinoLand U.S.A. – Look for the asteroid on Primeval Whirl (below the "The End Is Near" sign). There's a Hidden Mickey made of craters.
53. DinoLand U.S.A. – There's a blue dinosaur on the left side of Chester & Hester's Dino-Rama! sign. Look on his arm and you'll see a Hidden Mickey made up of his scales.

The Resort Hotels

54. Disney's All-Star Sports Resort – Look for a Mickey Head made of a baseball in the gift shop.
55. Disney's Animal Kingdom Lodge – In the grand center of the lodge, look for a Mickey in the many pieces of art. One depicts a monkey with orange and red swirls.
56. Disney's Animal Kingdom Lodge – The Jiko restaurant has carpet with cheetah spots–some that look like Mickey heads.
57. Disney's Animal Kingdom Lodge – In fact, most of the spotted flooring has Mickey heads, even in the hallways leading to the rooms and even the rugs.
58. Disney's Art of Animation – They are everywhere here! Look for one in the spots of the fish outside of the Finding Nemo building.
59. Disney's Boardwalk Inn – Mickeys decoratively appear in the wooden carving on the TV stands in the rooms.
60. Disney's Boardwalk Inn – The lobby has a Hidden Mickey located on the floral rug.
61. Disney's Grand Floridian Resort & Spa – Look for an entire Mickey Mouse (and Minnie) in the tile work in the grand lobby.
62. Disney's Grand Floridian Resort & Spa – The M. Mouse Mercantile has a Hidden Mickey on its sign.
63. Disney's Port Orleans Resort – Look for Hidden Mickeys on the chair designs in the rooms.
64. Disney's Polynesian Village Resort – In the gift shop, look for netting filled with certain round items that make a Mickey head.
65. Disney's Yacht Club Resort – In the rooms, look for Hidden Mickeys made of knotted ropes between the boats.

Disney Springs

66. Pin Traders – There's a large Hidden Mickey (maybe it's not-so hidden) located in the concrete just outside of this store.
67. Once Upon a Toy – Check out the build your own Mr. Potato Head section. The sandals have little Hidden Mickeys on them (there's also a Mickey Mouse hat he can wear).
68. T-Rex Café – Look for the truck in front of the sign. Inside of the truck, there is a lot of dirt–except in one area. Look closely and you'll see that the missing dirt is in fact a Hidden Mickey.
69. Tren-D – Look for a mannequin with short blonde hair. Under her left eye is a very familiar black design.
70. World of Disney Store – There are a few Hidden Mickeys in the store. The first is easy to spot, near the ceiling on the wall of the middle room, you'll see a row of Mickey Mouse heads.
71. World of Disney Store – Look for a massive mural depicting the Chinese Theatre. Near the top of the theatre is a circle with a Mickey head painted in the center.
72. World of Disney Store – The store's third Hidden Mickey is all over the place. Look on the wooden racks to see a metal emblem with "World of Disney" and a globe stamped in the center. Near the "W" and the "Y" are two Hidden Mickeys.

There are hundreds (maybe thousands) of more Hidden Mickeys to find around the parks. Once you find these, keep your eyes peeled around the Parks, stores, and Resort Hotels for Mickey Mouse's iconic look!

Chapter Nineteen

FastPass+ Tips

Introduction

One of the best features about the Walt Disney World Resort is that you can pre-book a place on your favorite rides. This is done through their FastPass+ system up to 60 days before the first date of your purchased reservation. FastPass+ reserved times give you an hour window to visit the ride and effectively cut the line to board faster than anyone else. WDW has this system down with separate FP+ lines that empty into the same ride at the end. Typically, you'll wait about 10-20 minutes from the FastPass line. Sometimes, on less popular rides, the line is virtually a walk-on for FP+ holders.

The FP+ works with your MagicBand or Park ticket to allow you easy scanning by cast members at the FastPass+ lines. The amazing thing about FP+ is that it's so easy to book timeslots to your favorite rides that even kids could do it. However, choosing your FP+ selections can be tricky. If you're not extremely familiar with the popularity of certain rides (or when you'll want to ride them), you might not select the appropriate FP+ selection.

Typically, you'll be allowed to choose 3 FastPass+ selections a day, one park at a time (even if you have a Park Hopper option). The four main parks have FP+ (Magic Kingdom, Epcot, Hollywood Studios, and Epcot) while the water parks do not. FastPass+ usually works with rides, however many of the more popular shows will have reserved seating or standing for FP+. Truthfully, you may not always get to pick each ride you'd like. Some of the more popular rides like Frozen Ever After in Epcot can run out of reservations weeks ahead of your visit. For these, we recommend booking as soon as possible to ensure you get your desired timeslot.

In this chapter, we explore the FastPass+ selection process and our recommendations on which to book and which aren't necessary. Planning with the best options will save you hours and hours or time waiting in lines.

How to Book Your FastPass+ Selections:

1. Purchase Park tickets.
2. Wait until it's 60 days before your Resort reservation or from the date of your ticket purchase (30 days if you aren't staying at a WDW Resort Hotel).
3. Visit https://disneyworld.disney.go.com/plan and login to begin on your computer, phone, or tablet. If you haven't set up an account, you'll need to on the WDW website. If you've purchased tickets via a 3rd party site, visit the link we provided and you'll be able to "Link Your Tickets".
4. OR download the My Disney Experience app, login with your Disney ID, and select FastPass+ on the drop-down menu.
5. OR call for help: (407) 939-4357

Tips for Planning with FastPass+:

1. Book Early – We can't stress this enough. 60 days before your trip the FP+ selections become available to you. If you buy a 5-day pass, you will be allowed 5 days of selections on the days that you choose during your stay.
2. Reserve Early Timeslots – We recommend booking all of your FP+ times before noon. Once you've completed all of your reservations, you can book additional selections one at a time. If you are planning on park hopping, WDW now allows you to book the additional FastPasses (after you've used your first 3), at other Parks around the Resort.
3. You Can Change Your Mind – If you've decided to switch Park days or times, you can do so as long as

there is availability. The website and app are quick and easy ways to make these changes.

4. Arrive at Opening – The best way to enjoy the attractions that you've missed on FP+ is to arrive early at the opening of the Park. Experience this attraction first as to avoid the long lines that form later. Sometimes you can get 3-4 rides done in the first hour!

5. Early and Late Arrivals – If you arrive too early to the FastPass queue, you won't be allowed to use your pass. The cast member will tell you how much more time you have and instruct you to wait. However, if you arrive late, you often have a 15-minute window. Of course, this can change on busier days, but Disney knows that sometimes traffic buildup and other factors can lead to late arrivals, so they allow you show up a few minutes afterward.

6. Always Ask – If for some reason you show up after or too early, you can always ask special permission from the cast member to use your Pass out of turn. They aren't obligated to assist you on this, but often times they are able to work something in your favor. Just be polite and you'll get far with Disney employees.

7. Keep Checking the App – When someone changes or cancels a FastPass+ selection, it becomes available to other guests. If you weren't able to book all of your top, they might become available at these seemingly random times. Keep checking the My Disney Experience app throughout the day to see if you can find the attraction or timeslot you're looking for.

FastPass+ Kiosks

In the event that your phone dies or you don't have data service, there are several FastPass+ kiosks throughout the Parks. These allow you to change your reservations and add additional ones with ease on a touch screen. Often, a cast member will be available to assist you.

Magic Kingdom Park
Mickey's PhilharMagic (Fantasyland)
The Diamond Horseshow (Liberty Square)
Jungle Cruise (Adventureland)
Buzz Lightyear Space Ranger Spin (Tomorrowland)
Stitch's Great Escape (Tomorrowland)

Epcot
Character Spot, east of the water fountains (Future World)
Innoventions Plaza, North of the Fountain (Future World)
Innoventions Breeze Way, West of the Fountain (Future World)
International Gateway, between France and the United Kingdom pavilions (World Showcase)

Disney's Hollywood Studios
After the Entrance (Corner of Hollywood Boulevard and Sunset Boulevard)
At the End of Sunset Boulevard (Sunset Boulevard)
Toy Story Midway Mania (Pixar Place)
Muppet*Vision 3D (Muppet Courtyard)

Disney's Animal Kingdom
Island Mercantile (Discovery Island)

Discovery Trading Company (Discovery Island)
Harambe Market, to the South (Africa)
Kali River Rapids (Asia)

★ **Magic Tip** ★

FP+ selections cannot be made during Extra Magic hours. Use these times to ride attractions when fewer visitors are in the Parks.

FastPass+ Attractions and Recommendations:

Here we list which attractions have FP+ availability as well as our recommendations:

• **Very High** – Make this a top priority FastPass+ selection.
• **High** – We recommend this highly as a choice.
• **Medium** – Lines vary with these attractions and depending on your craving to experience them, you may want to skip for a High or Very High recommendation.
• **Low** – Usually not necessary to reserve due to shorter lines.
• **Very Low** – Don't waste your FP+ selection on this.

Magic Kingdom Park

Barnstormer – Very Low
Big Thunder Mountain Railroad – High
Buzz Lightyear's Space Ranger Spin – High
Dumbo the Flying Elephant – Low
Enchanted Tales with Bell – Medium
Haunted Mansion – High
 "it's a small world" – Low
Jungle Cruise – High
Mad Tea Party – Low
The Magic Carpets of Aladdin – Very Low

The Many Adventures of Winnie the Pooh – Low
Mickey's PhilharMagic – Very Low
Monsters, Inc. Laugh Floor – Very Low
Peter Pan's Flight – Very High
Pirates of the Caribbean – High
Seven Dwarves Mine Train – Very High
Space Mountain – Very High
Splash Mountain – High
Tomorrowland Speedway – Medium
Under the Sea – Journey of The Little Mermaid – Medium

Epcot

Disney & Pixar Short Film Festival – Very Low
*Frozen Ever After – Very High
*Illuminations: Reflections of Earth (fireworks) – Medium
Journey Into Imagination With Figment –Very Low
*Living With the Land – Low
Mission: SPACE – Medium
The Seas with Nemo & Friends – Low
*Soarin' Around the World –High

Spaceship Earth –Low
*Test Track – Very High
Turtle Talk With Crush – Low

*Group A Selections: Epcot has 2 different categories for FastPass+ selections. Unfortunately, you can only choose 1 from Group A and 2 from Group B. We don't recommend selecting Living With the Land as it rarely has long lines.

Disney's Hollywood Studios

The Great Movie Ride – Low
Muppet*Vision 3D – Very Low
Rock 'n' Roller Coaster – Very High
Star Tours – The Adventures Continue – Medium
Toy Story Mania! – Very High
Turtle Talk With Crush – Low
The Twilight Zone Tower of Terror – High

Disney's Animal Kingdom

Expedition Everest – High
It's Tough to be a Bug! – Very Low
Kali River Rapids – High
Kilimanjaro Safaris – Medium
Primeval Whirl – Medium
DINOSAUR – High

Chapter Twenty

The Very Best of WDW – Top 7 Lists

Introduction

Now that you've nearly completed the guide, you may feel like there's a ton of information. Don't worry, it's not just you. It's true that WDW has what feels like an unlimited amount of options and we and completely understand that overwhelmed feeling. That's why we've come up with lists of the best things to do at the WDW Resort. You might feel burdened choosing a Resort Hotel or which rides to pick. You might not know the best dining spots or even which shows to see. After all, most everything sounds amazing to do and see at the Resort. Without further ado, here are our Top 7 Lists:

Listed in order (#1 being the most recommended):

Best WDW Resort Hotels
Based on price, amenities, theme, and location:
1. Disney's Beach Club
2. Disney's Polynesian Village Resort
3. Disney's Grand Floridian Resort and Spa
4. Disney's Animal Kingdom Lodge
5. Disney's Yacht Club
6. Disney's Port Orleans Resort – Riverside
7. Disney's Wilderness Lodge

Best Theme Parks (in Orlando)
1. Magic Kingdom (Walt Disney World)
2. Disney's Animal Kingdom (Walt Disney World)
3. Islands of Adventure (Universal Studios)
4. Universal Studios Orlando (Universal Studios)
5. Epcot (Walt Disney World)
6. Disney's Hollywood Studios (Walt Disney World)
7. Disney's Typhoon Lagoon (Walt Disney World)

Best Rides for Families
1.   Peter Pan's Flight (Magic Kingdom)
2.   Pirates of the Caribbean (Magic Kingdom)
3.   Seven Dwarfs Mine Train (Magic Kingdom)
4.   Soarin' Over the World (Epcot)
5.   Toy Story Mania (Hollywood Studios)
6.   Kilimanjaro Safaris (Animal Kingdom)
7.   Frozen Ever After (Epcot)

Best Thrill Rides
1.   Expedition Everest (Animal Kingdom)
2.   The Twilight Zone Tower of Terror (Hollywood Studios)
3.   Rock 'n' Roller Coaster (Hollywood Studios)
4.   Splash Mountain (Magic Kingdom)
5.   DINOSAUR (Animal Kingdom)
6.   Space Mountain (Magic Kingdom)
7.   Big Thunder Mountain Railroad (Magic Kingdom)

Best Rides for Kids
1.   Peter Pan's Flight (Magic Kingdom)
2.   Frozen Ever After (Epcot)
3.   Toy Story Mania! (Hollywood Studios)
4.   Kilimanjaro Safaris (Animal Kingdom)
5.   Pirates of the Caribbean (Magic Kingdom)
6.   Under the Sea– The Little Mermaid (Magic Kingdom)
7.   Dumbo the Flying Elephant (Magic Kingdom)

Best Shows
1.   Finding Nemo – The Musical (Animal Kingdom)
2.   Festival of the Lion King (Animal Kingdom)
3.   Indiana Jones Epic Stunt Spectacular! (Hollywood Studios)

4. Beauty and the Beast – Live on Stage (Hollywood Studios)
5. It's Tough to be a Bug! (Animal Kingdom)
6. Muppet*Vision 3D (Hollywood Studios)
7. Illuminations–Reflections of Earth (Epcot)

Best Restaurants

Based on food, theme, and value for price:

1. Be Our Guest (Magic Kingdom)
2. Victoria & Albert's (Grand Floridian Hotel)
3. Cinderella's Royal Table (Magic Kingdom)
4. Jiko – The Cooking Place (Animal Kingdom Lodge)
5. Yachtsman Steakhouse (Disney's Yacht Club Resort)
6. Via Napoli (Epcot)
7. Le Cellier Steakhouse (Epcot)

Best Food

1. Dole Whip (Magic Kingdom, Polynesian Resort, Animal Kingdom)
2. Mickey Waffles with Bananas Foster (Character Dining Breakfast Buffets)
3. The Gray Stuff Cupcake (Best Our Guest – Magic Kingdom)
4. Cabernet-Braised Short Rib (Captain's Grille – Yacht Club Resort)
5. Steaks (Le Cellier in Epcot, Jiko, Yachtsman Steakhouse, and the Flying Fish Café)
6. Casey's Corn Dog Nuggets (Casey's Corner, Magic Kingdom)
7. Kitchen Sink Sundae (Beaches and Cream – Beach Club Resort)

Chapter Twenty-Two
Pre-Planned Ride and Attraction Guides

Introduction

A big worry about attending the WDW Parks are seeing enough attractions while still avoiding long lines. With so many choices of things to do, it might be impossible to get everything done in one day without a plan. However, with our pre-made ride and attraction lists, you can enjoy the very best that WDW has to offer. These are proven to work using multiple tests, and we recommend following one of these in order to save yourself the hassle of hustling through enormous crowds. That's right, these pre-made lists work on even the busiest days!

Before you get started in the Parks, make sure you complete these steps:
1. Choose one of our pre-made ride and attraction lists to follow.
2. Book any recommended FastPass+ selections (we recommend 60 days before). Make sure that these selections begin around 30 minutes after the Park opens. If the Park has earlier Extra Magic Hours, then you can book in the first time slots.
3. Pre-Book any dining reservations (allows up to 180 days in advance).
4. Get to the Park before it opens.
5. Grab a map at the entrance to help guide you around.
6. Prepare to take a break when you need to in between rides.
7. Don't rush. Keep calm, enjoy the sights, and take in the magical feelings on your unforgettable vacation!

Must-See Attractions List

This list is perfect for families visiting with teens and tween, also for those who want to see the best that the Parks have to offer. We "cut out the fat" so-to-speak, in order to provide a list of the best attractions.

Magic Kingdom

Book Your FastPass+ Selections in this order: Pirates of the Caribbean, Space Mountain. Seven Dwarfs Mine Train.

1. **Magic Kingdom Welcome Show** (Entrance, before opening)
2. **Peter Pan's Flight** (Fantasyland)
3. **"it's a small world"** (Fantasyland)
4. **The Haunted Mansion** (Liberty Square)
5. **Pirates of the Caribbean** (Adventureland)
6. **Tomorrowland Transit Authority PeopleMover** (Tomorrowland)
7. **Space Mountain** (Tomorrowland)
8. **Seven Dwarfs Mine Train** (Fantasyland)
   Lunch: Be Our Guest Restaurant (Fantasyland)
9. **Under the Sea ~ Journey of The Little Mermaid** (Fantasyland)
10. **Barnstormer** (Fantasyland)
11. **Walt Disney World Railroad** (Fantasyland to Frontierland)
12. *** Big Thunder Mountain Railroad** (Frontierland)
13. **Splash Mountain** (Frontierland)
14. **Swiss Family Treehouse** (Adventureland)
15. ***Jungle Cruise** (Adventureland)
16. **Wishes fireworks** (Main Street, U.S.A.)

Other great attractions: Meet Mickey Mouse on Main Street, ride Stitch's Great Escape! in Tomorrowland, or carry along on the adorable Many Adventures of Winnie the Pooh.

* Book extra as FastPass+ selections if it becomes available when you initial 3 are completed.

Must-See Attractions List

Epcot

Book Your FastPass+ Selections in this order: Spaceship Earth, The Seas with Nemo and Friends, Frozen Ever After.

1. **Test Track** (Future World East)
2. **Mission: SPACE** (Future World East)
3. **Spaceship Earth** (Future World East)
4. **The Seas With Nemo and Friends** (Future World West)
5. **Journey Into Imagination With Figment** (Future World West)
6. **Frozen Ever After** (World Showcase – Norway)
   Lunch: Via Napoli in Italy or Chefs de France in France (World Showcase)
7. **Gran Fiesta Tour Starring The Three Caballeros** (World Showcase – Mexico)
8. *** Soarin'** (Future World West)
9. **Living With The Land** (Future World West)
10. **Ellen's Energy Adventure** (Future World East)

* Book extra as FastPass+ selections if it becomes available when you initial 3 are completed.

Must-See Attractions List
Hollywood Studios

Book Your FastPass+ Selections in this order: Star Tours, Toy Story Mania!, Rock 'n' Roller Coaster.

1. **The Great Movie Ride** (Hollywood Boulevard)
2. **Star Tours – The Adventures Continue** (Echo Lake)
3. **Muppet*Vision 3D** (Muppets Courtyard)
4. **Toy Story Mania!** (Pixar Place)
5. **Rock 'n' Roller Coaster Starring Aerosmith** (Sunset Boulevard)
6. **Beauty and the Beast–Live on Stage** (Sunset Boulevard)
   Lunch: Sci-Fi Dine-In Theater Restaurant (Commissary Lane)
7. **Indiana Jones Epic Stunt Spectacular!** (Echo Lake)
8. *** The Twilight Zone Tower of Terror** (Sunset Boulevard)
9. **Fantasmic!** (Sunset Boulevard)

* Book extra as FastPass+ selections if it becomes available when you initial 3 are completed.

★ Magic Tip ★

If you are planning a character breakfast event, we recommend booking it before your visit to Hollywood Studios. You can arrive to the Park after opening (even into the afternoon). This is often the least crowded Park at WDW with plenty of FastPass+ selections for the more popular rides. If you decide to do this, arrive at the Park at least a half hour before your FastPass+ selection for Star Tours so that you can experience The Great Movie Ride.

Must-See Attractions List
Animal Kingdom

This plan bounces you around a little bit, but it's the most efficient. You'll also be able to board the soaking Kali River Rapids in the middle of the day when it's the warmest so you'll dry faster.

Book Your FastPass+ Selections in this order: Expedition Everest, Kilimanjaro Safaris, Kali River Rapids.

1. **DINOSAUR** (DinoLand U.S.A.)
2. **Primeval Whirl** (DinoLand U.S.A.)
3. **Expedition Everest** (Asia)
4. **Maharajah Jungle Trek** (Asia)
5. **Kilimanjaro Safaris** (Africa)
6. **Gorilla Falls Exploration Trail** (Africa)
7. **Kali River Rapids** (Asia)
   Lunch: Yak & Yeti Restaurant (Asia)
8. **Wildlife Express Train** (Africa)
9. **Conservation Station** (Rafiki's Planet Watch)
10. **Habitat Habit** (Rafiki's Planet Watch)
11. **It's Tough to be a Bug!** (Discovery Island)
12. *** Finding Nemo–The Musical** (DinoLand U.S.A.)
13. **Rivers of Light** (Discovery Island) – *Opens Spring 2017*

* Book extra as FastPass+ selections if it becomes available when you initial 3 are completed.

With Kids

Kids might be the most excited to adventure into the Parks, but they often don't last very long. Because of this, we've added fewer attractions to some of the lists and included the best places to break when needed. These rides don't include many thrills or scary moments.

Δ – Rides we recommend most for Young Kids, ages 3-5

Magic Kingdom

Book Your FastPass+ Selections in this order: Peter Pan's Flight, Pirates of the Caribbean, Seven Dwarves Mine Train.

1. **Magic Kingdom Welcome Show** Δ (Entrance, before opening)
2. **Tomorrowland Speedway** (Tomorrowland)
3. **Stitch's Great Escape** (Tomorrowland)
4. **Peter Pan's Flight** Δ (Fantasyland)
5. **"it's a small world"** Δ (Fantasyland)
   Snack or Shopping Time
6. **Pirates of the Caribbean** (Adventureland)
7. **Swiss Family Treehouse** (Adventureland)
8. **Seven Dwarfs Mine Train** (Fantasyland)
   Lunch: Be Our Guest Restaurant (Fantasyland)
9. **Under the Sea ~ Journey of The Little Mermaid** Δ (Fantasyland)
10. **Dumbo the Flying Elephant** Δ (Fantasyland)
11. **Barnstormer** (Fantasyland)
12. **Festival of Fantasy Parade** Δ (Fantasyland)
13. **Mickey's PhilharMagic** Δ (Fantasyland)
    Snack or Shopping Time
14. **Jungle Cruise** Δ (Adventureland)

★ Magic Tips ★

1. If your child is more interested in meeting their favorite characters than rides, replace Pirates of the Caribbean's FastPass+ selection with a character meeting.
2. Young Kids should ride The Many Adventures of Winnie the Pooh instead of the Tomorrowland Speedway.

With Kids

Epcot

Book Your FastPass+ Selections in this order: Spaceship Earth, The Seas with Nemo and Friends, Frozen Ever After.

1. **** Test Track** (Future World East)
2. **Spaceship Earth** Δ (Future World East)
3. **The Seas With Nemo and Friends** Δ (Future World West)
   Snack or Shopping Time
4. **Journey Into Imagination With Figment** Δ (Future World West)
5. **Frozen Ever After** Δ (World Showcase – Norway)
   Lunch: Via Napoli for Pizza (World Showcase – Italy)
6. **Gran Fiesta Tour Starring The Three Caballeros** Δ (World Showcase – Mexico)
7. *** Soarin'** (Future World West)
8. **Living With The Land** (Future World West)
9. *** Epcot Character Spot** Δ (Future World West)
10. **Ellen's Energy Adventure** (Future World East)

* Book extra as FastPass+ selections if it becomes available when you initial 3 are completed.
** Many older Kids love this ride so we included it. You can also skip straight to Spaceship Earth if your child isn't tall enough to ride.

★ **Magic Tip** ★

   The Journey Into Imagination has a large play areas for Kids to experiment with science. You can easily burn up half a 20-30 minutes in each of this location.

With Kids

Hollywood Studios

Book Your FastPass+ Selections in this order: Star Tours, Toy Story Mania!, For the First Time in Forever.

1. **Muppet*Vision 3D** Δ (Muppets Courtyard)
2. **Star Tours – The Adventures Continue** (Echo Lake)
3. **Jedi Training: Trails of the Temple** Δ (Echo Lake)
   Snack or Shopping Time
4. **Toy Story Mania!** Δ (Pixar Place)
5. **The Great Movie Ride** (Hollywood Boulevard)
   Lunch: Sci-Fi Dine-In Theater Restaurant (Commissary Lane)
6. **For the First Time in Forever: A Frozen Singalong Celebration** Δ (Echo Lake)
7. **Indiana Jones Epic Stunt Spectacular!** (Echo Lake)
8. *** Fantasmic!** Δ (Sunset Boulevard)

* Book extra as FastPass+ selections if it becomes available when you initial 3 are completed.

★ **Magic Tip** ★

There isn't a whole lot to do for Kids in Hollywood Studios (at least not until they finish Toy Stoy Playland in a few years). If you are planning a character breakfast event, we recommend booking it before your visit to Hollywood Studios. You can arrive to the Park after opening (even into the afternoon). This is often the least crowded Park at WDW with plenty of FastPass+ selections for the more popular rides. If you decide to do this, arrive at the Park at least a half hour before your FastPass+ selection for Star Tours so that you can experience Muppet*Vision 3D.

With Kids

Animal Kingdom

We recommend booking a dining reservation at the Rainforest Café for lunch and then booking your third FastPass+ selection for DINOSAUR.
Book Your FastPass+ Selections in this order: It's Tough to be a Bug!, Kilimanjaro Safaris, DINOSAUR.

1. **The Oasis Exhibits** Δ (Oasis)
2. **It's Tough to be a Bug!** Δ (Discovery Island)
3. **Kilimanjaro Safaris** Δ (Africa)
4. **Gorilla Falls Exploration Trail** Δ (Africa)
   Snack or Shopping Time
5. **Wildlife Express Train** Δ (Africa)
6. **Conservation Station** (Rafiki's Planet Watch)
7. **Habitat Habit** Δ (Rafiki's Planet Watch)
   Lunch: Rainforest Café (Oasis)
8. **** DINOSAUR** (DinoLand U.S.A.)
9. **Primeval Whirl** (DinoLand U.S.A.)
10. **Finding Nemo–The Musical** Δ (DinoLand U.S.A.)
11. *** Kali River Rapids** (Asia)
12. **Maharajah Jungle Trek** Δ (Asia)
    Snack or Shopping Time
13. **Flights of Wonder** Δ (Asia)
14. **Rivers of Light** Δ (Discovery Island) – *Opens Spring 2017*

* Book extra as FastPass+ selections if it becomes available when you initial 3 are completed.
** DINOSAUR is scary to some Young Kids. In that case, substitute this ride with TriceraTop Spin. In that case, save your FastPass+ selection for the reserved seating at the Finding Nemo musical.

Thrill Riders

These are lists specially designed for those who enjoy high-speed roller coasters, thrills with drops, and other heart-pounding attractions. Keep in mind that not all of WDW's roller coasters are equally as thrilling, but we have included all of them for the coaster fans. We recommend getting to the Park at opening to ride a couple of the more popular attractions

Magic Kingdom
Book Your FastPass+ Selections in this order: Seven Dwarfs Mine Train, Space Mountain, Splash Mountain.

1. **Magic Kingdom Welcome Show** (Entrance, before opening)
2. **Pirates of the Caribbean** (Adventureland)
3. **The Haunted Mansion** (Liberty Square)
4. **Seven Dwarfs Mine Train** (Fantasyland)
5. **Barnstormer** (Fantasyland)
6. **Space Mountain** (Tomorrowland)
7. **Stitch Encounter** (Tomorrowland)
8. **Splash Mountain** (Frontierland)
   Lunch: Be Our Guest Restaurant (Fantasyland)
9. ***Big Thunder Mountain Railroad** (Frontierland)
10. **Jungle Cruise** (Adventureland)

* Book extra as FastPass+ selections if it becomes available when you initial 3 are completed.

Still have more time? Ride your favorites again, meet Mickey Mouse at the Town Square Theater, board a WDW classic like Peter Pan's Flight, or Park Hop to another Park.

Thrill Riders
Epcot / Hollywood Studios

We've included these Parks together because there aren't enough thrills in them each to fill a day. Since Epcot has the most difficult to obtain FastPass+ selections, we book these first. Once you've used them all, you can book at Hollywood Studios one at a time. Sadly, all of Epcot's thrill rides are in the same FastPass+ category, so you can't pre-book them.
Book Your FastPass+ Selections in this order: Soarin', optional: Spaceship Earth, Journey into Imagination with Figment.

Epcot:
1. **Test Track** (Future World East)
2. **Mission: SPACE** (Future World East)
3. **Soarin'** (Future World West)
4. ****Frozen Ever After** (World Showcase – Norway)
   Exit through the International Gateway between the United Kingdom and France pavilions. Take the free boat to Hollywood Studios.

Hollywood Studios:
5. **The Twilight Zone Tower of Terror** (Sunset Boulevard)
6. ***† Rock 'n' Roller Coaster featuring Aerosmith** (Sunset Boulevard)
   Lunch: Sci-Fi Dine-In Theater Restaurant (Commissary Lane)
7. **Indiana Jones Epic Stunt Spectacular!** (Echo Lake)
8. **The Great Movie Ride** (Hollywood Boulevard)
9. ***Star Tours – The Adventures Continue** (Echo Lake)

* Book extra as FastPass+ selections if it becomes available when you initial 3 are completed.
** If the line is too long, skip this one. Frozen Ever After has just a couple of short drops.
† If the line becomes too long and you can't get a FastPass+ selection, use the Single Rider option.

Fireworks: Watch the Star Wars ones at Hollywood Studios.

Thrill Riders
Animal Kingdom

Since there are only a few thrill rides in the Animal Kingdom, we have also included the animal walking trails and a couple of live shows.

Book Your FastPass+ Selections in this order: Expedition Everest, Kilimanjaro Safaris, Kali River Rapids.

1. **DINOSAUR** (DinoLand U.S.A.)
2. **Expedition Everest** (Asia)
3. **Maharajah Jungle Trek** (Asia)
4. **Kilimanjaro Safaris** (Africa)
5. **Gorilla Falls Exploration Trail** (Africa)
6. **Kali River Rapids** (Asia)
   Lunch: Yak & Yeti Restaurant (Asia)
7. **It's Tough to be a Bug!** (Discovery Island)
8. *** Primeval Whirl** (DinoLand U.S.A.)

* Book extra as FastPass+ selections if it becomes available when you initial 3 are completed.

Create Your Own Attraction List:

Names: _____   _____

 _____   _____

 _____   _____

Pre-booked FastPass+ Selections:

_____

_____

_____

1. _____
2. _____
3. _____
4. _____
5. _____
6. _____
7. _____
8. _____
9. _____
10. _____
11. _____
12. _____
13. _____
14. _____
15. _____
16. _____
17. _____
18. _____
19. _____
20. _____
21. _____

Create Your Own Attraction List:

Names: _____   _____

_____   _____

_____   _____

Pre-booked FastPass+ Selections:

_____

_____

_____

1. _____
2. _____
3. _____
4. _____
5. _____
6. _____
7. _____
8. _____
9. _____
10. _____
11. _____
12. _____
13. _____
14. _____
15. _____
16. _____
17. _____
18. _____
19. _____
20. _____
21. _____

Create Your Own Attraction List:

Names: _____   _____

_____   _____

_____   _____

Pre-booked FastPass+ Selections:

_____

_____

_____

1. _____
2. _____
3. _____
4. _____
5. _____
6. _____
7. _____
8. _____
9. _____
10. _____
11. _____
12. _____
13. _____
14. _____
15. _____
16. _____
17. _____
18. _____
19. _____
20. _____
21. _____

WDW Resort Vacation Checklist

- ❑ Park Tickets
- ❑ Ride List
- ❑ ID
- ❑ Credit Card / Cash
- ❑ Hotel Address
- ❑ Phone (and charging cable)
- ❑ Sunscreen
- ❑ Toiletries: toothbrush, toothpaste, etc.
- ❑ Swimsuit
- ❑ Jacket
- ❑ Comfortable Shoes
- ❑ Plastic bag for cellphone (water rides)
- ❑ Snacks
- ❑ Water bottles (if you aren't flying)
- ❑ Backpack or bag
- ❑ Restaurant Reservations
- ❑ WDW Guide Book by Magic Guides
- ❑ _____
- ❑ _____
- ❑ _____
- ❑ _____
- ❑ _____
- ❑ _____
- ❑ _____
- ❑ _____
- ❑ _____
- ❑ _____

Chapter Twenty-Two
Character Locations

Introduction

Disney is known for its iconic, heartwarming, and even villainous characters. That is why they bring them to life inside of the Walt Disney World Resort. You can meet most of your favorite Disney characters throughout the Parks and hotel. They are always happy to sign autographs, interact, and take a photo with guests (yes, even selfies)! Aren't sure if you should meet a character? We recommend it! After getting a hug from Mickey, Goofy, or a Disney Princess, people of all ages will get a smile that won't go away!

Magic Tips for Finding Characters the Easy Way:

1. Get the App – Download the My Disney Experience App on your mobile device to track the characters!
2. Grab a Map – Many of the characters have "show times" in certain locations Be sure to check the character times on the Park maps early in the day.
3. Book a Character Dining Buffet – The Resort Parks and Hotels have many characters who will interact with you while you eat. Sometimes you can meet 6 or more in one meal!
4. If you are looking to meet several Disney princesses, get a reservation at the Akershus Royal Banquet Hall in Epcot.
5. Keep Your Eyes Peeled – You may also see Disney characters unexpectedly walking around the Parks, in the shows, and parades.
6. You Can't See Them All – Sadly, not every character comes out each day. However, one of your favorites is sure to be there!

7. Book a FastPass+ – If meeting the characters is high on your list, consider using a FastPass+ selection to book a meeting time and avoid the long lines.

Character Locations (alphabetical)

Aladdin – Epcot (Morocco), Magic Kingdom (Adventureland

Alice – Epcot (United Kingdom), Magic Kingdom (Fantasyland), Wonderland Tea Party (Grand Floridian)

Anna – Epcot (Norway)

Ariel – Magic Kingdom (Fantasyland – Cinderella's Royal Table), Magic Kingdom (Fantasyland – Ariel's Grotto)

Aurora – Magic Kingdom (Princess Fairytale Hall), Epcot (Garden Grill in The Land and Akershus Royal banquet Hall Character Dining in Norway)

Baloo – Animal Kingdom (Asia)

Baymax – Epcot (Future World West – Innoventions West)

Beast – Magic Kingdom (Fantasyland – Be Our Guest dinner)

Belle – Magic Kingdom (Fantasyland – Enchanted Tales with Belle), Epcot (France and Akershus Royal banquet Hall Character Dining in Norway)

Buzz Lightyear – Magic Kingdom (Tomorrowland), Hollywood Studios (Pixar Place)

Captain Hook – Disney's Contemporary Resort (Pirates and Pals Fireworks Voyage)

Chip 'n Dale – Animal Kingdom (Oasis and Rafiki's Planet Watch), Magic Kingdom (Storybook Circus), Hollywood Studios (Commissary Lane)

Cinderella – Magic Kingdom (Cinderella's Royal Table), Epcot (Akershus Royal banquet Hall Character Dining in Norway)

Crush the Turtle – Epcot (Turtle Talk with Crush)

Daisy Duck – Magic Kingdom (Fantasyland – Pete's Silly Sideshow), Hollywood Studios (Hollywood and Vine character dining)

Donald Duck – Magic Kingdom (Fantasyland – Pete's Silly Sideshow), Epcot (Mexico Pavilion), Character Dining (Chef Mickey's at the Contemporary Resort, Cape May Breakfast Buffet at the Beach Club Resort)

Dug and Russell – Animal Kingdom (Discovery Island)

Eeyore – Magic Kingdom (Main Street – Crystal Palace Dining)

Elsa – Epcot (Norway)

Fairy Godmother – Magic Kingdom (Fantasyland)

Flik – Animal Kingdom (Discovery Island)

Gaston – Magic Kingdom (Gaston's Tavern)

Goofy – Magic Kingdom (Fantasyland – Barnstormer), Epcot (Mexico Pavilion), Character Dining (Chef Mickey's at the Contemporary Resort, Cape May Breakfast Buffet at the Beach Club Resort)

Green Army Men – Hollywood Studios (Pixar Place)

Indiana Jones – Hollywood Studios (Echo Park)

Jack Sparrow – Magic Kingdom (Adventureland near Pirates of the Caribbean. You have to talk to him after the show)

Jake – Hollywood Studios (Animation Courtyard)

Jasmine – Epcot (Morocco and Akershus Royal Dining in Norway), Magic Kingdom (Adventureland, Fantasyland at Cinderella's Royal Table Dining)

Jessie – Magic Kingdom (Frontierland near Splash Mountain)

Joy – Epcot (Future World West – Innoventions West)

Lilo – Polynesian Village Resort ('Ohana Dining Character Breakfast), Typhoon Lagoon

King Louie – Animal Kingdom (Asia)

Mad Hatter – Magic Kingdom (Fantasyland near the Mad Tea Party), Grand Floridian Character Dining Buffet)

Mary Poppins – Magic Kingdom (Main Street), Epcot (United Kingdom)

Mickey Mouse – Magic Kingdom (Main Street at the Town Square Theatre) Character Dining (Chef Mickey's at the Contemporary Resort, Garden Grill at Hollywood Studios,

'Ohana Breakfast at the Polynesian Village Resort), Animal Kingdom (Discovery Island – Adventurers Outpost)

Minnie Mouse – Magic Kingdom (Fantasyland – Pete's Silly Sideshow), Character Dining (Chef Mickey's at the Contemporary Resort, Hollywood and Vine at Hollywood Studios, Cape May Café at the Beach Club Resort), Animal Kingdom (Discovery Island – Adventurers Outpost)

Mulan – Epcot (China, Akershus Royal banquet Hall Character Dining in Norway)

Olaf – Hollywood Studios (Echo Lake – Celebrity Spotlight)

Peter Pan – Magic Kingdom (Fantasyland by Peter Pan's Flight), Disney's Contemporary Resort (Pirates and Pals Fireworks Voyage)

Piglet – Magic Kingdom (Main Street – Crystal Palace Character Dining)

Pluto – Magic Kingdom (Main Street), Hollywood Studios (Animation Courtyard), Animal Kingdom (DinoLand), Epcot (Future World – Legacy Plaza West), Character Dining (Chef Mickey's at the Contemporary Resort, Epcot's Garden Grill, and 'Ohana at the Polynesian Village Resort)

Pocahontas – Animal Kingdom (Discovery Island)

Rafiki – Animal Kingdom (Rafiki's Planet Watch), Magic Kingdom (Aventureland)

Sadness – Epcot (Future World West – Innoventions West)

Smee – Disney's Contemporary Resort (Pirates and Pals Fireworks Voyage)

Snow White – Magic Kingdom (Main Street – Near City Hall), Epcot (Germany and Akershus Royal banquet Hall Character Dining in Norway)

Stitch – Magic Kingdom (Main Street), Typhoon Lagoon, Polynesian Village Resort ('Ohana Dining Character Breakfast)

Stormtroopers – Hollywood Studios (Echo Lake)

Tarzan – Animal Kingdom (Discovery Island)

Thumper – Animal Kingdom (Discovery Island)

Tiana – Magic Kingdom (Fantasyland – Princess Fairytale Hall)

Tigger – Magic Kingdom (Fantasyland next to The Many Adventures of Winnie the Pooh)

Tinker Bell – Magic Kingdom (Main Street – Town Square Theater)

Winnie the Pooh – Magic Kingdom (Fantasyland next to The Many Adventures of Winnie the Pooh and the Crystal Palace Character Dining), Grand Floridian (1900 Park Fare Character Dining Buffet)

Woody – Magic Kingdom (Frontierland near Splash Mountain), Hollywood Studios (Pixar Place)

Characters Exclusive to Mickey's Not-So-Scary Halloween Party and Mickey's Very Merry Christmas Party:

Abu

Boo

Cruella de Vil

The Evil Queen

Jack Skellington

Jafar

Maleficent

Piglet

Prince Charming

Prince Naveen

Queen of Hearts

Sally *

Santa Claus

Scrooge McDuck **

Seven Dwarfs

Terk *

Wendy **

White Rabbit *

Halloween Party Only
** *Christmas Party Only*

Index

A

Activity Centers (see Children's Activity Centers)
adult guide, 290-301
Adventureland, 84-88
Aerosmith (see Rock 'n' Roller Coaster Starring Aerosmith)
Affection Section, 144-145
Africa, 140-143
air conditioning, 14-15, 20, 68, 295, 297
airplane, 51, 63-64
alcoholic beverages, 73, 75, 295-297
Alice in Wonderland, 94, 349
All-Star Resorts, Disney's, 193-195
AMC 24 (movies), 301
American Adventure, The, 116
Animal Kingdom (see Disney's Animal Kingdom)
Animal Kingdom Lodge and Villas, Disney's, 172-174
Animation Courtyard, 126-127
Annual Pass, 20, 23, 55-56
app, 20, 66-67, 73, 83, 320-321, 348
Ariel's Grotto, 98
Art of Animation, Disney's, 195-197
Asia, 145-148
Astro Orbiter, 102
author, information, 6
AVATAR (see Pandora–The World of *AVATAR*)

B

Baby Care Center, 284-285
babysitters, 294

Barnstormer, The, 95
Bay Lake Tower, Disney's, 178-179
barber, 84
Be Our Guest Restaurant, 214
Beach Club Resort and Villas, Disney's, 174-176
Beauty and the Beast – Live on Stage, 130
best days to visit, 34
Bibbidi Bobbidi Boutique, 98, 206, 305
Big Thunder Mountain Railroad, 88, 285, 323
Blizzard Beach, Disney's, 14, 77, 152, 160-164, 253-254
Boardwalk Inn and Villas, Disney's, 176-177
boats (see ferries)
Boneyard, The, 150
Brave "Play and Greet", 99
breast feeding, 284
buffets,
       'Ohana, 268
       1900 Park Fare, 264-265
       Cape May Café, 258
       Chef Mickey's, 261
       Crystal Palace, The, 216
       Garden Grill, The, 227
       Garden Grove, 273-274
       Hollywood and Vine, 241
       Trail's End Restaurant, 263
       Tusker House Restaurant, 250
       Wave… of American Flavors, The, 261-262
Build-A-Dino, 206
bus,

Disney's Magical Express, 15, 55, 59-60, 63-64, 167
Greyhound, 65-66
Orlando Bus Station, 65-66
WDW bus system, 68, 205-206
Buzz Lightyear's Space Ranger Spin, 101-102, 311, 323

C

cabs (see taxi)
camera, 90, 96, 145
Camp Dolphin, 293-294
car, driving by, 64-65
car rental, 50-51, 53
Caribbean Beach Resort, Disney's, 188-190
carrousel (see Prince Charming Regal Carrousel)
Carousel of Progress, Walt Disney's, 103
Casey Jr. Splash 'N' Soak Station, 97
Cash, 73
castle, 13, 15, 44, 78-80, 83, 215
Character Dining, 287
    Ohana, 268
    1900 Park Fare, 264-265
    Akershus Royal Banquet Hall, 224
    Biergarten Restaurant, 224
    Cape May Café, 258
    Chef Mickey's, 261
    Cinderella's Royal Table, 215
    Garden Grill, The, 227
    Garden Grove, 273-274
    Hollywood and Vine, 241
    Mickey's Backyard BBQ, 264
    Tusker House Restaurant, 250
character locations, 347-352
checklist, 346
Child Swap (see Rider Switch)
Children (see kids)

Children's Activity Centers, 292-294
China, Reflections of, 115
Christmas, 31, 34-35, 42-46, 51, 85, 95, 352
Cinderella Castle, 96
Cinderella's Royal Table, 41, 96, 215
Cirque du Soleil, La Nouba by, 23, 208-209, 301, 304
Contemporary Resort and Bay Lake Tower, Disney's, 178-179
Conservation Station, 145
corn dog, 214, 220, 223, 248, 250-251, 253, 261, 278, 329
Coronado Springs Resort, Disney's, 190-191
credit cards, 73
Country Bear Jamboree, 90-91

D

Dapper Dans, 84, 304
Dining, 210-279
    All-Star Resorts, 255-256
    Animal Kingdom, 244-251
    Animal Kingdom Lodge and Villas, 256-257
    Art of Animation, 258
    Beach Club, 258-259
    Blizzard Beach, 253-255
    Boardwalk Inn and Villas, 259
    Contemporary Resort and Bay Lake Tower, 260-262
    Coronado Springs, 262-263
    Disney Springs, 277-279
    Disney's Boardwalk, 276
    Disney Dining Plan, 20, 279
    Dolphin, 273-275
    Epcot, 224-237
    Fort Wilderness, 263-264
    Grand Floridian, 264-266
    Hollywood Studios, 238-244
    Magic Kingdom, 213-223
    pricing, 212
    not recommended, 279

Old Key West, 267
Polynesian Village Resort
and Villas, 267-269
Pop Century, 269-270
Port Orleans, 270
Saratoga Springs, 271
Swan, 273-275
Typhoon Lagoon, 251-253
Wilderness Lodge and
Villas, 271-272
Yacht Club 258-259
Dino-Sue, 149-150
DinoLand U.S.A, 148-150
DINOSAUR, 148
discounts, booking with, 23, 52-55
Discovery Island, 137-139
Discovery Island Trails, 139
Disney, Walt, 13-16
Disney & Pixar Short Film Festival, 107
Disney Dining Plan, 20, 279
Disney Festival of Fantasy Parade, 97
Disney's All-Star Resorts, 193-195
Disney's Animal Kingdom, 14, 16, 19,
21, 27, 30, 32-33, 45, 4, 76, 133-150,
244-251, 284, 286, 315
Africa, 140-143
Asia, 145-148
DinoLand U.S.A, 148-150
Discovery Island, 137-139
Hidden Mickeys, 315
Oasis, The, 136-137
Pandora–The World of
AVATAR, 135-136
Rafiki's Planet Watch, 144-
145
Disney's Animal Kingdom Lodge and
Villas, 172-174
Disney's Art of Animation, 195-197
Disney's Beach Club Resort and Villas,
174-176
Disney's Blizzard Beach, 14, 77, 152,
160-164, 253-254
Disney's Boardwalk Inn and Villas,
176-177
Disney's Caribbean Beach Resort, 188-
190
Disney's Contemporary Resort and

Bay Lake Tower, 178-179
Disney's Coronado Springs Resort,
190-191
Disney's Fort Wilderness – Cabins and
Campgrounds, 186-188
Disney's Grand Floridian Resort and
Spa, 179-181
Disney's Hollywood Studios, 14, 16,
19, 21, 27, 30, 32-33, 45, 50, 76, 119-
132, 238-244, 284, 286, 314-315
Animation Courtyard, 126-
127
Echo Lake, 122-124
Hidden Mickeys, 314-315
holidays, 45
Hollywood Boulevard, 122
Mickey Avenue, 128
Muppets Courtyard, 124-
125
Pixar Place, 125-126
Star Wars Land, 27
Sunset Boulevard, 128-132
Disney's Magical Express, 15, 55, 59-
60, 63-64, 167
Disney's Old Key West Resort, 197-198
Disney's Polynesian Village Resort,
181-183
Disney's Pop Century Resort, 195-197
Disney's Port Orleans Resort
(Riverside and French Quarter), 191-
193
Disney's Saratoga Springs Resort and
Spa, 199-200
Disney's Typhoon Lagoon, 14, 77, 152,
156-159, 251-253
Disney's Wilderness Lodge, 183-184
Disney's Yacht Club, 185-186
Disneyland Resort, 13
dogs, 74-75
Dole whip, 84, 213, 249, 254, 269, 329
Dolphin, Walt Disney World, 200-202
Donald Duck, 114, 250, 350
Downtown Disney (see Disney
Springs)
Dumbo the Flying Elephant, 94, 324

E

Earl of Sandwich, 174
early entry (see Extra Magic Hours)
eating (see Restaurants)
Echo Lake, 122-124
elephant, 140
Ellen's Energy Adventure, 108
Enchanted Tales with Belle, 99
Enchanted Tiki Room, Walt Disney's 87
Epcot, 14-15, 19, 27-28, 49-50, 104-118, 284, 286, 312-314
    American Adventure, The, 116
    China, Reflections of, 115
    France, 115
    Future World, 106-111
    Germany, 116-117
    Hidden Mickeys, 312-314
    Italy, 117
    Japan, 115
    Morocco, 116
    restaurants, 224-237
    United Kingdom, 116
    World Showcase, 111-118
esplanade, 226
ESPN Wide World of Sports Complex, 14, 55-56, 306,
Expedition Everest–Legends of the Forbidden Mountain, 146, 286, 315, 325
Extra Magic Hours, 20, 46, 52, 81-82, 106, 153, 167, 291, 299, 323, 331

F

Fairytale Garden: *Brave* "Play and Greet", 99
Fantasmic!, 130-131
Fantasyland, 92-100
FastPass+, 20, 318-325
Festival of Fantasy Parade, 97
Festival of the Lion King, 141-142
Figment the Dragon, 208

Finding Nemo–The Musical, 149
fireworks, 39, 35, 41, 44-45
    Illuminations: Reflections of Earth, 117-118
    Star Wars: A Galactic Spectacular, 132
    Wishes: Nighttime Spectacular, 83-84
Flights of Wonder, 147-148
food (see dining)
Fort Wilderness – Cabins and Campgrounds, Disney's, 186-188
Fossil Fun Games, 150
France, 115
Frontierland, 88-91
Frozen Ever After, 114
Frozen Holiday Wish, A, 35, 44-45
Future World, 106-111

G

Gay Days, 37-38
Ghirardelli Ice Cream & Chocolate Shop, 278
gorilla, 142
Gran Fiesta Tour Starring the Three Caballeros, The, 114
Grand Floridian Resort and Spa, Disney's, 179-181
Great Movie Ride, The, 122

H

Habitat Habit!, 145
Halloween, 29, 39-42
    Mickey's Not-So-Scary Halloween Party, 29, 40-42, 74, 352
hamburgers, 216, 219-222, 226, 231, 233, 235, 238, 239, 240, 242, 248, 251-252, 254, 257-258, 262-268, 266, 270, 271-275, 277-278
Harmony Barber Shop, 84
Haunted Mansion, 91-92, 305

Hidden Mickeys, 308-317
history, 13-14
holiday celebrations, 31, 34-35, 42-46, 51, 85, 95, 352
Hollywood Boulevard, 122
Hollywood Studios (see Disney's Hollywood Studios)
hopper tickets, park, 21, 56-57, 59, 60-61
hot dogs, 214-220, 231-233, 242, 245, 251-255, 264, 267-268, 271, 278
hotels, 165-203
    All-Star Resorts, 193-195
    Animal Kingdom Lodge and Villas, 172-174
    Art of Animation, 195-197
    Beach Club Resort and Villas, 174-176
    Boardwalk Inn and Villas, 176-177
    Caribbean Beach Resort, 188-190
    Contemporary Resort and Bay Lake Tower, 178-179
    Coronado Springs Resort, 190-191
    Dolphin, 200-202
    Fort Wilderness – Cabins and Campgrounds, 186-188
    Grand Floridian Resort and Spa, 179-181
    Old Key West Resort, 197-198
    Polynesian Village Resort, 181-183
    Pop Century Resort, 195-197
    Port Orleans Resort (Riverside and French Quarter), 191-193
    Saratoga Springs Resort and Spa, 199-200
    Shades of Green, 202-203
    Swan, 200-202
    Wilderness Lodge, 183-184
    Yacht Club, 185-186
hotel reservations, 22-23

Hyperion Theater, 123

I

ice cream, 45, 213, 221-223, 226, 228, 230-233, 236, 238, 240-241, 243-245, 249-2551, 254, 258, 278
Illuminations: Reflections of Earth, 117-118
Imagination!, 108
Indiana Jones Epic Stunt Spectacular!, 123-124, 304
"it's a small world", 34, 44, 95
It's Tough to be a Bug!, 137-138
Italy, 117

J

Japan, 115
Jedi Training: Trials of the Temple, 27, 124, 304
Jiko – The Cooking Place, 256-257
Jingle Cruise (Jungle Cruise Holiday), 85
Jungle Cruise, 85

K

Kali River Rapids, 146-147
kennels, pet, 74-75
Kilimanjaro Safaris, 140-141
Kimonos, 296
Kiss Goodnight, The, 80-81

L

La Nouba by Cirque du Soleil, 23, 208-209, 301, 304
Land, The, 109
Le Cellier Steakhouse, 230-231
LEGO Store, The, 207
Liberty Square, 91-92

Lilo's Playhouse, 293
lion, 142
Lion King, Festival of the, 141-142
Little Mermaid, The, 96, 98, 110, 127, 195, 300, 305, 310, 324, 328, 332, 336
lockers, 76, 155

M

Mad Tea Party, 94
Magic Carpet Rides of Aladdin, The, 87
Magic Kingdom, The, 13, 15-17, 19, 21, 32, 49, 76, 78-103, 284, 285, 310-311
    Adventureland, 84-88
    Fantasyland, 92-100
    Frontierland, 88-91
    Halloween, 40-41
    Hidden Mickeys, 310-311
    Liberty Square, 91-92
    Main Street, U.S.A., 81-84
    restaurants, 213-223
    Tomorrowland, 100-103
Magical Express, Disney's, 15, 55, 59-60, 63-64, 167
MagicBand, 15, 19-20, 22, 52, 55, 73, 82, 167, 201-202, 319
Main Street, U.S.A., 81-84
Maharajah Jungle Trek, 147
Many Adventures of Winnie the Pooh, The, 94
marathons (see runDisney)
Memory Maker, 20
MGM Studios, 14, 21, 120
Mickey Avenue, 128
Mickey's PhilharMagic, 96-97
Mickeys, Hidden, 308-317
military discounts, 54, 203
Mission: Space, 108
monorail, 68-69, 118, 168, 178-184
Monsters, Inc. Laugh Floor, 103, 324
Morocco, 116
Muppets Courtyard, 124-125
Muppet*Vision 3D, 125
My Disney Experience App, 20, 73, 83, 320-321, 348

N

Nemo (see The Seas: With Nemo and Friends)

O

O Canada!, 114
Oasis, The, 136-137
Old Key West Resort, Disney's, 197-198
one-day ticket, 22
opening ceremony (see Rope Drop)
Orlando, 13-16, 59-60, 63-64
Orlando International Airport, 51, 63-64
Orlando Train Station, 68

P

Pandora—The World of *AVATAR*, 135-136
Pangani Forest Exploration Trail, 142-143
parades,
    Disney Festival of Fantasy Parade, 97
    Halloween, 41
    Christmas Fantasy Parade, A, 44
PeopleMover, 102-103
Park Hopper tickets, 21, 56-57, 59, 60-61
Parking, 65
Pete's Silly Sideshow, 98
Peter Pan's Flight, 93
pets (see kennels)
phone number list, 22-23
PhotoPass, 20
Pinocchio Village Haus, 220-221

Pirate's Adventure (Treasures of the Seven Seas), 87
Pirate's League, 88
Pirates of the Caribbean, 86
Pixar Place, 125-126
Pizza, 194, 196, 221, 223-224, 237, 239, 247-248, 252, 257, 260, 262, 263-265, 270-271, 273-275, 278
Polynesian Village Resort, Disney's, 181-183
Pop Century Resort, Disney's, 195-197
Port Orleans Resort, Disney's (Riverside and French Quarter), 191-193
Priceline.com, 54, 65
Primeval Whirl, 148-149
Prince Charming Regal Carrousel, 128, 195
Princess Fairytale Hall, 99
princesses, Disney, 31, 35, 44, 83, 98-99, 116, 206, 215, 224, 305-206

Q

queues, 39, 94, 100, 111, 129, 146, 285, 313, 315, 321

R

Rafiki's Planet Watch, 144-145
Rafts, 90, 146-147, 156, 259-160,
railroads,
    Big Thunder Mountain Railroad, 88, 285, 323
    Orlando Train Station, 68
    Seven Dwarfs Mine Train, 93
    Walt Disney World Railroad, 82, 91
    Wildlife Express Train, 144
rain, 13-14, 37, 73-74
Rainforest Café, 136, 247-248, 278, 339

reservations (hotels, dining, and shows), 22
restrooms, 72, 99-100, 284
restaurants, 210-279
rhinoceros, 141
ride levels, 24
Rider Switch, 285-286
Rivers of America, 88, 91-92
Rivers of Light, 138
Rock 'n' Roller Coaster Starring Aerosmith, 129-130, 286
roller coasters,
    Barnstormer, The, 95
    Big Thunder Mountain Railroad, 88, 285, 323
    Expedition Everest, 146, 286, 315, 325
    Primeval Whirl, 148-149
    Rock 'n' Roller Coaster Starring Aerosmith, 129-130, 286
    Seven Dwarfs Mine Train, 93
    Space Mountain, 100-101
rope drop, 21
    Animal Kingdom, 136
    Epcot, 106
    Hollywood Studios, 121
    Magic Kingdom, The, 80
Rose and Crown, 233-234
runDisney, 30-31

S

Safaris, Kilimanjaro, 140-141
Sandcastle Club, 292-293
Santa Claus, 34, 43-44, 352
Sanuk, 181
Saratoga Springs Resort and Spa, Disney's, 199-200
Seas with Nemo & Friends, The, 109-110
Season of the Force, 29, 136-137
selfie sticks, 77
Sephora, 181, 225, 227
Seven Dwarfs Mine Train, 93

360

Shades of Green, 202-203
Shootin' Arcade, Frontierland, 91
shopping (see Disney Springs)
Shula's Steak House, 274
shuttles, 59-60, 67-68
Simba's Cubhoyse, 292
Single Rider Line, 20,
        Test Track, 111
        Expedition Everest, 146
Sleeping Beauty Castle, 14, 106, 130, 247
slow-moving rides, 305-306
Soarin', 32, 105-106, 109
Space Mountain, 100-101
Spaceship Earth, 110
Splash Mountain, 73, 89-90
Star Tours – The Adventures Continue, 123, 286, 325
Star Wars Land, 27
Star Wars Launch Bay, 132
Star Wars: A Galactic Spectacular, 132
Starbucks locations in Theme Parks,
        Creature Comforts (Animal Kingdom), 244
        Fountain View (Epcot Future World), 227
        Main Street Bakery (The Magic Kingdom), 220
        Trolley Car Café, The (Hollywood Studios), 243
Steakhouses,
        Capa (Four Season), 118
        Captain's Grille (Yacht Club), 259
        Jiko – The Cooking Place (Animal Kingdom Lodge), 256-257
        Le Cellier Steakhouse (Epcot, World Showcase), 230-231
        Shula's Steak House (WDW Dolphin), 274
        Yachtsman Steakhouse (Yacht Club), 259
Stitch's Great Escape!, 102
storage (see lockers)
strollers, 72

Sunset Boulevard, 128-132
Sushi, 228, 236, 260
Swan, Walt Disney World, 200-202
Swiss Family Treehouse, 85

T

T-REX, 278
Tangled Rest Area, 99-100
taxis, 67
Teppan Edo, 136, 295
terms (see phrases)
Test Track, 111
tickets, 22-23
Tiger, 147
thrill riders, 24, 340
Tom Sawyer Island, 90
Tomorrowland, 100-103
Tomorrowland Speedway, 101
Tomorrowland Transit Authority PeopleMover, 102-103
Tower of Terror (see The Twilight Zone Tower of Terror)
Town Square Theatre, 83
Toy Story Mania!, 125-126
Trader Sam's Grog Grotto, 183, 268-269
trains (see railroads)
travel packages, 50-55
Tree of Life, 134-136, 138
TriceraTop Spin, 149
Turtle Talk with Crush, 110
Typhoon Lagoon, Disney's, 14, 77, 152, 156-159, 251-253
Twilight Zone Tower of Terror, 128-129

U

umbrellas, 155
Under the Sea ~ Journey of The Little Mermaid, 96
United Kingdom, 116
Universal Studios Orlando, 27, 53, 120

V

Via Napolo Ristorante e Pizzeria, 237
Victoria & Albert's, 43, 266, 295, 239
Village Haus (see Pinocchio Village Haus)
Voyage of the Little Mermaid, 127

W

walking distance, hotels within, 174-176, 185
Walt Disney, 13-16, 128
Walt Disney: One Man's Dream, 128
Walt Disney World Railroad, 82, 91
Walt Disney's Carousel of Progress, 103
Walt Disney's Enchanted Tiki Room, 87
water bottles, 72, 346
water parks, 151-164, 151-155
waterproof case, 73
weather, 14, 29-30, 34-44
websites, 22-23
Wilderness Explorers, 139
Wilderness Lodge, Disney's, 183-184
Wildlife Express Train, 144

Wishes: Nighttime Spectacular, 83-84
World of Disney (store), 208, 305, 317
World Showcase, 111-118

Y

Yacht Club, Disney's, 185-186
Yachtsman Steakhouse, 259

Z

zebra, 141-142, 257,

# #

2017, Visiting in, 26-27

Notes:
• We did not index every restaurant as they are available in alphabetical order by resort area from pages 210-279.
• We also haven't indexed individual character meeting spots as they are located on pages 347-352.

Conclusion

Thank you for the purchase of this guide. We sincerely hope that this book is a valuable resource for you. As noted at the beginning, we are Walt Disney World fans and we've created this book from our firsthand knowledge and research over many years and visits. Walt Disney once said that "we keep moving forward, opening new doors, and doing new things, because we're curious and curiosity keeps leading us down new paths." With those words, we hope that you find yourself on adventures both expected and unexpected. That you try new attractions, dining experiences, and return from your vacation filled with happy memories!

Want even more tips and discounts
including free information for the
Universal Studios Orlando Resort?
Sign up for our Free E-Mail List on our Website:

www.magicguidebooks.com

#MagicGuidebooks

Love Disney Pictures?
Follow us!

Or scan this code with
your mobile device to
sign up for free
updates and discounts!

**Instagram
@magicguides**

Wishing you a magical vacation!
Magic Guidebooks

Made in the USA
San Bernardino, CA
04 May 2017